NICK CAVE

Studies in Popular Music

Series Editors: Alyn Shipton, journalist, broadcaster and lecturer in jazz history at the Royal Academy of Music, London, and at City University, London, and Christopher Partridge, Lancaster University

From jazz to reggae, bhangra to heavy metal, electronica to qawwali, and from production to consumption, *Studies in Popular Music* is a multi-disciplinary series which aims to contribute to a comprehensive understanding of popular music. It will provide analyses of theoretical perspectives, a broad range of case studies, and discussion of key issues.

Published

Open Up the Doors: Music in the Modern Church
Mark Evans

Technomad: Global Raving Countercultures
Graham St John

Send in the Clones: A Cultural Study of Tribute Bands
Georgina Gregory

The Lost Women of Rock Music: Female Musicians of the Punk Era
Second edition
Helen Reddington

Dub in Babylon: Understanding the Evolution and Significance of Dub Reggae in Jamaica and Britain from King Tubby to Post-Punk
Christopher Partridge

Global Tribe: Technology, Spirituality and Psytrance
Graham St John

Heavy Metal: Controversies and Countercultures
Edited by Titus Hjelm, Keith Kahn-Harris and Mark LeVine

Forthcoming

Falco and Beyond: Neo Nothing Post of All
Ewa Mazierska

NICK CAVE

A STUDY OF LOVE, DEATH
AND APOCALYPSE

ROLAND BOER

SHEFFIELD UK   BRISTOL CT

For Robert Smith, my music teacher so many years ago.

Published by Equinox Publishing Ltd.

UK: Unit S3, Kelham House, 3 Lancaster Street, Sheffield, S3 8AF
USA: ISD, 70 Enterprise Drive, Bristol, CT 06010

www.equinoxpub.com

Paperback edition published 2013.

British Library Cataloguing-in-Publication Data
A catalogue record for this book is available from the British Library.

Library of Congress Cataloging-in-Publication Data
Boer, Roland, 1961-
  Nick Cave: a study of love, death and apocalypse / Roland Boer.
    p. cm. -- (Studies in popular music)
  Includes bibliographical references and index.
  ISBN 978-1-908049-67-4 (hb)
  1. Cave, Nick, 1957---Criticism and interpretation. 2. Bible--Influence. 3. Music--Religious aspects. I. Title.
  ML420.C39B74 2012
  782.42166092--dc23

ISBN: 978-1-908049-67-4 (hardback)
       978-1-781790-34-2 (paperback)

Typeset by CA Typesetting Ltd, www.publisherservices.co.uk
Printed and bound in the UK by Lightning Source UK Ltd., Milton Keynes and Lightning Source Inc., La Vergne, TN

Contents

Preface

This is at one level a very intimate book, for an indispensable feature of my writing is that I must listen to music while doing so, usually the same relatively small selection of music that allows me to enter the intimate space of a very familiar home of thought. With anticipation, a sigh and a deep sense of pleasure, I enter more deeply into that world, and as I do so the concerns of the world about me slip into the distance for awhile. More than once, that approach has enabled me to deal with difficult periods, providing a blessed relief. But it is also deeply sustaining in all circumstances. Occasionally – to gloss Adorno – I move around the various items of that world, which I envision as a room or shack, but they are deeply familiar and well worn-in: chair, a simple table, a picture, a book or two and a few familiar musicians.

One of those musicians is Nick Cave, a singular, idiosyncratic and brilliant Australian who has not always enjoyed wide acclaim. This book is an effort to understand Cave's appeal, specifically through the lens of his extended biblical and theological engagements. I do so not merely in terms of his written work, the novels and plays and poetry and lyrics that he continues to produce, but also the music itself – even though that division between the lyrical and the musical is, as I will argue, a result of the reified and fragmented (that is, capitalist) system in which we live. Above all, I am interested in how Cave reads the Bible, the total depravity of his imaginary world, its apocalyptic patterns, the welcome focus on death, love, the concern with Christ and the changing nature of the music (specifically in terms of forms of the song) he has produced.

More of that soon enough, but for now allow me to sketch out how this study emerged. It began in 2005 with an invited lecture in the Centre for the Study of the Use of the Bible in the Faculty of Theology at the University of Copenhagen. As I was pondering a topic for that lecture, Christina Petterson suggested I might talk about Nick Cave. So on a long road trip from Melbourne to Newcastle, in Australia, I listened to all of Cave's musical works and then wrote a paper that became the basis of the first chapter in the book. By the time I arrived in Copenhagen, in September of that year, Cave himself was in town, performing at the Opera House at the request of the Crown Princess, Mary. If one thought that Cave might be over-awed by the occasion, nothing could have been further from the truth. He swore, cursed and threw himself, almost ecstatically, into the performance in a way that continues to astound audiences. Over the next few years, a couple more papers appeared, one on apocalyptic and another on the love song, for collections on the Bible and culture. Until at last in 2008, Chris Hartney of the University of Sydney asked me whether I was working on a book on Cave – immediately after delivering a paper on Cave's love song (the basis of Chapter 5) and after being introduced to one of Chris's students, who was writing an honours thesis on Cave. I had not thought so until that point, but it seemed obvious when he mentioned the possibility. So it is to Christina and Chris that I owe the impetus for this book. Finally, in January 2009 I attended the 'All Tomorrow's Parties' music festival on Cockatoo Island in Sydney Harbour. Cave had invited a group of older and newer musicians and groups, all of whom had been influential for his own music or who pursued types of music in which he is interested – punk, psychedelic, krautrock, experimental, proto-industrial, primitive rock, blues, spiritual and so on. Above all, Rowland Howard, guitarist with The Birthday Party back in 1980–83, performed his amazing guitar-work at one of his last performances before he died, and The Saints, back together after 33 years, belted out those pieces that had been at the roots of the heady emergence of punk itself, especially the stunning debut single of 1976, '(I'm) Stranded', that had been so influential on Cave himself and which I remember hearing when it first came out while I was still in high school. Upon completing their set, Chris Bailey, the chain-smoking lead singer of The Saints, introduced a full Bad Seeds line-up as 'The Best Fucking Band in the Universe'. No other reason need be given for a study of Cave.

I began writing this book on a container ship, the CMA-CGM ship, MV La Tour, which took me half way around the world, from Melbourne to Tilbury via two oceans, five seas and the Panama Canal. Thirty-seven days it took, from late June to the end of July, 2010, travelling in a way that human beings have done for millennia before this strange and brief period of air travel. And I completed the book on the journey home, six months later, this time travelling by train, ship and train, from Copenhagen to Beijing, the last leg on the Trans-Mongolian, which takes six days from Moscow to Beijing, via Ulan Bator.

This study has also called on me to return to some of my own musical experiences, especially when I played, rather intensively, rock, then jazz and classical guitar, coupled with a reasonably large dose of musical theory. Too long have those experiences laid dormant, left on the side for children, studies of a swathe of ancient languages, biblical criticism and Marxist philosophy and social thought. So Cave has encouraged me to recover that earlier love, to pull out my old axe and renew the strings. I have no idea whether he will even bother to read this book, although he does have a reputation for devouring anything that is written about him. If he does, he may think it a piece of academic wanking, but I would hope the engagement from a deep theological background might provide a point of engagement.

Finally, I would like to thank those who have encouraged me, wittingly and unwittingly, to develop this study. Early on Søren Holst and Geert Hallbäch of the University of Copenhagen provided a forum for some initial exploration. Mary Ann Beavis of *The Journal of Religion and Culture* was brave enough to publish an early and unformed piece called 'Under the Influence'. As well, John Walliss of Liverpool Hope University and Chris Partridge of Lancaster University have pushed me to think on matters apocalyptic, while Elaine Wainwright and Philip Culbertson ensured that Christology was not forgotten in considering Cave's work. But to Christina Petterson I owe the ultimate thanks for suggesting I write about Cave and his artistic production in the first place.

Roland Boer
On the No. 4 train (Trans-Mongolian)
Somewhere in Siberia, between Moscow and Beijing (via Ulan Bator)

Introduction

The best fucking band in the universe.
(Chris Bailey, lead singer of The Saints, introducing Nick Cave
and the Bad Seeds on Cockatoo Island, Sydney, 2008)

We leave religion to the psychos and fanatics.
(Grinderman 2007)

The story goes that Arnold Schoenberg was once asked, 'Do you have perfect pitch?'

'Thank God, no', he said.

On that matter and that matter alone do I stand on the same ground as Schoenberg. Yet, in order to bring out the value of such a shortcoming, let me invoke another sense, now in regard to Ernst Bloch. Chronically long-sighted, so much so that his glasses were like pebbles and in his last years he went completely blind, Bloch turned this inability to see close-up to his advantage. Instead of constantly trying to focus on the immediate and the close, he turned his gaze to the distant horizon, to seek what could barely be discerned – the utopian possibilities of what we would normally miss. That is, he always sought to discern more deeply, to gain the skill of both 'clair-voyance' (*Hellsehen*) and 'clair-audience' (*Hellhören*) in regard to his philosophy and musical analysis (Bloch 1974: 163; see also Korstvedt 2010: 153). I would like to think that Schoenberg, too, turned his lack of pitch, the lack of a conventional musical ear, to his own advantage, thereby being able to discern and create the whole movement of New Music that enticed Adorno so much.

At a much more modest level, I too seek to develop such a reading of Nick Cave's musical and literary production, coming at this material from my background in biblical and theological analysis, along with both a sustained concern with Marxist criticism and an older love that has come back into favour, namely, an intense concern with all manner of guitar-work and the attendant theory that goes with such study. But the initial question to be asked is, why Nick Cave? He is not a mainstream musician, or indeed a mainstream novelist, poet, film-script writer or playwright. And he is not very well known in that increasingly insular and fearful place between Canada and Mexico, the USA (although the Grinderman albums are making inroads there [Grinderman 2007; 2010]). That is to say, the claim by the originators of punk (The Saints) that Nick Cave and the Bad Seeds is the 'best fucking band in the universe' needs a couple of words of justification. I might begin to answer the question by observing that Cave remains one of the most original and arresting of alternative musicians in the last three decades, from leadership in the punk wave of the late seventies and early eighties to the unique avant-garde movements that followed. But what interests me about Cave is not merely that he is a musician and songwriter, but that his artistic creation also includes novels, poetry, film-scripts, plays, lectures and the occasional short story. Further, all of that creative work is infused with arresting reinterpretations of the Bible and theology more generally. Obviously, that feature is crucial for a study such as this.

In the seven chapters that follow I deal extensively with key biblical and theological dimensions of Cave's work, such as the modes in which he engages with the Bible, the total depravity of the worlds invoked in his novels and other written work, the consistent invocation of apocalyptic themes, his restoration of death as a valid dimension of life, the twists on the love song, the role of a sensual and heretical Christ and then a detailed analysis of his musical forms. Yet I also work with a certain theoretical background that sustains my analysis, so let me outline the major points of that background.

The best way into that discussion is by means of negation, that is, by stating what one will not find in this book. I do not seek to provide a comprehensive theory of rock, for that is the challenging and perhaps systemically impossible task of those with an interest in such matters (Moore 2001), even when relying on collaboration to provide at least a sense of comprehensiveness (Covach and Boone 1997, Frith and Goodwin 2005). Further, my approach is not predominantly oriented to sociology (Friedlander 2006, Wicke 1990), cultural studies (Bennett *et al.* 1993, Broadhurst 1999, Grossberg 1997: 27–121; Jayasinghe 2009),[1] gender (Whiteley 1997) or musicology (Covach and Boone 1997). The concern of this study is a particular artist, which, despite the traps of such an approach in fostering the perception of individual genius and the great men (and women) of history, it at least provides some well-defined boundaries within which to undertake my analysis. Comparable recent examples include musicological analyses of Björk (Dibben 2009), Elvis Costello (Griffiths 2007) and Bob Dylan (Negus 2008), as well as an informative study of a band, the influential Velvet Underground (Witts 2006), except of course that my study is not primarily musicological. Its concern is religion, or more specifically theology and the Bible, in Nick Cave's work. All the same, I do not focus exclusively on the lyrics, as is the habit of some of those who do deal with religious and biblical matters, such as Symynkywicz (2008), Cousland (2005), Kessler (2005), McEntire (2010), Culbertson (2010), Erskine (2010),

Sample (2010), Turner (2006) and Gilmour (2009, 2011), who tends to sacrifice depth of analysis for encyclopaedic collection.

For those who come to this work from biblical criticism, I should also say that it is not an exercise in what is increasingly called 'reception history', in English-language biblical criticism at least.[2] The problem here is that this term relies on a spurious distinction drawn from German historical-critical biblical scholarship: one first engages in exegesis of the original biblical text, usually with three steps – translation, paraphrase (restating the key moments of the text in question) and exegesis proper, the 'leading out' of the meaning of the text. Needless to say, such an approach produces the intractable assumption that there is one true meaning of the text, a meaning that may be identified by this singular method. After exegesis comes reception history (*Rezeptionsgeschichte*) and the history of the text's use (*Wirkungsgeschichte*), although the latter is usually subsumed within the former. This reception history is understood as secondary to the originary text and its exegesis; in that reception history may be lumped all those other approaches, like feminist, Marxist, postcolonial, psychoanalytic, ideological, queer and so on, all of which are supposedly anachronistic (without seeing that historical-critical 'exegesis' itself is just as anachronistic, since it developed in a historically specific period well after the Bible was written). But the proponents of this approach also understand any interpretation of the text outside exegesis by biblical scholars as secondary, especially the way the Bible is interpreted in art, literature, film, politics or music. For these reasons, my study of Cave is not an instance of this type of 'reception' criticism, for I simply take Cave as offering yet other interpretations, which are as valid (or not!) as those who seek to maintain the fortress of biblical criticism or theological interpretation. Far more interesting are the patterns of interpretation in which Cave engages, the creative reconstructions of the theology and biblical motifs (in which neither the Bible nor theology has priority), rather than any concern for the legitimacy or otherwise of those reconstructions.

So what approach do I follow? I draw upon a select number of theorists who provide the methodological possibilities of digging deep into the theological nature of Cave's work, whether literary (novels, plays, poems) or musical (moving from lyrics to music). Ernst Bloch is the methodological foundation stone of the analysis that follows, with Theodor Adorno providing some useful support (others, such as Theodore Gracyk [1996] and Jacques Attali [1985], will also make appearances). After much consideration of the considerable and deeply insightful musical analysis of both Ernst Bloch and Theodor Adorno, I have opted to make more extensive use of the former. As I shall make clear in the last chapter, a deep affinity connects Bloch with Nick Cave, making Bloch the natural theorist who underpins much of my analysis. I am most interested in his extraordinary opening section, bar one of *The Spirit of Utopia*, called 'The Philosophy of Music' (Bloch 2000: 31–164; 1985c: 49–208; also published in Bloch 1985b: 1–139; 1974: 7–164).[3] Since I offer a concise statement of Bloch's approach in Chapter 7, I will not pre-empt that discussion here, suffice to emphasize here his sensitivity to the utopian and redemptive possibilities embodied in music, his bold efforts at dialectical reading, his emphasis on the human dimension of music, especially hearing and singing, and above all his realization of the interweaving of religion and music – all of which renders Bloch's philosophy of music extremely useful for my engagement with Cave.

Adorno is of course present in a lighter mode, especially his concern with the social location of music, in which the very autonomy and even alienation of music and the musician (authenticity and desire to avoid 'selling out') is a far more telling register of social and economic location than any direct reference (Adorno 1999 [1959]: 1–14; 2002: 391–430; 2006 [1949]: 99–102); as well as his argument that music (not merely popular music[4]) is by and large part of the 'culture industry', and that only in the briefest moments when music resists – through what I have elsewhere called 'political iconoclasm' (Boer forthcoming[b]) which he draws and develops from the ban on images in the Second Commandment[5] – does it offer the briefest utopian glimpse, a moment of redemption. Such examples appear throughout his work, not merely in his extensive analysis of music. So we find the effort to recover the old philosophical term, *restitutio in integrum*, 'of making whole once again the pieces into which it has been smashed' (Adorno 2008 [2003]: 191; 2007 [2003]: 237), but especially the comments on his music teacher in Vienna, Alban Berg: Adorno designates him 'the foreign minister of the land of his dreams (*Außenminister seines Traumlands*)' (Adorno 1991 [1968]: 33; 2003 [1968]: 366), for whom the 'greatest works of art do not exclude the lower depths, but kindle the flame of utopia on the smoking ruins of the past' (Adorno 1999 [1959]: 79; 2003 [1959]: 96).[6] And Adorno was not averse to noting the inescapable theological dimension of music, although he was more wary than Bloch of making the connection. Music, suggests Adorno, is different from the language of intentionality, for it 'contains a theological dimension', revealing and concealing at one and the same moment, becoming 'demythologized prayer', attempting and failing to 'name the Name' (Adorno 1998 [1963]: 2).

Nonetheless, Adorno does provide me with an insight into the vexing problem of the separation of music and lyrics in popular music, especially in his unfinished *Current of Music* (Adorno 2009 [2006]). Rather than taking the problem as a given that must be dealt with or resolved in some way, he asks

why it is a problem in the first place: reification and especially fragmentation are the key. Inescapably part of the capitalism under which we all live,
reification becomes the cultural and philosophical form of commodification,
entailing not only a 'thingification', in which the products of labour take on
the forms of human relations, while those human relations become more and
more like the interaction of such products, but also a fragmentation, a Tay-
lorization of life into ever-smaller and apparently discrete realms (academic
specialization is but one small aspect of this reality). For Adorno, the philosopher and musicologist, reification meant not only the baleful separation of
thought and action, but also of music and lyrics in popular music: 'Music and
lyrics remain largely disassociated, and fulfil their function rather as two com-
plementary media rather than as a strict unity of content, emotional or other'
(Adorno 2009 [2006]: 392).[7] In our current social and economic formation,
it is well nigh impossible to overcome such a fragmentation, for the achievement of a thorough integration is not characteristic of a mythical golden age
that has passed, but of a time that has not yet come (to gloss Bloch).

For what it is worth, my treatment of Cave both recognizes that fragmentation and seeks to deal with in as best a fashion as one might. So I begin
with literary analysis, casting aspersions on Cave's written and spoken word as
means of controlling interpretation, dealing with his novels, poetry and plays,
before passing onto his song lyrics – on the themes of apocalyptic, death, love
and Jesus. But even in those thematic considerations, I already broach questions of musical form, especially in the fourth and sixth chapters, on death and
Christology respectively. Those initial forays lead into the last, detailed and
long chapter on the changing forms of the song in three decades of musical
production. More specifically, I distinguish between three forms (along with
some variants): the anarchic/discordant song, the hymn (and its associated
lament) and the dialectical song. As the last form indicates, this is a dialectical
analysis, profoundly informed by Bloch's philosophy of music.

A few introductory comments are also in order concerning scholarly work
on Nick Cave and religion, of which there are but scattered efforts. The recent,
uneven collection, *Cultural Seeds: Essays on the Work of Nick Cave* (Welberry
and Dalziell 2009), is at least a start, for it has a few essays on the question
of religion. To begin with, Eaglestone (2009) begins promisingly, arguing that
Cave provides an instance of the refusal to bracket religion off in a discrete
segment from the rest of life, for religion suffuses all his work. But then the
argument becomes derailed, for it relies on Cave's own word to see his shift
from Old Testament to the New Testament as one that turns on the contrast
between the rhetoric with which we discuss God and a dreamed of direct relationship with him. The shift to the New Testament is of course marked by

the appearance of Jesus in Cave's lyrics, but for some reason that is beyond me, Eaglestone espies such a shift with the 1986 album, *Your Funeral... My Trial* (Cave 1986b). A perusal of my Chapter 6 will show why I disagree with Eaglestone. The piece by Wiseman-Trowse (2009) has a small and superficial treatment of religion in the context of a larger argument in which he attempts to join the dots connecting four points: Cave, Elvis Presley, Jung's archetype of the *Puer Aeternus* and the lead character in *And the Ass Saw the Angel* (Cave 1989), Euchrid. And Dalziell (2009) offers an eclectic, somewhat rambling and impressionist analysis that seeks to uncover – fully realizing the traps and impossibilities of doing so – the pattern of artistic construction in Cave's work with a specific focus on the themes of love and melancholy. She touches upon novels, plays, songs, via a focus on an exhibition at the Arts Centre in Melbourne (November 2007 to April 2008) in which the various paraphernalia of Cave's artistic life were on display (notebooks, photographs, sketches, paintings), arguing in the end that Cave is a collector of fragments, just like her.

A sparse number of other assessments of Cave and religion appeared a little earlier, such as the wayward item by McEvoy (2007), who argues that the rise of melancholy in Cave's music also marks the privileging of lyric over music, the emphasis on Cave rather than the Bad Seeds, and thereby the 'demise' of Cave as he descends into a concern with personal expression rather than the art form, resulting in an outpouring of violence and murder. A little earlier, Cousland (2005) focused on the grotesque in Cave's lyrics, using it as a means of showing how Cave deploys divine absence to point to transcendent beauty – a form of aesthetic redemption I will find wanting. A similar conclusion, albeit moving along a different path is found in Kessler (2005), who focuses on the oppressive album, *The Boatman's Call* (Cave 1997a), arguing that here we find an inward turn towards an interactive rather than an interventionist God; that is, by means of our imagination, God – otherwise silenced – is enabled to speak.

Despite their shortcomings, these works at least provide some backdrop for my study. But I have kept one recent study until last, that by Lyn McCredden (2009). Of the few studies undertaken thus far, this analysis is the most useful, despite its tendency to focus on the lyrics (as do all of the treatments I have mentioned). McCredden offers a survey of sacred and theological themes in Cave's lyrics and I have drawn upon her work from time to time. Cave refuses to separate sacred and profane, she argues, for they suffuse all of life – flesh, erotics and violence. In the process, he produces an 'embracingly contemporary theology of the fleshed or carnal sacred...caught up in desire for a divine source or balm' (McCredden 2009: 167–68). As will become clear soon enough, I read 'balm' in terms of the search for redemption in all its variety.

Lastly, throughout the writing process I have kept in mind as far as possible the fact that writing itself is a poor medium to deal with the expanse of music. As Elvis Costello once said, 'writing about music is like dancing about architecture' (Gracyk 1996: vii). Or in Adorno's terms, 'To interpret language means: to understand language. To interpret music means: to make music' (Adorno 1998 [1963]: 3).

1 Searching the Holy Books

I've searched the holy books.
(Cave 1994)

I would just look it up to find a quote and find myself reading it
for the next two days.
(Cave in Dwyer 1994)

This chapter undertakes three tasks: one exploring and thereby introducing the extensiveness of Nick Cave's engagement with the Bible and theology; another examining some distinctive features and problems that arise with that engagement, especially Cave's effort to control interpretation of his life and work through a complex of autobiography, the dominance of the word and Christology; and a third seeking moments when, in the very effort at controlling interpretation, such authorial dominance begins to break down. The discussion closes with some methodological considerations that arise from that effort at dominance and its breakdown, focused on the issue of what may be called strategies of containment. In that discussion, I seek to answer the following questions: how are we to understand these appropriations and interpretations of the Bible? In particular, what are the implications of the breakdown of Cave's own effort at control for those interpretations?

Synopsis: Nick Cave and the Bible

I've got to stop quoting from the Bible because it's irritating.
(Cave in Mulholland 1996)

As mentioned in the Introduction, Cave has for many a long year been an avid reader of the Bible, drawing deeply upon it for inspiration in his song-writing, novels, poetry, plays and film-scripts. A preliminary overview of his engagements with the Bible and theology will provide a map by which to navigate the analyses that follow in this and the following chapters. One may roughly distinguish between three moments: Cave's own overt statements; the obvious items of content, where the Bible and religion more generally appear; and the formal nature of Cave's appropriation, a topic that is a little suppler than matters of content. As for his own observations, we find Cave averring, 'I know the Bible reasonably well' (Pascoe 1997), or his explicit engagement with the Bible in his introduction to the Gospel of Mark in the Canongate Bible series (Cave 1998),[1] or his comment that the Song of Songs and above all the Psalms have influenced his song-writing very deeply (Cave 2004b: 398). Although I will throw some suspicion on Cave's own word later in this chapter, these observations are manifested in the overt content of band and song titles, as well as the writing itself. For example, the second part of the album title from The Birthday Party days, *Mutiny! – The Bad Seed* (Cave 1983), comes from Psalm 58:3, a title that would soon enough become the name of the new band from 1984. So too does the title *Kicking against the Pricks* (Cave 1986a) come from the Bible, this time Acts 26:14. The list goes on: *The First Born Is Dead* (Cave 1985) is drawn from the story of the divine slaying of all the Egyptian first-born sons on the eve of the Israelite escape in the eleventh chapter of Exodus, but it also has christological associations; *The Good Son* (Cave 1990) comes from both the story of Cain and Abel in Genesis 4 and the parable of the Prodigal Son, albeit now focused on the faithful son who works hard all his life for his father in Luke 15:11-32; *Dig!!! Lazarus Dig!!!* (Cave 2008) refers of course to the story of the raising of Lazarus in John 11:1-44; finally, the novel *When the Ass Saw the Angel* (Cave 1989) is a direct reference to the narrative of Balaam's ass in Numbers 22.

When we turn to the lyrics themselves, even from the earliest days of The Boys Next Door and The Birthday Party, almost every second song contains an explicit biblical, theological or religious reference or allusion, so much so that it would be somewhat tedious to list them all here (and would take up the rest of this book). To draw examples from but one album, *Mutiny! – The Bad Seed* (Cave 1983), we find many theological references in the track 'Mutiny in Heaven', explicit lyrics such as 'Lucy, ya made a sinner out of me/Now ah'm burnin' like a saint' from 'Swampland', or the line 'Raisin' up like Lazarus' from 'Vixo', as well as the following lyrics from 'Wild World':

> Post crucifixion baby, and all undone...
> Church bells ring out the toll of our night

Similarly, the novel, *And the Ass Saw the Angel* (Cave 1989), and the film, *The Proposition* (Hillcoat 2005), are saturated with the theological doctrine of total depravity (see my discussion in Chapter 2). The poetry, too, is drenched with biblical references. For instance, in the play 'Salomé' an allusion to the Song of Songs 4:1-7 and 7:1-9 appears: 'Her breasts are hillocks of honeycoloured sand. Her quim is shielded by fine lace' (Cave 1988a: 87). The whole play is of course drawn directly from the story of the execution of John the Baptist in

Matthew 14:1-2, Mark 6:14-29 and Luke 9:7-9. Similarly, in the poem 'Opium Tea', the repeated line, 'I am what I am and what will be will be' (Cave 1997b: 176), is taken from the statement of God's identity, addressed to Moses in Exodus 3:14. Here Cave shows some sophistication in his adaptations from the Bible, for the ambiguous phrase in that Hebrew Bible (Old Testament) text may have a present or future tense: the Hebrew *ehyeh asher ehyeh* designates an incomplete and thereby continuing action or state, referring to either past, present or future – hence Cave's 'am' and 'will be'. One last example: in the poem 'Little Empty Boat' the following lines appear, alluding to the Gospel of John 3:1-21 and 11:25:

> I respect your beliefs, girl
> And consider you a friend
> But I've already been born once
> I don't wanna be born again
> Your knowledge is impressive
> And your argument is good
> But I am the resurrection, babe
> And you're standing on my foot
> (Cave 1997b: 166)

This is enough content to show that the Bible and theology saturate all of Cave's writing. A good deal more items will appear in the various expositions in the remainder of this book. But let us now turn to the way the Bible and theology also influence the form of Cave's writing. In the seventh chapter of this book I offer a detailed examination of the forms or genres of Cave's music, highlighting three key forms in a dialectical analysis: the anarchic or discordant song, the hymn (and its associated lament) and the dialectical song. There is no need to provide the details of that full analysis here, suffice to point out that the hymn and lament are genres that come straight out of the theological, if not ecclesiastical, tradition of Christianity. These forms are characterized by a significantly slowed tempo, conventional harmonics, a dominant keyboard (often an organ), collective singing that is reminiscent of a choir or congregation singing and (in the case of the lament) a held and falling note that gives voice to longing. Cave himself is explicit concerning the influence, observing that 'The Song of Solomon, perhaps the greatest Love Song ever written, had a massive impact on me', and then, 'The Song of Solomon is an extraordinary Love Song but it was the remarkable series of love song/poems known as the Psalms that truly held me... In many ways these songs became the blueprint for many of my more sadistic love songs' (Cave 2004b: 398). However, as I will argue in a later chapter on the love song, Cave is not always the best guide to his own work. In this case, he is referring to the content of his love songs, but I would suggest that the formal influence is far stronger: the genres of hymn and lament in his work show not only the afterlives of church singing, but also the formal influence of the biblical Psalms. But now we have come a full circle, for the hymns of the many ecclesiastical traditions were and continue to be shaped by those very same Psalms.

To sum up, Nick Cave's writing in all its shapes – band names, track titles, song-writing, poetry, plays, talks and films – manifests a profound and ongoing interaction with the Christian Bible and theology. However, such a survey merely lays the groundwork for more sustained analysis, which begins in the next section and continues throughout this book. In what follows, I raise some critical issues from this engagement: the slippery terrain of autobiography, christological motifs in the songs themselves, the attempt by Cave to control the interpretation of his work, the chinks in this comprehensive effort at control and then the theoretical issues that arise from such engagements.

The Life of Nick

> I felt a genuine rage in those days, a disgust at myself and the world around me. (Cave in Ellen 1998)

On the matter of autobiography, I shall focus more explicitly on the Bible, for autobiography and Bible have a symbiotic relation in Cave's carefully crafted narratives concerning his own life. Before we explore that relation further, let me come clean with two assumptions: autobiography is the highest form of fiction and it constitutes a singularly effective form of control.[2] Both apply to Cave's engagement with the Bible. Whenever the authorial 'I' appears – and my frequent use of the first-person pronoun in this chapter is no exception – then my radar of suspicion goes into high gear.[3] But what interests me more is that whenever Cave writes, sings and speaks about the Bible, he is very keen to control how that engagement is interpreted. The first sign of that control is the autobiographical narrative that appears time and again.

Let us focus on two examples of autobiographical control: in the widely copied introduction to the Gospel of Mark that was published by Canongate (Cave 1998), Cave quickly links his reading of the Bible to stages in his life. So he begins with his first Bible and the appeal the Old Testament had for an angry young man in his twenties: 'the Old Testament spoke to that part of me that railed and hissed and spat at the world'. Or as he puts it in a BBC talk, 'all I had to do was walk out on stage and open my mouth and let the curse of God roar through me' (Cave 1997b: 138; see also Sierksma 1997). But with a desire growing to give away the drugs (begun in the 1990s and achieved by the turn of the millennium), with a certain mellowing and perhaps maturity, the more temperate Cave ceases to find a vengeful God as appealing as he did in his angry, drug-crazed youth. The quieter Cave turns to the New Testament: then his eyes are opened by the Gospels of Mark and Luke (the name of his second son) and the rest of the New Testament. Here he encounters the dim, sad light of Christ calling to him, as in the Holman Hunt painting, 'The Light of the World' (without naming it). Cave zeroes in all too quickly and symptomatically on Christ; his brief characterization of Mark's Gospel in all its urgency brings him to the call of Christ. This Christ speaks to him with a 'softer, sadder, more introspective' (Cave 1997b: 139) voice out of the Gospels. Christ comes to him outside the damaging control of a church for which Cave has no time.

I suggest that the focus on Christ is symptomatic of what is happening with Cave's biblical interpretation, but before I develop that point, let me dwell with his autobiographies a little longer. For they are in fact plural, multiple autobiographies that run over one another.[4] Alongside the introduction to the Gospel of Mark, we find the same points with a few twists appearing in the interview with Jim Pascoe (Pascoe 1997): the childhood choir in Wangaratta in country Australia, the insipid Christ peddled by the Church, the Church itself as a manipulator of the Bible for its own ends, reading the vengeful Old Testament in his twenties, the softer New Testament later and the identification of Christ as a human being who struggles over questions of faith, life, imagination and misunderstanding. In the talk, 'The Flesh Made Word', made for BBC radio on 3 July, 1996, the same points recur, although now with the significant addition that God is in fact Cave's muse: in retrospect, Cave sees that his dark and creative imagination came from God, a God that he did not find in the church of his childhood. Indeed, the creative Jesus that appeals to him is one who railed against the religious establishment.[5]

With these thumbnail autobiographies widely available, one may be tempted to scurry for the biographies, especially those by Ian Johnston (1996), Robert Brokenmouth (1996), Maximilian Dax and Johannes Beck (1999) and Amy Hanson (2005). Too soon do we fall into the old pattern of interpreting the music, or rather the lyrics, from the perspective of Cave's biography. But what strikes me about these biographies is that whereas for Cave himself autobiography and Bible are closely linked, for his biographers the Bible is only a minor element. A few passing comments on Cave's Bible-reading habits, a note concerning an album title or two, but that is all; it is certainly not as interesting as, say, the drug habits of a tormented soul who made it big on his own terms. What a contrast to Cave's autobiographies, for here the Bible takes centre-stage – Bible and autobiography are inextricably connected. This situation stands out even more sharply when we realize that Cave does not restrict his engagement with religion to the Bible. He writes and sings about faith, God, the Church, the saints and so on. But in these cases there is minimal autobiography, for only when he turns to the Bible does autobiography come to the fore.

I did promise another example of autobiographical control, this time from his music. Let us follow Cave's own lead for a moment and take his autobiographical word as it stands: he states that *The Boatman's Call* (Cave 1997a) is an unmediated and non-metaphorical – as far as that is possible – narrative of crucial events in his life when he was in a very important relationship (with P. J. Harvey, soon after his breakup from Viviane Carneiro, the mother of his second son, Luke) that he knew would not last (Calkin 2001, Fontaine 1997, Mordue 1997, Nine 1997). But it is also the album in which Cave wears his heart on his sleeve, singing a succession of what can only be called hymns (see further Chapter 7). Here, then, in the music itself we find the intersection of autobiography and Bible. The album is replete with biblical allusions (the boatman calling from the lake, the hand that protects me, turning the other cheek), overtly religious hymns like 'There is a Kingdom' or the more sardonic 'Idiot Prayer', and theological paradoxes, such as that of faith and its necessary lack, or the Pauline tension between sin and the desire to do good, or the Reformed doctrine of total depravity and its consequences, or Cave calling on the interventionist God in whom he does not believe to do precisely that, intervene. The Bible seems to evoke Cave's inner, especially his sexual, life like no other.

Thus, in the central 'Brompton Oratory' we find the lyrics laced with the Bible, especially Luke 24, in which Christ returns after the resurrection to his loved ones. We will work through this track in more detail in my discussion of the love song in Chapter 5, suffice to point out here that the piece reflects on a contrast: some are indeed fortunate, for their loved ones return, but this return does not apply to Cave himself, for his lover will not return. The fortunate ones turn out to be the disciples in Luke 24, who experience the post-resurrection appearances of Jesus and are exceedingly happy. Cave is less fortunate: no matter how much he may yearn, how much everything in this moment of worship (the context is a Pentecost church service) reminds him of the woman he has lost, how the wine recalls her smell, how her beauty is as impossible to define, believe or endure as that of God, how neither God nor the devil can have the effect that she has had on him – no matter how much the Bible, worship and God may remind him of his lover, she is gone for good.[6]

Other biblical passages on the same album follow a similar line. For instance, 'He who seeks finds and who knocks will be let in', spoken by the 'man who spoke wonders though I've never met him', becomes the intense bodily expectation of a lover in 'Are You The One That I've Been Waiting For?' Finally, in 'Far from Me', biblical words become Cave's words to his lover:

> For you dear, I was born
> For you I was raised up
> For you I've lived and for you I will die
> For you I am dying now...
> Did you ever
> Care for me?
> Were you ever
> There for me?

The first four lines come directly from the words directed at the child at baptism – 'for you, little child, he was born' and so on – and the second four are a gloss on the parable of the sheep and goats in Matthew 25:44, in which the signs of one's devotion to Christ are those acts of altruism and not overt religiosity. The pattern has become somewhat clearer: not only does Cave's life become one with the biblical texts, but there is also a far more interesting substitution taking place: in the first four lines I quoted, Cave simply substitutes 'he' (Christ) for 'I', and in the second lot of four lines the 'me' becomes Cave himself in place of Christ.

Two angles are now coming together – one from Cave's written texts, interviews and talks, and one from his songs. The first is the clear connection that Cave makes between the Bible and his autobiography. The second, however, is more intriguing: when his songs do invoke the Bible, they so not merely in an autobiographical fashion, but also with a christological focus. In short, Bible, autobiography and Christology come together in a potent mix.

Now, we might attribute all this to the well-known line from 'Nobody's Baby Now' – 'I've searched the holy books, I tried to unravel the mystery of Jesus Christ, the saviour' (Cave 1994) – but this is a rather soft option. The BBC talk from 1996, 'The Flesh Made Word', is far more revealing. In this talk, the underlying theme is no less a comparison between Cave's own relationship with his father and that between Christ and his Father, the God of the Hebrew Bible. And in the same way that Jesus came 'to set right the misguided notions of his Father' (Cave 1997b: 140), so also Cave sees himself realizing the thwarted literary and creative energies of his own father. Just as God evolved in Jesus the son, so also Cave's father evolves in him, for 'like Jesus, there is the blood of my father in me... Like Christ, I too come in the name of my father, to keep God alive' (Cave 1997b: 141, 142; see also Baker 2003). With statements like these, as well as the claim that God speaks through him, music critics began to worry about Cave's mental and spiritual health – perhaps all that heroin was finally catching up with him.

I suspect that Cave's mental and spiritual health is a good deal better than many of us, so I have no worries on that score. However, I do have some misgivings about such a christological focus, especially in the way it relates to the personality cult or star system of which Cave is very much a part. I draw these misgivings from Max Horkheimer and Theodor Adorno's *Dialectic of Enlightenment* (2002: 145–47; 2003 [1947]: 206–209). Briefly put, for Horkheimer and Adorno, the roots of the personality cult lie squarely with the christological reflections of the early church.

This point emerges in the midst of the long discussion of anti-Semitism, which they trace back to the differences between Judaism and Christianity – the latter generating hatred of the Father by the followers of the Son. The paradox for Adorno and Horkheimer is that, in its efforts to overcome Judaism, Christianity recovers and renews idolatry, giving it a potency it never had before. The paradox grows, since Christianity is supposed to mark a shift from law to a grace that was inherent in the Hebrew covenant, replacing a religion of sin and guilt, of abstract horror and duty, with one of love. Yet precisely in this shift does idolatry resurge and the culprit is none other than Christology.

How so? Christology presents us with 'pretensions of the finite' (Horkheimer and Adorno 2002: 145; 2003 [1947]: 206), that is, the raising of the very human Christ to divine status. In Christ, the worship of a human figure receives religious sanction. But this is only a beginning, for now they deploy the dialectic of Christology itself: in the same way that the absolute is made human in Christ, so human beings may be deified like Christ. It is an inverse ratio: only through the humanization of the divine in Christ does it become possible to divinize other human beings. Thus, as soon as we recognize someone with charisma, who convinces us with stunning oratory or perhaps simple sayings of deep wisdom, who promises much if we will only trust him or her, we are lost. I do not merely mean that such leaders will disappoint, leading us to a mosquito-infested marsh or treacherous jungle to eke out a slave-like existence, or that they end up seducing the young boys and girls while owning a fleet of Rolls-Royces, or that the Swiss bank account will swell while we become penniless. Rather, I mean that the process of deification has already taken place, that the human being has become like god, an idol in whom we have invested our own powers and resources. That process, suggest Horkheimer and Adorno, has been enabled in a way not seen before by Christology.

In other words, the deep dialectic of Christology gives us the logic of the personality cult, for when Christ is most completely God – as one of the trinity, dwelling in heaven, an all-powerful creator, omniscient, the source of love and so on – only then does his humanity push its way through all the theological categories, through all of the attributes of God, and claim its presence. So also with his divinity: when the humanity of Christ is dragged to the remotest and most inaccessible point, when it can travel no further, is puffing and sweating and ready to drop, then the divinity of Christ begins to show up. The first step enables the second, which is where the personality cult picks up the dialectical swing, for as Christ has become man and then returns to the heavens, human beings may now join him on the return journey, becoming deified in the process – or at least they become so in the eyes of their adorers. Being a god–human (according to traditional Christology) opens the door for others to reverse the equation and become a human–God, that is, an idol. The finite stands in for the infinite, the lie for truth, the illusion for knowledge.

To return to Cave: statements like 'In Christ the spiritual blue-print was set so that we ourselves could become God-like' (Cave 1997b: 139) take on a rather different sense in light of Horkheimer and Adorno's observations. As the name 'Nick Cave' increasingly gained iconic status, first as an underground figure and then on the edges of mainstream music, increasingly the subject of and curator of exhibitions (for example, Barrand and Fox 2007), so also did he become more interested in Christ. It has become an extended parleying of the personality cult, no matter how explicit that agenda may be.

The 'Word' of Cave

> I can let the words speak for themselves. (Cave in Pishof 2001: 84)

Thus far we have a complex and comprehensive effort to control interpretation – a songwriter who invokes the Bible in an autobiographical, even christological mode. There is, however, a second dimension to such control, namely the *Word* itself. That there is now a trail of christological associations following behind any reference to the 'Word' should hardly come as a surprise, for while the Bible may be the 'word of God', Christ becomes the 'Word of God'.

It is not just that so many of us trained to interpret written texts gravitate to lyrics, to Cave's word, but that Cave himself plays up the role of his words.[7] Not content with writing lyrics for songs, he tries his hand regularly at poetry and brief scripts for plays, has written a couple of novels and screenplays and is known to speak in perfectly formed English sentences (Doran 2010); one does not need to look far to locate all of this in a variety of easily accessible media. The lyrics are occasionally available on the internet and are now also published, formatted as though they were poetry, in print as *The Complete Lyrics* (Cave 2007). One may also find them, along with poetry, some short plays, the text of radio talks, facsimiles of Cave's own scribbling from his notebooks and so on in the double-volume *King Ink* (Cave 1988a, 1997b).

Yet Cave is above all a songwriter, and – to state the bleeding obvious – these songs are performed and sung with his current bands, The Bad Seeds and Grinderman. But what happens when we listen to what is now a substantial opus? Most of the time, we can understand the lyrics rather well (even with many of the tracks during the overtly punk phase of The Boys Next Door and The Birthday Party from 1979 to 1983). In other words, when it comes to the mixing room, the lyrics are mixed so that they come through with extraordinary clarity. And Cave tends to sing them relatively clearly, just in case we may be a little slow or hard of hearing. So, for instance, as I write this chapter I listen to one of the many albums he has put out over the years, conveniently checking the printed lyrics on the rare occasion that a word is unclear in the song.

However, when it comes to explicitly biblical and theological engagements, a split opens up between the tendency to clarity and one that can only be described as an obscuring of the lyrics, between mixing them up and mixing them down. Among the former may be included 'Brompton Oratory' (discussed above) or 'There is a Kingdom' from *The Boatman's Call* (Cave 1997a), or 'Tupelo' with its drawing upon the flood narrative of Genesis 6–9 in *The First Born Is Dead* (Cave 1985), or 'The Good Son' from the album of the same name (Cave 1990), or indeed the eponymous track 'Dig!!! Lazarus Dig!!!' (Cave 2008).

Yet the second group of tracks is far more interesting, for the more closely they work with the Bible, the more do the lyrics threaten to disappear into obscurity, so much so that it is often difficult to decipher what Cave is singing. Most of these pieces come from *Tender Prey* (Cave 1988b). There are a few exceptions, such as 'Up Jumped the Devil' and 'Sunday's Slave', but the rest hover on the edge of uncertainty. 'The Mercy Seat', 'Mercy', 'Deanna' and 'Slowly Goes the Night' threaten to lose their lyrics in the mix: in 'Deanna', multiple voices and music surging forth and threatening to swamp the words; 'The Mercy Seat' splits between two voices, one difficult to understand and the other clearer; 'Slowly Goes the Night' begins rather clearly but then becomes progressively more difficult to understand. As for the rest – 'Watching Alice', 'Sugar Sugar Sugar' and 'New Morning' – the lyrics are about as clear as many a Rolling Stones song. Now the Stones have many reasons to mix their lyrics down, but Nick Cave? What is going on here?

I suggest that this album manifests the impossibility of complete control, the instability of the author's hegemony in the midst of his work, a tension between control and its loss. Four tracks in particular reveal this uncertainty:

on the one hand, 'The Mercy Seat' still shows all the signs of a christological autobiography, while in 'City of Refuge', 'New Morning' and 'Mercy' this clarity and control slip away into an obscure alley, dragged there by the lyrics. But even 'The Mercy Seat' bears this instability or tension within itself, between the dominance of the 'word' and its disappearance. On the one hand, the chorus is quite clear, largely due to a repetition in which music and words mesh to drive the same message through time and again; on the other hand, the two verses are not at all clear for they are muttered sotto voce. Let us see what we can understand:

> And the mercy seat is waiting
> And I think my head is burning
> And in a way I'm yearning
> To be done with all this measuring of truth.
> An eye for an eye
> A tooth for a tooth
> And anyway I told the truth
> And I'm not afraid to die.

Fifteen times is this chorus repeated over a track that lasts seven and a quarter minutes, albeit with variations as the electric chair heats up and cooks its victim – his head and then the seat burns, glows, smokes, melts, while his blood boils in successive versions of the chorus until we return to the version I have quoted above. And of course the biblical references are laid out before us,[8] the one from the high point of the Yom Kippur ritual of the Hebrew Bible when the blood of the bull is sprinkled over the mercy seat while incense wafts over it (Leviticus 16:11-19, overlaid with the holocaust, the technical terms for burnt offering, in Leviticus 1), and the other from the law of blood guilt – an eye for an eye, a tooth for a tooth.

Nonetheless, if we want a closer engagement with the Bible, then it comes in the only other words of the song that are legible:

> I hear stories from the chamber
> How Christ was born into a manger
> And like some ragged stranger
> Died upon the cross
> And might I say it seems so fitting in its way
> He was a carpenter by trade
> Or at least that's what I'm told...
> In Heaven His throne is made of gold
> The ark of his Testament is stowed
> A throne from which I'm told
> All history does unfold.

Down here it's made of wood and wire
And my body is on fire
And God is never far away.

Here the mercy seat, or ark of the covenant, of Leviticus 16:13, Christ's manger and cross, his throne in heaven, and the electric chair all merge into one. But two items stand out: these verses are sung with exactly the same melody and musical sequence of the chorus I quoted earlier. Are they verses or chorus? They are sung with the melody of the chorus but their content is not at all that of the chorus. Above all, they can be clearly understood. Second, it is precisely when the lyrics are clear – here assisted by the music – that the references remain distinctly christological. Word and 'Word', if I may put it that way, remain tightly bound together.

That bond begins to unravel with two songs, one a version of Cave's obsession with the story of John the Baptist (see also the comments on the play 'Salomé' above [Cave 1997b: 69–75]): 'Mercy' takes on the voice of John while in prison awaiting his call before Herod to answer the gruesome request of Herodias' daughter (see also McCredden 2009: 174). The immediate biblical texts, as noted earlier, are Matthew 14:1-12, Mark 6:14-29 and Luke 9:7-9, but in this song the words continually slip out of recognition in John's plaintive lament. Cave recovers himself every now and then before the words disappear yet again. In the other song, the hymn-like 'New Morning', with its eschatological evocation of the promise of a new day, we take a step further, for here only the occasional word emerges from the mix to make some sense.

Everything comes apart, however, with 'City of Refuge' – a stark contrast with 'The Mercy Seat'. If 'The Mercy Seat' holds its own against the instability that interests me, and if 'Mercy' begins to give way, then 'City of Refuge' brings it to the fore with a vengeance. On the first hearing or two, one's impression is that the song is merely one long repetition of the refrain 'You better run, You better run, You better run to the City of Refuge' (I have lost count of how many times it recurs). On repeated listening, I did detect a few verses, but the only way to make sense of them is... yes, to look at the lyrics. Like 'The Mercy Seat', 'City of Refuge' is a close engagement with the Bible. The key text is Numbers 35, where the legislation for the cities of refuge is laid out at some length: 'When you cross the Jordan into the land of Canaan, then you shall select cities to be cities of refuge for you, that the manslayer who kills any person without intent may flee there' (Numbers 35:10-11). Various situations in which one might involuntarily cause death follow. The cities' role is to short-circuit the blood guilt – the need to avenge a death with another death. But echoes of the cities of refuge run through Exodus 21:12-13, Joshua 20 and 1 Kings 1:50-53; 2:28-31.

As far as the song itself is concerned, the incessant repetition of 'You better run' evokes the urgency of flight. A mournful mouth-organ begins the song, being joined by an acoustic guitar when the first 'You better run' comes through in a slow and soft voice. A crescendo of flight builds with bass, drums and chunky rhythm guitar joined by multiple desperate voices as the flight gains momentum. One can feel the massing chase behind the refugee – at this point he or she may as well be a slave, an ancient Israelite fleeing blood guilt or indeed a refugee seeking safe harbour from a war-ravaged Middle East that suffers under the weight of Western imperialist forces out to secure dwindling oil supplies. However, apart from the incessant chorus, the verses are illegible: they evoke apocalyptic scenes of standing 'before your maker', stained with the blood of crime and darkness, or facing the final 'days of madness' when even graves will no longer be places of rest. Yet, in order to understand the lyrics one must resort to the printed version. In the sung version, the overwhelming effect is the *absence of lyrics*: they are negated both by unceasing repetition and by sliding into the background of the music mix.

I mentioned earlier that this loss of clarity manifests an instability in Cave's control over the material, showing up but a partial control that always threatens to slip away. But what has happened to the two other features – autobiography and Christology – closely enmeshed with this effort at control? These songs deal with biblical narratives – mostly Hebrew Bible but also John the Baptist – and not the favoured New Testament stories of Christ characteristic of Cave's most explicit biblical engagements. In other words, these biblical engagements lose the distinctly christological focus of those autobiographical moments; when the words disappear, so do the christological references and autobiography. While we might attribute one or the other absence to the particular instance of the song, the loss of all three at once is rather spectacular, especially in light of the way they mesh so closely in much of Cave's material.

Conclusion, or, Strategies of Containment

> It was a world I'd invented which I could escape into. (Cave in Nine 1997)

So what are we to make of this chink in Nick Cave's formidable armour? He overwhelms us with a potent mix of word, autobiography and Christology, and it takes some time to find the break, the gradual unravelling that I have traced in *Tender Prey*. I have made it quite clear that I am less than comfortable with the authorial Cave, the Cave for whom the 'Word' is central, who directs our interpretation via his christological autobiography.

But rather than letting that discomfort determine my response, let me sit down with Nick Cave and discuss with him his relation with the Bible, particularly his modes of interpreting that curious collection of texts. What might the results of that discussion be? Assuming he is making some active, conscious effort to interpret the Bible, then what kind of interpretation is it? It by no means falls in with any of the known canons of biblical interpretation, ranging from scholarly work in all its myriad ways through sermons to popular re-readings. He is entirely idiosyncratic in his use of the Bible and indeed theology.

As a way of dealing with this apparent unconventionality, I would like to focus on the chink in Cave's authorial control traced above, a chink that takes us in two directions.[9] To begin with, it seems to me that the break signals the presence of what might be called, to borrow a term from Fredric Jameson (1981), a 'strategy of containment'. Such a strategy is basically a comprehensive ideological effort at cohesiveness and control – hence containment. The catch is that such control relies on a range of items that must be excluded in order to maintain the impression of control and cohesion. For example, in the continual effort of capitalist societies to maintain the impression of social cohesion, any challenge to the dominant order must be labelled variously as criminal, mentally disturbed, eccentric and so on. To admit that it was actually organized opposition, or even constitutive resistance, to social cohesion would be tantamount to admitting that there is no cohesion in the first place. As far as the interpretation of Nick Cave's music is concerned, such a strategy sets parameters, opens up certain possibilities and closes down others. That is, it indicates the various means by which an authorial voice sets the agenda for interpretation, which it can manage only by blocking out other possibilities.

As I argued above, Cave attempts to control interpretation of his engagement with the Bible by means of a potent mix of autobiography, the dominance of the (sung and written) word and Christology (the authorial Word *par excellence*). He gives the impression that everything that needs to be said about his work may be said within the confines of this triumvirate. But this strategy of containment also has its limits; it closes down other possibilities and gives the impression of providing all of the possible moves that might be made. And so the breaks in such a strategy become crucial, signalling not merely that a strategy of containment is in operation but also where it is inadequate. And the crack in Cave's effort at comprehensive control shows up in those songs on *Tender Prey*, where the lyrics by and large disappear behind the music. This break signals the limits of Cave's own effort at control or containment.

The immediate response to the break in his control would be to take the opposite position – an anti-authoritative one. This can have many versions, such as the search for a Derridean realm beyond the text, or intertextual free play, or Negri's constitutive resistance, or a call to move beyond the Church or indeed any religious system and institution that has a stake in controlling interpretation, or an anarchist move, in all the best senses of the word. And we might be tempted to see the chink in Cave's authorial armour as indicating such a move. I could point out that for all Cave's polemic against the Church, such anarchy is precisely what he fears.

Yet such a response still falls into the logic of that which it opposes: quite simply one rejects the authoritative voice in order to slip in another. There is, however, a second option that opens up with the breakdown of Cave's authorial control. Again the crucial point is what that chink designates. That soft underbelly of Cave's control over meaning indicates, I would suggest, the conditions that make a strategy of containment like Cave's possible in the first place. What are those conditions? The answer to that question – liberalism and the music industry's ideology of authenticity – will have to wait until the chapter on Christology.

2 The Total Depravity of Cave's Literary World

> All they wanted was the usual holiday snap of hell.
> (Cave in Nine 1997)

My primary concern in this chapter is the imaginary world of Nick Cave's literature rather than his music and song-writing, a world whose unifying theme may best be understood in terms of that irreproachable Calvinist doctrine of total depravity. The argument, therefore, has two overlapping features: to outline the contours of this relatively consistent world through the variety of his literature; and to explore how the theological doctrine of total depravity functions, inadvertently,[1] both as the consistent theme of that world and as the trigger for undeserved redemption. In what follows, I simultaneously construct the framework of that world – in terms of the deranged house of incest, substance abuse, the spread of depravity to nature itself and the way the Bible is woven into that world – and fill in its content from the full range of Cave's literature, albeit with a focus on the novels. As that world gains some body, its dialectical relation to redemption begins to emerge, although with a problematic twist.

Before proceeding, three preliminary comments require attention concerning Cave's literature, the imaginary worlds of literature and the doctrine of total depravity. To begin with, my focus here is primarily Cave's literature rather than his music. Although one or two songs will appear in my discussion, I treat them in this case as poems, as lyrics without music. The justification for doing so is not only that his song lyrics often function as poetry in their own right,[2] but that he has also written a reasonable amount of poetry per se. My main concern, however, is the array of literary production outside the music. This includes poetry, scattered plays (usually very short, miniatures if you will), short stories, a film-script or two, the occasional essay, or rather public lecture, since these essays are really performance pieces, and – above all – two very different novels, *And the Ass Saw the Angel* (Cave 1989) and *The Death of Bunny Munro* (Cave 2009).[3]

Further, by an imagined world I mean a constructed, literary world characteristic of certain types of fiction. Science fiction and fantasy construct, as a central generic feature, alternative worlds, often in a distinctly physical sense. Cave's literature belongs to neither genre, but I take the uncontested position that fiction as such creates an imagined world, no matter how much it may resemble our own, into which it invites the reader. Finally, I understand the notion of total depravity in a distinctly Calvinist sense: since we have sinned and fallen short of the glory of God, we are utterly and totally depraved and damned (see Calvin, *Inst.* 1.4.1–4; 1.5.11–15 and especially 2.1–5; *OS* 3:40–44, 55–60, 228–320).[4] We can do nothing good or worthwhile on our own, let alone take any steps towards our own salvation. For that we need God and his grace, which comes to us in our depravity and the recognition thereof. Why such a heavily theological tone in the organizing category of Cave's literature? As anyone who has read it will know, and indeed as this book makes clear, theology is never far from the surface in Cave's work, albeit a theological perspective with Cave's own unique, individualist and heretical twist, informed in its language and thought forms by the Bible.

Cave World

> A world full of retribution and desire and violent, vengeful gods.
> (Calkin 2001)

Given the disparate and dispersed nature of Cave's literary production, how can one argue for a consistent imaginative world? In form and substance the various products seem far apart. *And the Ass Saw the Angel* and *The Death of Bunny Munro* (hereafter *Ass* and *Bunny Munro*), for instance, hardly seem to have been written by the same writer: the former is overdone and forced, with too much alliteration and packed with rare words (Cave apparently surrounded himself with dictionaries, old books and Bibles as he wrote in order to find a bag-full of new terms [Tavolodo and Tamas 1997]).[5] Indeed, it shows many of the effects of trying too hard and yet losing his nerve with a first novel, opting out for the omniscient narrator's voice where the first person narrative becomes too much of a challenge.[6] By contrast, *Bunny Munro* is sparse and fast, free from many of its forebear's dense flaws, but now falling into the trap of having been written a little too rapidly. In short, while the earlier novel is the product of a heroin addict and alcoholic, the later work is the slightly frenetic product of one who has given up even his beloved cigarettes.[7]

At other moments, they draw closer to one another, as with the sudden experience of turning a page in a novel and feeling as though one is in the midst of one of Cave's songs (for example, see Cave 1989: 137),[8] or even the sense that a novel like *Bunny Munro* is really a ballad that has broken out of its formal restrictions to become a different genre. So too do the variegated productions merge in terms of the imaginary world Cave creates. Despite its different names – the Ukulore Valley, the very English seaside town of Bunny

Munro, the plains and mountains of the film *The Proposition*, or even the emergency ward of the Star of Bethlehem Hospital (Cave 1988a: 73) or the racetrack home of Golden Horn Hooligan (Cave 1988a: 76–77) – the contours of a distinct and continuous world begin to appear. Not a world, however, to which one willingly escapes, for it is grim, deranged, fevered, stark, sordid, violent, treacherous and perverse, in short, utterly depraved.

Often it overlaps with our own world, a few items pushed a little further yet still recognizable, but at other moments it is a strange world that seems a distant country or perhaps another planet from our own. For example, in the spare *Bunny Munro* that world may well be any seaside town, perhaps an English one like the Brighton in which Cave himself lives. But then its similarity begins to fray: Munro drinks enough to kill himself from toxic shock; he is impossibly successful with women, engaged in gratuitous sex with floppy-arsed waitresses, tattooed pussies, nymphomaniac housewives, worn out and slack-mouthed prostitutes and semi-conscious and painfully skinny addicts on page after page,[9] although the way his charm becomes unstuck is a sign of his own unravelling; the idyllic seaside township with which the novel opens is but an illusion, for soon the eerily heavy apocalyptic rain comes, a serial killer gradually makes his way towards the town, the apartment blocks turn out to be drearily filthy and poor, the people blasted by fate, substance abuse, poverty and a complete lack of altruism.

On other occasions that world is even much further away. In Cave's over-cooked *Ass* it becomes a separate valley, distant both physically and experientially. It does have vague hints of the southern USA, mingled in with some distinctly Australian outback themes and a touch of Brazil (Sonn 1992), and its sense of being another world is explicitly enhanced by both the narrative of pilgrimage, at the direction of the prophet Jonas Ukulore, and the name of the valley, which is of course Ukulore. The inhabitants themselves are Ukulites, or at least those who are faithful to the words and directions of the prophet and his successors. An old and still successful literary ploy, the remote valley enables Cave to create a perverse backwoods world. Here is the town of somewhat devout but self-serving faithful, usefully sitting on a gold mine of sugar cane production (so lucrative that when – back in the early days – the prophet Jonas received a new vision to move yet again he was shot by an unknown sniper and his slick brother Joseph, with a quick eye for profits rather than prophets, took over the leadership). Other cane workers – drunks, drug addicts, mean bastards and bitches – come into the valley during harvest time, but the Ukulites form the core of a larger, if somewhat isolated, whole. This valley is also home to the feared and revered swamp. Located at the northern end, the swamp is a space of mythological creatures of fearsome proportions; the Ukulites firmly believe that the swamp would belch forth and swallow them up should they veer from the straight and narrow. Children are beaten into psychological submission by threats about the evil swamp, hardened cane workers tell stories about it in hushed whispers around a late fire after a slug of White Jesus too many, and the fearful populace crowd into the valley's southern reaches to avoid the swamp. Close by the swamp, at the northern edge of town, slightly up the hill, is Euchrid's home, itself isolated, a place of 'idjats'. But more of that later.

Other elements of Cave's world coalesce from the scattered moments of his writing. It may be the junkyard sex of the petrol station waitress and the drifter (Cave 1988a: 75), the mad priest who chops off four of his remaining sinful fingers one by one (Cave 1988a: 68–70), or the masturbatory scene of death and sensuality in his short play on John the Baptist and Salomé (Cave 1988a: 88–92). And in the film, *The Proposition* (Hillcoat 2005), that world is once again remote, violent, riddled with utmost sinfulness and is almost irredeemable.[10] Despite the obvious effort to locate it in frontier Australia in the early days of the English penal settlement, with its stressed superintendent, Captain Stanley, the outlaw Burns brothers, brutal soldiers and wily Aborigines, the feel of that world is remarkably similar to *Ass*. No heroes here, only victims; a world pervaded by perverse deals (a 'proposition' in which the commander holds and punishes the youngest Burns brother in order to entice his psychopathic older brother out of hiding in the hills), sheer brutality, the harshest environment and a pervasive presence of flies. In short, this world is one of utter sinfulness and degeneracy, whether in the film or novels or snippets of other pieces.

That House on the Edge of Town

A carnival of the obscene and the absurd. (Johnston 1996: 71)

For my sins (and like Cave), I too grew up in a small Australian country town. Or rather, I grew up in a number of them, for my father moved often as a clergyman, first in the Reformed and then the Presbyterian Churches. Orange, Braidwood, Tumbarumba, Maitland, Terrigal, Gloucester – the names all speak of my father's utopian country parish, one in which the members were devout and faithfully read their Bibles, which they knew deeply and intimately. Always searching, he never found it, for the people who were part of small country churches were members for a range of reasons, most of which my father deemed to be not genuine.

But I remember that house on the edge of town. Poor, teeming with adults, teenagers, children, cats, dogs, chickens, the odd sheep, goat and cow (for milk and whatever), all dressed with hand-me-downs or charity from the opportunity shops, somewhat dull-eyed and lantern-jawed. The children would drop out of school early and go to work at the most menial jobs in town. Sometimes the adults drank, sometimes not; sometimes they came to church, mostly not. But the rumours were well established: they were in-breds, those Mallerbys. It all began with a brother and sister, people would say, who are now the grandparents. A few strange kids, the father fucking his daughters and producing yet more, the sons each other and their sisters, so that by now it was a hopeless mix. As kids ourselves, we kept away, casting looks from a distance when one of the Mallerbys rode by on a bicycle. In another town it might have been the MacInnerneys, or the Winchesters, or the Smiths, but the story was largely the same. The fact that the Department of Community Services finally decided that the cosy secrets of country towns were less than healthy and put the children of these families into care suggests a glimmer of truth in the old rumours.

My perspective was always that of an outsider; in *Ass* (on which I focus more closely now) Cave attempts to provide an insider's view through the – mostly – first person of Euchrid Eucrow. Scion of the notoriously depraved Morton family – which boasted the green-toothed cannibalistic highway robber, Toad or 'Black' Morton, among its number, a string of Old Testament names such as Ezra, Nun and Gad, all part of a family tree that was 'as twisted and tangled as the briars that tortured the hills' (Cave 1989: 20) – his father Ezra had changed his surname to Eucrow to escape the local version of the Department of Community Services: Sheriff Cogburne's 'clean-up' campaign. With an ear shot off and a mule as his only help, Ezra had staggered into the arms of the fastest lush in the West, Crow Jane (herself the title of a song by Cave from the *Murder Ballads* album [Cave 1996b]).[11]

Ezra and Jane's only surviving son, Euchrid, is mostly the first-person narrator of our story, his brother having died soon after childbirth. Mute, bent in his back, given to visions of angels and hearing the word of God in his ear, Euchrid remains relatively 'normal' for much of the novel. An outcast in town, persecuted for his abnormality, Euchrid's handicaps are also the source of his special powers – an ability to communicate with animals, a stealth that sees him slip about town as the consummate voyeur, the ability to enjoy his own company. Here too is a hint of what may be called the dialectic of depravity, for only in Euchrid's incest-bred 'idjacy' does he gain these powers. That dialectic will lift itself to a whole new level as the novel reaches its sordid and deranged conclusion.

One trigger for that unravelling, in which Euchrid goes completely mad and thereby sets in train an ambiguous redemption, comes when his father kills his mother in a moment of sheer exasperation and then dies later when he 'falls' into the tank of wild and venomous beasts – those which his father has trapped and collected finally undo him. Euchrid begins fall to pieces: he traps like his father and drinks from his mother's moonshine-still – the proverbial White Jesus that rips the back out of one's throat. Arguably, the madness is enhanced by another trigger: the fact that the townspeople had destroyed his one sanctuary, his creative centre deep in the swamp, where he kept his weird and wonderful collection of keepsakes, the precious detritus of a life on the edge of madness. That sanctuary will return a little later, under my discussion of eschatological madness, so it will keep.

The locus of this crazy, well-nigh apocalyptic onslaught with its redemptive edge is that same house on the edge of town. What was simply a rundown shack on a muddy hill is now transformed into a deranged fortress – Doghead (a play on Godhead and perhaps God's kingdom [Wiseman-Trowse 2009: 164]). Unable to bear the thought of living in the same house in which he cowered from his mother's drunken rages and in which she was killed by his father, unable, in fact, to live with the enthusiasm with which he greeted her death, Euchrid guts the inside of the house, leaving only its shell. Within the house he sleeps on a filthy pile of rags, surrounded by the decaying carcases of animals he had trapped, swarms of blowflies and uncured skins hanging from the ceiling. Surrounding the house he creates a new sanctuary to replace the one destroyed in the swamp, a makeshift fortress protected both by a complex pattern of booby-traps and a watchtower he occupies during his waking hours. Wearing an old sea-captain's coat and a scythe in his belt, unwashed and perpetually drunk on White Jesus, Euchrid watches the town through the captain's telescope.

In a depraved world, in a depraved valley, that house on the edge of town is the most depraved of all.

A Slug of White Jesus

> But what it does is shut everything down, and other people can't get in, and I can't really tolerate that for any length of time. Having life robbed of its detail. (Cave in Robinson 1998)

> I take it to shut things down. (Cave in Paytress 1998)

Given the range of addictions explored by Cave – erstwhile heroin addict, heavy drinker and chain smoker (all of which he has given up) – it comes as no surprise that substance abuse is another telling marker of the pervasive depravity and dissoluteness of his world. That abuse is the defining feature of so many characters, if not the perpetual concern of his earlier literary output. We find it in the first-person account, set among lowlifes in a graveyard of trains, of a bender with 'Maine Kelly' (Cave 1988a: 74); or perhaps the bar-room setting for the murder ballads 'Stagger Lee' and 'O'Malley's Bar' (Cave 1996b); or the fond farewell embodied in the poem 'The Sweetest Embrace' (Cave 1997b: 178–79). In *Ass*, Euchrid's mother – 'a piss-eyed hell-bag with a taste for the homebrew' (Cave 1989: 14) – seems to supply the whole valley from her three stills, Apple Jack, White Jesus and Stew – in descending order of drinkability and cost. She seems to make her living selling the stuff to the hobos and drunks and cane cutters and any lowlife who cares to have a swig or three. Eventually, Euchrid too will gain a liking for his mother's favourite, White Jesus, slugging from the earthenware bottle just as she had done.

The only characters in *Ass* who do not rely on Crow Jane's wicked brews are the Ukulites, but then they are caught up in a far more vicious addiction to a perverse and stark religious cult, a cult that has obvious echoes with the American predilection for visions, prophets and new religious movements, but one that for me evokes the world described by E. P. Thompson (1993) in seventeenth- and eighteenth-century England. Here we find the Moravians, Irregular Methodists, Seekers, Universalists, Quakers, Fifth Monarchy Men, Philadelphians, French Camisards, Sandemanians, Hutchinsonians, Sabbatarians, Seventh-Day Men, Thraskites, Adamists, Brownists, Tryonists (vegetarians), Salmonists, Heavenly-Father-Men, Children of the New Birth, Sweet Singers of Israel and Thompson's favourites, the Muggletonians (see also Hill *et al.* 1983). Not only would the Ukulites fit in well with these groups, but the propensity for prophet after prophet also fits the bill.

The Ukulites may be the opposite of the insipid and lukewarm religion that Cave recalls and rejects from his days as a choirboy in Warrnambool (a country town on the south coast of Victoria), but that does not mean he endorses their perverse and sexually repressive enthusiasm. Or rather, he can understand the seduction, the gullibility, the inability to break free, the promise of a quick fix to the knot of life's problems, even the close-knit and self-perpetuating community of addicts. Here Cave agrees with the misinterpretations of Marx's famous comment (1975 [1844]: 176) concerning opium: religion – or at least this version of it – is a drug. Or to put it in terms of the novel itself, they too swill massive drafts of their own version of White Jesus.

Alcohol also sloshes its way through *Bunny Munro*, who drinks himself into a state of complete collapse and ultimate death. Sundry other products appear as well: with his sleeping tablets, uppers for the morning, chain-smoking and swilling his way from pussy to pussy, Bunny is an addict of the first order. The difference is that by now Cave himself, father of twin boys, as well as two sons from former relationships (Jethro and Luke), had kicked all his habits, replacing them with a frenetic pace of artistic production. And so now the convoluted glimmer of redemption in *Ass* becomes in *Bunny Munro* a full-blown redemptive conclusion with its own twist.

Rain in the Valley

> The emotional shredland where primitive passion slashes razor sharp with the heart's deepest desires and fears. (Gee 1997a)

> Rain and madness. (Cave in Sonn 1992)

But we are not ready to be redeemed quite yet... The human beings in *Ass* may be incestuously tortured, physically and psychically deformed (not merely Euchrid and his clan, but also the prophet Jonas and his band of Ukulites), yet Cave is deeply true to another dimension of the theological doctrine of total depravity: human sin also affects the natural world of which we are a part. I think not merely of the animals trapped and kept, often with a limb missing, by Euchrid and his father Ezra before him, of the way they are starved to death, nor even of the high-pitched whine of flies that attend their corpses towards the end of the novel or that dominate the sound-track of *The Proposition*[12] – a mark of the biblical Beelzebub, the Lord of the Flies, which was itself a derisive pun on the Canaanite god, Baal Zebul.

Above all, the signs of natural depravity in *Ass* are the swamp and the rain. As we saw earlier, the swamp looms large in the novel, a place of fear and dread for most, but of blessed escape and visions for Euchrid. Fumes and gases, plants that wetly slap and grasp, ancient 'treasures' belched forth from time to time, new ones taken: the swamp is not so much a mono-valent sign of total depravity as a sign of its ambivalence. Evil and sucking (quick-sand) it might be and have, but once one recognizes that we are all utterly and totally depraved, then the swamp becomes a refuge, a place of self-awareness and the possibility of meeting God. Euchrid seems to know, momentarily, that he cannot do a thing to save himself. At that moment the angel comes to him, deep in the swamp, a wisp of light air, goodness and redemption.

Another dimension of moisture is equally ominous and equally inscrutable: the rain. Neither seasonal nor monsoonal, the rain is so dominant that it becomes the name of the first part of *Ass*. For three years, from 1941–43, the heavens empty out, destroying crops and lives, chasing all but the most faithful from the valley. The wise investments of Joseph Ukulore ensured that the sect members would, during hard times, all have incomes for three years (the mythical, biblical term of famine), but that does stop them beating themselves to find the source of their sin, the women, semi-naked, flagellating themselves on the streets, the men deep in personal remorse. But the rain stays and people gradually begin to lose hope. Once again, nothing they do seems to help. The mad preacher, Abie Poe, comes and goes with his message of utter sinfulness, the need for repentance and foolish promises of an end to the rain.[13] The townsfolk round on the prostitute whom all the men enjoy and whom Euchrid loves, Cosey Mo, but still the rain buckets down. Finally, the break comes from entirely outside human agency: a crippled woman (Cosey Mo after her lynching) leaves a baby, Beth, at the feet of the prophet's memorial. For no apparent or fathomable reason, Beth's arrival signals the end of the rain. The Ukulites believe she has brought redemption and treat her so. But not the readers, for we are by no means left with the impression that she is the real cause.

Bible

> A chilly thing. The Bible. Sometimes. (Cave 1989: 130)

As I have indicated in the previous chapter, the reader of Cave's literature – and indeed the careful listener to his songs – cannot miss the pervasive presence of the Bible. Of course, the title of *And the Ass Saw the Angel* comes from Numbers 22,[14] and the text of Balaam's encounter with his long-suffering and ultimately wordy ass opens the book as an epigraph. (Cave reputedly read the Bible incessantly while writing the novel.) As we wind our slow path to the dialectic of redemptive depravity, I focus on two features of Cave's in-depth encounter with the Bible. One deals with form (lamentations of woe), and the other with content (the calling of eschatological madness).

Lamentations of Woe

> 'To eat at the same ball of vomit year after year.' (Cave in Sullivan 1998)

Apart from an incessant creativity, Cave shares another close bond with Bertholt Brecht. In a newspaper interview in 1928 Brecht was asked, 'what book has made the strongest impression on you in the course of your life?' His answer: 'You're going to laugh: the Bible [Sie werden lachen: die Bibel]' (Jameson 1998: 162). For Brecht, the answer applies as much to content as to form. In Cave's case, *Ass* is one of his most biblically influenced literary creations. Here we stumble across direct quotations from the Bible, such as Psalms 29 and 58, as well as a text from the prophet Isaiah (Cave 1989: 173, 159–60 and 149). But the more intriguing moments are those textual pieces that bear traces of their biblical models. Thus, the descriptions of women (for example, Cave 1989: 124), both positive and – so often for Cave – negative, have echoes of the Song of Songs, especially those texts that describe allegorically a woman's body (Song of Songs 4:1-5; 5:10-16; 7:1-5).

But I am most interested in those that slide towards depravity, such as the mock (biblical) patriarchal narrative in the early pages of *Ass*. Not so much Abraham, Isaac, Jacob and Joseph from the biblical book of Genesis, but now the twisted clan story of Ezra Morton-cum-Eucrow: 'And Ezra, son of Nun, went down into the valley' (Cave 1989: 21), it begins, before going on to tell how Ezra escaped the clan curse with a mule for company, how he finished off a bottle of moonshine only to find his ear shot away, slumped faint upon his mule's back, and was then revived by none other than the sozzled Crow Jane.

Degenerate, too, is the preaching of the fragile prophet Abie Poe (who bears an echo of the younger Cave of the Birthday Party days, who would walk on stage, open his mouth and 'let the curse of God roar' [Cave 1997b: 138]). That language draws heavily on biblical models of prophetic condemnation and apocalyptic expectation, pushed now to a ludicrous degree (but still, I hate to admit, perfectly recognizable in preachers of our own day). Above all, the abjection of Euchrid appears in the 'The Lamentations of Euchrid the Mute'. Interspersed at four moments close to the centre of the novel, Euchrid narrates, sequentially, an experience of pack rape by three boys, his multitude of deformities, being beaten up and chased out of town, and finally the deepest burden of all, his mother, who was 'mah true and unspeakable foe' (Cave 1989: 108–109, 113, 118–19, 122–23). Modelled on the biblical book of Lamentations, which was purportedly uttered by the prophet Jeremiah after the fall of Jerusalem in 587 BCE, Cave's own lamentations also show a deep trace of the book of Job, which has intrigued more than its share of creative and literary figures. In *Ass*, the effect of the lamentations is not only to register the bewilderment of Euchrid as to his lot in life, but also the brutal and sordid ordinariness of his afflictions.

The Calling of Eschatological Madness

'The father of the antichrist maybe.' (Rollins in Barber 1997)

On one feature of utter dissoluteness both *Ass* and *Bunny Munro* could not agree more: it involves the life-wrecking spiral into madness, a madness that ushers in the end of the world. But the novels are by no means the only time Cave deals in such insanity. Many of the perversely appealing characters on the *Murder Ballads* album are presented from the inside, the psyches of serial killers chillingly and amusingly intimate – Stagger Lee, Loretta of Millhaven, but even more intimately the unnamed first persons of 'Song of Joy' and 'O'Malley's Bar' (Cave 1996b)[15] in which the killer narrates his own mad rampage. Here, of course, musical and literary production overlap, but eschatological derangement also appears in more strictly literary pieces like 'Golden-Horn-Hooligan', where the racetrack hero speaks, fearfully, of the breath on his neck and the voice in his head, whispering premonitions of his own death in a 'whirring ball of flames' (Cave 1988a: 77), much like the debilitating sense of doom expressed by the sweating and anxious Ex-Valentine in 'American-Speedway-Fever-Trash' (Cave 1988a: 78–79).

As far as *Ass* is concerned, I have already commented above on the way the derangement of Euchrid is triggered as much by the death of his parents as by the destruction of his creative sanctuary in the swamp (at the hands of the town's men), but here I would like to comment on four features: the sanctuary itself; the connection with a sense of calling and the imminence of predestination; the eschatological nature of that madness; and the overwhelmingly individual focus of that eschaton.

The swamp-sanctuary is Euchrid's last refuge of creative sanity. Constructed from moss, branches, odds and ends of cardboard and tin, within Euchrid stores his collections of old bones, shells, pieces of soiled bandage (coming from the time when he tried to ascertain whether his blood was black or red), parts from Cosey Mo's destroyed caravan, along with tresses of her hair, a picture stolen from the church of her daughter Beth.[16] And the destruction of that sanctuary, free as it was from the rants of his mother and taunts of the townsfolk, becomes a fulcrum for the novel. Here the doubled description of its destruction serves to underline its importance. On nearly every other occasion in the novel, the resort to a third-person narrative signals a loss of nerve on Cave's part, a fall-back when the first-person point-of-view becomes too difficult. But not here (Cave 1989: 140–45), for we read first of the destruction from Euchrid's frantic description and then from the perspective of a detached observer of the town's menfolk, who happen upon the sanctuary while chasing a spooked horse. Not a little of Cave himself is to be found in Euchrid, seeking desperately a way to give voice to his irrepressible creativity: 'For me, Euchrid is Jesus struck dumb, he is the blocked artist, he is internalised imagination become madness' (Cave 1997b: 141). It would not be the first time Cave has compared himself to Jesus (see Chapter 1), or at least seen himself reflected in the creative genius of Jesus in the New Testament. But unlike Euchrid, Cave seems to have managed to forestall bursting like a creative blocked pipe.

Yet Euchrid does burst, becoming soon enough 'the mad king of Doghead' (Cave 1989: 178). It is an explosion tied in closely with a profound sense of calling, itself not without a few overtones of predestination. Throughout the novel, we find variations on the theme that Euchrid is on a divinely appointed mission, one that fits in with God's greater plan: 'Only the Great One, in all his omnipotence, could have foreseen how crucial it was that ah, His Servant, His cog, should break the lock and lift the lid…and in God's measured time, expose the core of mah calling' (Cave 1989: 43). Not only does he take on the task of John the Baptist, a mediator for the messiah (on this score Beth mistakenly sees Euchrid first as God and then as Christ [Cave 1989: 222–24]), but that sense grows in direct proportion to the snowball of Euchrid's madness. The problem, of course, is that myriad deranged people have claimed such a status. How many occupants of psychiatric hospitals claim to be Jesus on his second coming? How many paranoids fear they have done something that will destroy the world and thereby need to do something to avert the disaster? For that matter, how many Hollywood films are thereby paranoid? Cave's genius here is to examine this hoary question from a fresh angle, to trouble the simple attributions to madness of such claims, indeed, like Foucault, to trouble the category of madness itself.

However, when we come to our third feature of Euchrid's madness – its eschatological nature – we also return to the underlying theme of total depravity, for his decline into insanity is inseparable from a wider sense of impending doom. In other words, the personal is also collective; the imminent end of one is also the end of the other. In *Ass*, of course, the collective is represented by the community in the Ukulore Valley. But how is this connected with the doctrine of total depravity? In the same way such sinfulness pervades the whole of history, society and nature, so also does Euchrid's eschatological madness sweep that very same history, the same society and the same nature into its orbit.

Similarly in *Bunny Munro*, where Bunny's spiralling madness also functions like the doctrine of sin, it is not restricted to that particular human being, Bunny Munro, but it leaks in to affect the whole realm of nature. Bunny may be drinking, smoking and fucking his way to death, but other humans also become more and more depraved as the novel goes on – listless hooded teenagers in desolate blocks of flats, overweight and over-drugged colleagues, the junkyard of a junkie's house with whom he has his last screw. Overwhelmed too by the pervasive affect of depravity is the ageing, spluttering car, the Punto, as is the serial killer dressed as the devil who descends upon this brittle coastal idyll, as is nature: the apocalyptic wind and rain lash the town with impossible speeds and volumes, until the (imagined?) lightning flash that sears Bunny's soul at the close of the story. The effect – at this level Cave succeeds – is to make the reader feel as though the world as a whole is coming apart.

Finally, it is a very individual madness, an individual depravity, an individual eschatology. Rain and storms may come, killers may descend, the valley may slide inexorably towards a climactic destruction, nature may be responsible for one's deformities, history itself may be enlisted, but it begins with and centres around an individual, whether Euchrid Eucrow or Bunny Munro. In other words, the extra-personal features I have traced – the way nature seems swept up into depravity and how history itself spirals into eschatological lunacy – are really extensions of the self, of that still private and sacrosanct individual. At one level this is consistent with total depravity, for it enters into the world through the sin of one man and woman, Adam and Eve. Yet, at another level it is far indeed from this collective personality of biblical myths, for Cave buys deeply into the conventional liberal ideology of the private individual, the ego at the centre of the universe (and Cave's ego is rather large). I will deal more extensively with the creation and history of this sacrosanct individual in Chapter 6, as well as the way Cave's claims to artistic authenticity and heretical path of theological expression fit squarely within this tradition, so I do not need to pre-empt that analysis here, save to point out that Cave is in this respect a good old liberal, a private artist seeking to give voice to his authentic soul. So also with the novels and their eschatological madness, for it is a private madness that sucks nature and history into its orbit.

Conclusion: The Dialectic of Redemptive Depravity

> It has taken all the darkness and guilt of the world on itself. (Adorno 2006 [1949]: 102)

The doctrine of total depravity avers that since we are so utterly sinful, we can do nothing good on our own, indeed that all our efforts to do so only end up being evil in and of themselves. So it is with Cave's world. Perverse, abusive and abused, destroyed by alcohol and drugs, emptily self-serving, frequently violent, sexist, addled with insanity, utterly unattractive; like a 'stream of filth spewed from its nether-regions' (Cave 1989: 49), it is a world Cave depicts again and again. Focused above all on the human individual, it draws the earth and heavens into its utter sinfulness.

But does he offer the possibility of redemption? I have suggested as much above, but now wish to explore three dimensions of that redemption, namely, its ambivalence, dialectical nature and deeply biblical nature. It may have been four dimensions if I had included those instances when no redemption is offered or wanted. Euchrid's cry speaks for them all: 'Ah don't wanna be cleaned! Mah natural state is unclean! Ah am a very filthy being' (Cave 1989:

71). It may apply to the main character in 'Salomé', who is herself so depraved, getting a rise only from the great Freudian couple of sex and death, that she is 'beyond redemption' (Cave 1988a: 88). So too, the poem 'Right Now, I Am A-Roamin' ' (Cave 1997b: 169–71) has the protagonist unable to redeem himself: it matters not whether it involves cleaning up his house, straightening out his affairs, giving up the booze and drugs and eating some food, calling on his mother and cooking her a meal, seeing his little boy or unpacking his bags and washing his rags; none of these will happen just yet, for he has not quite done with roaming. Yet the poem also gives voice to a deeper theological truth, born out in the wonderful text of Paul in Romans 7: no matter how aware he is of sin, how bad it is, how it condemns him under the Law, how it leads to death and destruction, the author still sins, for the seduction is too great:

> For I do not do what I want, but I do the very thing I hate. Now if I do what I do not want, I agree that the law is good. So then it is no longer I that do it, but sin which dwells within me. For I know that nothing good dwells within me, that is, in my flesh. I can will what is right, but I cannot do it. For I do not do the good I want, but the evil I do not want is what I do. Now if I do what I do not want, it is no longer I that do it, but sin which dwells within me. (Romans 7:8-18)

The dialectical genius of Paul's text (and Cave's poem, 'Right Now, I Am A-Roamin', if I may put him in such august company) is that the moment of abjection, of the recognition of one's complete depravity, is precisely when God begins to act.

It may be a very ambiguous and unresolved redemption, but it is the first hint of what would become a full-blooded search in Cave's later works. Thus, in the brief early play called 'The Five Fools' (Cave 1988a: 68–70), the mad priest who carefully and systematically chops off the sinning fingers of his left hand – those of the right already having met a similar fate – leaves behind the thumb. Ostensibly to 'provide warning, punish and intrude' (70), the sole surviving thumb provides a perverse moment of hope and possible redemption, although what that might be is left entirely unresolved. The same may be said of the line 'look to the sky, Daddy-O' in the poem 'There is a Light' (Cave 1997b: 126), for that look skyward in a midst of a drugged-up, gambling underworld offers nothing more than the look itself. In a very different story, 'Bline Lemon Jefferson', redemption takes the form of murdering the overseer and escaping across the Mississippi from Arkansas to Tennessee, albeit not without losing his sight on the way, replaced with 'bran new cataracts small n whit n round like the body of Christ... O Eucharist!... O Sacrament!...wafer thin and holy' (Cave 1988a: 131).

The same applies to *Ass*, where the ambiguous redemption is dialectically consistent with the notion of total depravity, carried off brilliantly through a formal flourish, and deeply biblical. To begin with, the redemption is closely tied up, dialectically, with the depravity of the people, for it comes as a direct and unexpected counterpoise to that depravity. The line of redemption begins with the addicted prostitute, Cosey Mo. Showing up the hypocrisy of the menfolk, beaten and disfigured, yet she bears a child, Beth, who will embody the perverted hopes of the Ukulites. But Beth does not play by the rules, seeing in the peeping Euchrid an embodiment of God and then more specifically Jesus – anathema to the formidable body of women who seek to protect Beth for her expected messianic role. Now the formal flourish comes into play: Euchrid in his growing madness receives a message to kill Beth. He sharpens his sickle, prepares his fortress Doghead for its final destruction and sets out to meet Beth at the appointed hour, when 'ah put mah sickle inside her' (Cave 1989: 242). Dead she seems; Euchrid makes for the quicksand in the swamp and menfolk chase him down to put him to a quick end. But the sickle, as the afterword makes clear, was his cock and not his sharpened blade (hinted at in Beth's earlier 'At last, Jesus, you have come'), and Beth dies while bearing his child, all under the direction of a cripple. Is it Cosey Mo? We do not know and are left guessing. A hint of redemption, yes, undeserved even, but its nature is thoroughly ambiguous.[17]

But what of the biblical echo? Here it is the outcast and maltreated that become the vehicles of redemption, the stone that the builders rejected which has become the cornerstone. As with the biblical prostitute Rahab, so does Cosey Mo become a crucial step in the genealogy of redemption (Rahab features in the genealogy of Jesus in Matthew's Gospel). And her daughter born out of prostitution, Beth, herself becomes pregnant to a filthy, crazy, drunken mute, the child of their union offering the glimmer of ambivalent hope at the close of the novel. Since the depravity is so total, redemption must come from an entirely unexpected quarter.

However, for a full-blooded moment of redemption we must wait 20 years after the publication of *Ass* (in 1989). At the close of *The Death of Bunny Munro* we come across a similar literary tactic – the doubled ending – but now much more clearly with a redemptive agenda. Bunny's mad run to destruction ends when his beaten up Punto runs headlong – in the pouring rain – into a cement-mixer truck; Bunny Junior survives and at first it seems as though Bunny, flung from the truck, survives too. Lightning streaks down, sears him and heals him, giving Bunny time – a long time (from pp. 253–77) – to meet all those he has wronged, take their venom and aggrieved hatred and then apologise, reconciling himself to the world and to himself. And then, when he has achieved reconciliation, he dies. Not once, but twice: first, in the extended scene of reconciliation, he slips slowly into death; second, on the road in the belting rain, the cement-mixer on its side and the Punto smashed, he lies motionless, embraced by a son who now becomes a man.

Yet the very existence of a father–son relationship at the centre of the novel should have alerted us to a redemptive structure. Obviously giving voice to a desperate effort to resolve the trauma of Cave's own complex relationship to his dead father (who died in a car accident when the teenage Cave was being bailed out of prison by his mother), it also speaks of his own relations with his sons, two earlier ones (Jethro and Luke) and the other two – twins – more recently. *Ass* may be an overblown effort to compensate, creatively, for his perception of his father's failed dreams and aborted efforts, especially the failure to write that long-planned novel (see Cave 1997b: 141), but *Bunny* embodies that effort in its very structure: for Bunny Junior is at the accident at which Cave wishes he had been, ready to pick up the mantle of his dead father, cleaned up and detoxed. Indeed, I would argue that Cave's father casts a very long shadow over his work (as Cave's obsessive repetition of the narrative of his father's death and failed literary ambitions shows all too well). Cave's father did not understand or appreciate popular music, let alone the music to which Cave was attracted, and disapproved of Cave's clear love of playing in bands. Of course, for a teenage boy, that would be just the incentive to pursue such a career even more diligently...until he comes to realize that he would never have an opportunity to reconcile with his father over these differences. And so we find Cave, weighed down with guilt and longing, writing more and more in a way that would have gained the approval of his long-dead father.[18]

What are we to make of this growing sense of redemption from a world of total depravity? Has Cave gone soft in his old age, finding solace in religion and responsibility as a parent? Would it have been better to stay with a stark, un-redeemed and depraved world? As should have become clear by now, all of Cave's literary work is in some sense a search for redemption, no matter how small or ambivalent the hint. Yet Cave has also realized that in a depraved world, redemption cannot be achieved on our own, for it must come from beyond human agency.

3 Some Routine Atrocity, or, Apocalyptic

> I saw some ordinary slaughter
> I saw some routine atrocity.
> (Cave 2004a)

Closely related to the total depravity of Cave's literary output is a distinct apocalyptic feel to his music. But what exactly does it mean to describe his music as apocalyptic? I take two paths here: a rather conventional one that outlines the generally agreed upon notions of apocalyptic and one that is far less conventional, for it seeks the way Nick Cave constructs his own apocalyptic world from the building blocks of biblical apocalyptic.[1]

Three Modes

> A vehicle for some of the cruellest...scenarios in music. (Nine 1997)

We can delineate the various senses of apocalyptic rather quickly, since there is reasonable (although never complete) consensus. Three overlapping senses may be identified, referring to genre, worldview and social movement. Originally literary, the genre of apocalyptic refers to a body of knowledge revealed (*apokalupto*) to a chosen person by means of vision, dream or visitation. This knowledge provides an insight into history, especially a future cataclysm in which God is the central player. At this point an ambiguity arises between the technical meaning of apocalypse and its content: scholars insist that it means a revelation, but more widespread usage understands apocalypse as referring to all matters pertaining to the catastrophic end of history with its coded accounts of the vast clashes between the forces of good and evil. I will play with both sides of this ambiguity.

It is worth noting the nature of apocalyptic language within this genre. Heavily metaphorical, saturated with images, deeply mythological, it can be a highly creative genre. Yet all too quickly, these metaphors and images solidify, become items to imitate again and again, and thereby lose their creative edge. Indeed, we can roll off the terms all too easily, especially in light of their deeply biblical heritage – the Beast, the Whore of Babylon, 666, the New Jerusalem and so on. To my mind, the better artists are those for whom apocalyptic does not involve cementing the images in place but in exploring how they move about and generate new connections and possibilities.

A second sense refers to a worldview (see Collins 1997: 7–8; 2001: 25–38), although the better term is ideology, which should be understood in this context as a descriptive or functional term (over against a critical use in which ideology is false consciousness that must be unmasked) designating the necessary ideational and cultural dimension of human existence by which we map our own collective and individual existences into the much vaster context of economic systems and sweeps of history (Barrett 1991: 18–34; Larrain 1983b, 1983a). While we have only two properly apocalyptic texts in the Bible – Daniel and Revelation – and many extra-canonical apocalypses, an apocalyptic worldview permeates some other texts. For instance, some of the Gospel sayings put in the mouth of Jesus (such as Matthew 24, Mark 13 and Luke 21) have a distinctly apocalyptic note, with their revelation of tribulation, war and rumours of war. But what does such an ideology mean? In terms of form, it refers to the way language is used, including the metaphors of an inner group and of conflict, powerful images that frame a world of oppression and miraculous release. In terms of outright content, we find a strong moral opposition between good and evil and a pervasive air of anticipation. The present time of troubles and gloom may be bad, but they have been foreseen and will be short. The inner circle (the 'good') will soon be vindicated in a much hoped for, if somewhat risky, redemption, when the bad will be vanquished. Suffering, pain, death, chosenness, reckoning, faithfulness, vindication – all of these make up an air of heavy anticipation. We might regard the ideology of apocalyptic as providing both a story to live by now and motivation for the future (see Boer 2008).

The final element of apocalyptic is the movement. The power of any piece of literature or ideology lies in the people who gather around it, the people for whom the text or the idea expresses their deepest beliefs, hopes and wishes. Indeed, the first big breakthrough in studies of biblical apocalyptic was the move away from purely literary influence and the use of sociological comparative studies to argue that apocalyptic is characteristic of severely oppressed and disempowered groups (see Wilson 1984). Apocalypse is the last resort, a final effort to make sense of a world that has gone horribly wrong. Jewish apocalyptic emerged when the population of Yehud found itself in a forgotten corner of the Persian and then Hellenistic empires. Later apocalyptic movements, of which there are myriad, followed a similar pattern – whether Joachim of Fiore and those who followed his preaching, Wilhelm Weitling at the time of early communism in the nineteenth century (Haefelin 1986, Hüttner 1985, Knatz 1984, Wittke 1950) or the Jon Frum movement in the Pacific Islands of the twentieth century (Billings 2002, Krieger 1994), to name but three. In this context, one's last hope is in the chariots of God.[2]

This brief sketch is enough to provide me with some compass points for dealing with Nick Cave, especially in terms of biblical apocalyptic. One might pursue the argument that the many fans of Nick Cave actually form an apocalyptic movement, with their charismatic prophet who, through his music and writing, foretells a new age free from all oppression. Then we would have the quaint image of a gathering of Cave fans at an appointed hour awaiting the end of history, if not the Second Coming of Jesus. However, I would suggest that the last category of apocalyptic – the movement – does not actually apply to the work of Cave.

By contrast, the other two categories do apply, albeit with a few twists. It seems to me that many of Cave's songs have a distinct apocalyptic worldview. This is a world or murder, mayhem and atrocity, a grim world of unrelieved pain and sadness – in short, it is saturated with evil. Some of the material may also be described as apocalyptic in genre: in some cases we do have a revelation about a cataclysmic end. The catch is that this revelation usually belongs to a religious crackpot whose persona Cave both creates and inhabits. In all of this, a highly creative process is underway. Old and new apocalyptic images, metaphors and symbols appear, but in unexpected combinations. In the process of drawing creatively upon apocalyptic, Cave transforms it in his own unique fashion.

God's Anger: The Flood

> I was far more acquainted with destructive forces than constructive ones. (Cave in Anonymous 1996)

> All I had to do was walk out on stage and open my mouth and let the curse of God roar through me. (Cave 1997b: 138)

We can roughly map the apocalyptic dimension of Cave's music in terms of three overlapping zones – God's anger, Cave's Trinity and then the Resolution. They overlap in terms of musical form and content as well as in terms of time. The first really comes from Cave himself, for as he once put it, 'all I had to do was walk out on stage and open my mouth and let the curse of God roar through me' (Cave 1997b: 138). As we saw in Chapter 1, in his self-representation, he puts this down to an earlier, angry young man phase, fueled by drugs and alcohol and an exacerbated sense of sadness and rebellion. But let me drag this description away from Cave's autobiography and apply it to the apocalyptic side of his music. This anger is both derived *from* God and directed *at* God. Apart from his early days with the Gothic punk of The Birthday Party, the main aspects of this apocalyptic anger are the continuing anarchic, punk-influenced songs that still appear today, and the thread of murder, mayhem and atrocity that runs through his work. I consider both in turn.

As far as God's anger is concerned, a synoptic view of all of the material written and sung by Nick Cave produces a surprise or two. If we expected the book of Revelation or even Daniel to turn up as the prime source of images, then we are in for a disappointment. Instead, the major apocalyptic source is the story of Noah and the Flood from Genesis 6–9, a story not usually associated with apocalyptic. Yet, in those biblical chapters God speaks directly with Noah, the world is characterized as uncompromisingly evil over against Noah's goodness and we have a catastrophic if somewhat watery end to the world as the basis for a new beginning. In light of Cave's appropriation, if not its implicit use in various catastrophic scenarios today, I would suggest that Genesis 6–9 is an apocalyptic vignette that we often overlook. The fact that it is another creation story, situated within the mythology of Genesis, tends to obscure its apocalyptic concerns. Yet, the story of the Flood touches on both the creation and end of the world, linking myths of origin with apocalyptic myths of the final cataclysm.

The Flood is a recurring motif in a series of songs – 'Tupelo' from *The First Born Is Dead* (Cave 1985), 'Muddy Water' from *Kicking against the Pricks* (Cave 1986a), 'The Carny' from *Your Funeral... My Trial* (Cave 1986b) and 'Papa Won't Leave You Henry' from *Henry's Dream* (Cave 1992).[3] A few comments about the musical form of these songs is needed before considering their content. To begin with, they are all much closer to Cave's anarchic punk roots. With its snarling disharmonies, sheer noise, and the fore-grounding of all those things you are taught not to do as a guitarist, punk was both a moment in that perpetual return to the origins of rock and an effort to undermine it. If we take Jacques Attali's definition of music as organized noise (Attali 1977, 1985), then punk – best understood as a cacophonous assault on the ears – is the least organized of all. Throw in anger, a cocktail of drugs and violent shows in seedy venues and punk starts to gain an apocalyptic edge.

The four Flood songs are heavily indebted to Cave's punk past, good instances of what I will call the anarchic song in Chapter 7. Perhaps the best description is 'post-punk' – a term that basically describes punk rockers if they survive the binge of drugs and alcohol and are able to explore their creative genius for a little longer. Each of the songs is raw and somewhat ragged. Yet, in contrast to the earlier material from days of The Boys Next Door and The Birthday Party, the music of these four songs is a little understated rather than becoming an implement to bash one over the head. That said, the music remains ominous, full of foreboding, fear and threat.

The form turns out to be a fitting partner for the content of the songs, a content that is, with its images and metaphors, a mix of recognizable apocalyptic items from the Bible, such as the Beast, new arrangements and connections such as the Flood story, and then a whole new collection of items that Cave drags in from elsewhere. For instance, with the cover song 'Muddy Water' (Cave 1986a) we encounter the rise of a river over a lowland farm and the end of a poor farmer's livelihood. But it is just a little more cataclysmic than your garden variety inundation: 'This flood will swallow all you've left behind/Won't be back to start all over'. On a slightly more sinister note both 'Papa Won't Leave You, Henry' (Cave 1992) and 'The Carny' (Cave 1986b) spew out a much grimmer image of the watery destruction brought by the flood. In the former, the rains from the 'firmament' (a reference to Genesis 1:7) signal a time of troubles, of 'lynch-mobs, death squads, babies being born without brains'. In 'The Carny' (shorthand for 'carnival worker'), the foreboding that comes with the rains dominates the song. Here the fearful and legendary Carny has slipped away from the freak show with which he was travelling. His departure and the attempt by dwarves called Moses and Noah to bury his old nag (called 'Sorrow') trigger the deluge. The other freaks take shelter in fear, the forlorn ground rapidly floods and the company heads for higher ground. But not before we get a vivid picture of the rising flood:

> The whole valley reeking of wet beast
> Wet beast and rotten soft hay
> Freak and brute creation
> (Cave 1986b)

The best and most sustained example of an apocalyptic flood song is 'Tupelo' (Cave 1985) from the album *The First Born Is Dead* (not the last time a title draws from a biblical theme). The song opens with sounds of thunder, lightning and rain. From beneath the storm rise the driving bass guitar riff and then the drum line that will anchor the song through its howling frenzy. With its jagged guitar cuts and the urgent quavering voice of Cave, it is not a song to which one would relax at the end of the day with one's pipe, slippers and hot chocolate. In fact, I used to turn it on at full blast at the doorways of my teenage sons' rooms if they had slept in. Somehow the song achieved what no alarm clock could do – wake them up. I must admit they cursed me to no end, thumping the 'off' button and returning to bed.

In this song, Cave takes on a mad persona – something he does so well. Here it is a mad preacher from the Mississippi town of Tupelo – variously the birthplace of Elvis Presley and a name of a flowering tree that produces fine honey.[4] For this preacher, the thunderstorm is the first sign of the end of the world, of God's judgement and Jesus' second coming. But the mishmash of biblical texts is both uniquely Cave *and* an extraordinarily good example of precisely this type of preaching. Cave-cum-mad-preacher assume they hold the truth (through a dirty little deal with God), and so, with unique access to divine truth, he proclaims that the storm is *that* storm of the last days. From mundane observations – the hen won't lay and the nag is spooked and crazy – to more ominous signs – black raindrops in which the birds won't fly, a sucked up river in which the fish won't swim – the storm marks the arrival of the Beast himself. Salvation lies with a child born to a poor mother, 'in a clap-board shack with a roof of tin'. But the child's role is ominous. As a scapegoat, he will carry the burden of Tupelo out of town, but he will also be its saviour.

A series of motifs are drawn under the umbrella of the Flood: evil and good, the signs of the end, the final struggle between the Beast who rolls in on thunder and rain and the child who is born to a poor, drunken mother in a shack, the dual scapegoat from the Hebrew Bible. Rather than a secondary item that has been dragged into the apocalyptic fold, the Flood actually becomes the structuring device of an apocalyptic scene. And it functions at the different levels of apocalyptic I traced out earlier: the content of conflict at the end of history, the divine knowledge gained by an insider, and the symbolism of ominous and fearful destruction. But Cave stretches each one, rearranging it to come up with something quite distinct. The history-closing conflict becomes less a coded prediction of events than a nightmare-ridden foreboding. Divine revelation becomes the dubious knowledge of a madman. And the symbolism is a mix of recognizable items (Beast, lethal rain, death), new conjunctions (the Flood) and the wholly new (the freaks, the Carny, the dwarves called Moses and Noah, the babies born without brains and on and on).

All of which should remind us of the pervasive rains in the dense novel *And the Ass Saw the Angel* (Cave 1989), which I discussed in Chapter 2. Not only was the song 'Tupelo' written around the same time as the novel, but we can now see that the ominous mood of apocalyptic finds a ready partner in the total depravity of the novel. In my discussion of the novel, I argued that the almost unceasing rains indicated the utter corruption that pervades its alternative world. But now I may fill out the picture a little further, for apocalyptic both arises from a situation of enervating desperation and depicts a world so thoroughly depraved that all one can hope for is the complete and usually grim destruction of that world and the salvation of a small, faithful remnant.

Murder, Mayhem and Atrocity

> Known...for mayhem-filled performances and a lexicography of glee-
> ful savagery. (Nine 1997)

Some of these Flood songs might qualify as apocalyptic at the level of genre, but another group is more clearly apocalyptic in terms of worldview or ideology. These are the songs of murder, mayhem and atrocity, among which three sub-themes may be discerned, namely, conventional biblical apocalyptic, the deployment of apocalyptic in relation to drugs and love songs, and the overlap with songs of murder.

So we find the deeply biblical evocations of a world on the brink of collapse and ruin, occasionally with an ecological dimension. A listen to the relatively recent *Abattoir Blues* – the title is already an indication – produces track after track dwelling on the routine atrocity of destruction.[5] But traces of this depiction of a world on the course of unavoidable destruction appear at earlier moments in Cave's corpus. Thus, in 'Big Jesus Trash Can' (*Junkyard* [Cave 1982]), Texas, with its filthily rich oil barons, becomes a site of apocalyptic destruction: 'screams from heaven's graveyard/American heads will roll in Texas (roll like daddy's meat)/roll under those singing stars of Texas' (Cave 1982). Or in 'Saint Huck' in *From Her to Eternity* (Cave 1984), Huck's death takes place as the 'mo-o-o-on, its huge cycloptic eye/watches the city streets contract/twist and cripple and crack'. So also in 'Jangling Jack' from *Let Love In* (Cave 1994), where apocalyptic creeps in as Jack is killed by the barman as he goes for a drink: 'He sees the berserk city/Sees the dead stacked in piles/Sees the screaming crowd.'

However, Cave has a tendency to steer away from the collective dimension of apocalyptic and focus on its individual implications. A signal instance is the deployment of apocalyptic themes to depict the trial of giving up drugs. One thinks here of two tracks from *No More Shall We Part* (Cave 2001), the first of which, 'Fifteen Feet of Pure White Snow', speaks of the sheer struggle to give up heroin, with its constant temptations on the brink of destruction and days worse than anyone might experience. And 'Hallelujah' evokes the buckets of tears brought on by the process, tears that need twenty big buckets, twenty pretty girls, and 'twenty deep holes to bury them in'.[6]

This individualizing tendency also emerges in the way apocalyptic motifs are woven in with some of the love songs. Occasionally, love appears as a small redemptive note in the midst of an apocalyptic scenario (as I will discuss in more detail in the next chapter), but more common are those tracks that express in apocalyptic terms the brutality of love, both present and lost. We find this element particularly in another couple of pieces, now hymns, from *No More Shall We Part* (Cave 2001) – 'As I Sat Sadly by Her Side' and 'Darker with the Day'.[7] The latter is more conventional, with its smoke, little fires bursting on the lawns, great cracks appearing in the pavement and the earth itself yawning. But the former has a more individual twist that one comes to expect from Cave. Here the singer notes, while looking through the window, the earth and moon and stars, along with planets and comets with tails blazing, all 'forever falling'. But now the lover comes in and chides him with a characteristically liberal response: when will you ever learn, she asks, that what happens is none of your concern, that you heart is not a home for those of your brothers, that you have no right to sit in judgement on the world God has created, no matter how 'ugly, useless and over-inflated' it might be.

However, the most notable apocalyptic pieces are those that explore the motivations, contexts, nature and end result of murder. I will examine these songs in more detail (and provide full lists) in the next chapter, but for the purposes of this discussion a few key matters need to be emphasized. Although a few of these murder tracks appear on other albums, they come together with a unique concentration on the extraordinary *Murder Ballads* (Cave 1996b). Here a good collection of slightly mad but all-too-familiar characters make up the perpetrators – the regular patron at the local bar, the aggrieved lover, an old woman, a small girl, a visitor from out of town and a doctor. Most of them are serial killers, some are caught, others not. Many of the murders are set in quiet small towns or isolated hamlets. And Cave takes on the persona in question one after another. In the process, we enter into the intimate, warped and coldly rational minds of the killers.

The signal tracks on the album are those that blend an upbeat, dance-like rhythm, giving an almost light-hearted feel, with lyrics that are graphically gruesome. Stagger Lee wreaks his destruction at a place called the Bucket of Blood, filling the head of Billy Dilly with lead as the latter sucks on his dick. In the small town of Millhaven, little Loretta nails dogs to doors, staves in heads of little boys, burns down slums and beheads the odd handyman, all the while singing 'all God's children, they all gotta die', and the unnamed killer of the long 'O'Malley's Bar' narrates in lascivious, self-absorbed and near-orgasmic detail the slaughter of each person in the bar, all the while making biblical and theological allusions as he asserts his divine mission.

But is this apocalyptic? We might dismiss these songs and their poetry as the obsessions of a troubled artist who has more than enough demons with which to struggle. This is where a crucial couple of lines from 'Nature Boy' from *Abattoir Blues* (Cave 2004a) suggest a deeper logic to these murder ballads, to the songs of anger, senseless killing and death:

> I was just a boy when I sat down
> To watch the news on TV.
> I saw some ordinary slaughter,
> I saw some routine atrocity.

The song goes on to ask how this ordinary slaughter and routine atrocity might be overcome: in an echo of the Cave's obsessively repeated story of his father's death (see Chapter 2), Cave mentions in the song his long-dead father's belief that beauty is the answer. In other words, slaughter, destruction and atrocity may be the way the world is, but it should not be so. In short, we have here a strong doctrine of sin and evil, one that we have already met in the previous chapter in terms of total depravity. Instead of a mild theory in which evil is a negation of goodness, or merely a necessary but somewhat anaemic precursor to redemption, Cave trawls his way through the rotting corpses of evil in all their putrid detail. Indeed, as with the apocalyptic Flood and its over-lap with total depravity, so also is a strong sense of the palpable reality of evil a distinctive marker of apocalyptic literature and its worldview.

Glimpses of Redemption

> When the big bomb goes off, all that's going to survive are goths and cockroaches. (Cave in Sullivan 1998)

As with the scenario of total depravity, this world of murder, mayhem and atrocity eventually bends towards the constant desire for redemption, although Cave takes his time finding it and offers no neat solutions. I will explore the range of Cave's redemptive forays in the conclusion, but here our concern is the redemptive expectation built into the world of apocalyptic. Only once does Cave veer close to the conventional mode of apocalyptic salvation, in which the long-expected maelstrom of catastrophic destruction brings about a trium-phant victory of God, ably assisted by his fiery chariots swooping down from the clouds. That moment is the track 'New Morning', from *Tender Prey* (Cave 1988b), in which we find ourselves in a post-apocalyptic world, where irony and prophecy rub shoulders with one another (Scanlon 1988). The song opens with a blood-covered kingdom, which is nothing other than heaven itself in which the corpses of the conflict of the night before strew the battlefield. The spears of the sun, draped in banners of fire, overlook the field in blinking vic-tory from the battle of the night before. And the world of the new day prom-ises to be absent of sorrow, sadness and – rather curiously – narrow roads.

Yet that rather banal piece stands out as an exception, a moment of quite conventional apocalyptic redemption that is not repeated in Cave's work.

More significantly, in his late music Cave may place us in the midst of that final catastrophe, which often turns out to be the here and now, but redemption turns out to be a far more enigmatic affair, offering a glimpse, the merest possibility, a modest act that heralds hope and a new beginning. That approach appears in a small collection of tracks on *Abattoir Blues* (Cave 2004a), which provide a hint of redemption in the midst of the world-ending calamity with the simplest of acts, usually in the context of love – 'Messiah Ward', 'There She Goes, My Beautiful World', 'Nature Boy' and 'Abattoir Blues'.[8] Each song offers a different possibility, whether overcoming catastrophe through beauty, or getting out and doing something instead of complaining, or in simple acts of hope in the midst of the contradictions of a world on the skids.

For instance, as we saw earlier, 'Nature Boy' turns on the lines, 'in the end it is beauty/That is going to save the world, now' (Cave 2004a). The routine atrocity and murder of the opening lines finds a possible answer in beauty. And that is the trigger for an evocation of the world-changing arrival of a lover; or, in 'There She Goes, My Beautiful World', a number of threads in the song that look to the end of the world and simultaneously push towards redemption. One is semi-autobiographical: the singer lies on his bed with an empty head and empty ears and worries whether the great poets and authors wrote while 'under the influence' (Cave has said that a major reason he gave away the drugs was that he would lie for days and not do a thing, the old source of inspiration now proving to be debilitating). So the question becomes, has his beautiful world of inspiration gone, too? At another level, it is nature that is going and perhaps has gone through environmental collapse, especially if we remember the evocation of natural beauty at the beginning. And then it is a woman – the ambiguous 'she' who is going – and even God of whom he asks for nothing except one thing: 'Give me ever-lasting life'. Yet, all of these items must encounter the redemptive close of the song:

> So if you got a trumpet, get on your feet, brother, and blow it
> If you've got a field that don't yield, well get up and hoe it.

Redemption will not appear as a *deus ex machina*, an other-worldly solution beyond one's agency. Instead, if you are faced with apocalyptic catastrophe, then pull your finger out and do your bit.

In 'Messiah Ward' we get a more consistent end-of-the-world theme: the refrain keeps reminding us that 'they're bringing out the dead' and we learn that the stars have been torn down and that the moon has been banned from shining. Yet in the pitch dark of this mayhem, the author suggests to the woman, 'You can move up a little closer/I will throw a blanket over' (Cave 2004a). A small act perhaps, but in the midst of the cataclysm it offers a simple hope. But is it enough to forestall and overcome the mayhem and destruction of Armageddon?

Finally, in 'Abattoir Blues' the cataclysmic scenario is the most extensive of any song Cave has produced: air heavy with doom, a world dissolving according to plan, fire in the sky, mountains of dead, crashing stock exchanges, the culture of death and mass extinction. No future vision this, for it is the present, the lived reality of everyday life. Yet that present is suffused with the deep contradictions of such a life: the boring and frivolous routines of those in wealthy nations – rising at first light with the sparrows, a frappucino in one's hand the moment after waking, the drive into work, the need for validation through such work – clashes with the scenes of woe that come from elsewhere in the world. That contradiction weaves its way through the song, thrown together in line after line, showing up in a jammed moral code, confusion, a sense of hypocrisy and the juxtaposition of hoping to be a Superman but turning out to be such a jerk. But these are not mutually exclusive items, for they turn out to be intimately related, 'Entwined together in this culture of death' (Cave 2004a) – in a way that becomes an implicit criticism of capitalism itself. How to respond? The song offers no final solution to the abattoir of today's life, preferring to throw out possibilities. Is it to be a lifeline from God? What about escaping with the two of them? Or is it through a simple request: 'Slide on over here, let me give you a squeeze'?

These songs trace what may be called the tension of apocalyptic hope. No longer do we follow a desultory path to a grim end; instead, another option begins open up. The sky might be on fire and the dead might be heaped up, but Cave searches for some path other than the one that ends in meaningless oblivion or in glorious apocalyptic victory. We may not be able to stop such a cataclysmic end, but there are one or two things that may offer a glimpse of hope – the smallest act of love in the midst of pain and suffering may actually make a difference. Or perhaps we may not be able to stop the pain and sadness, but there are one or two things that might lessen them. These shards offer no grand resolution, or a claim that love will save us, no carefully worked-out schema of redemption – just the occasional hint that things need not go completely to hell.

Conclusion

> Some gloomy old git who sits at the piano moaning on about this and that. (Cave in Calkin 2001)

Cave's apocalyptic has turned out to be inextricably enmeshed with the theme of total depravity, so much so that it serves to fill out the picture of an utterly corrupt world with yet another deeply theological and biblical theme, yet his approach to apocalyptic is by no means conventional. Less a mere deployment of that theological genre and ideology, his engagement is an idiosyncratic blending of both expected and unexpected items. So the implicit apocalyptic dimensions of the biblical Deluge are brought to the fore, enhanced by the addition of travelling carnivals, freaks and thunderstorms; mayhem, atrocity and murder become the subject matter of some extraordinary, upbeat and slightly tongue-in-cheek material; and the Last Days become not the site of a desperately hoped-for glorious victory by forces beyond our control, but the moment when a small act may make a difference – although that act's beneficence is left unresolved and unstated. Once the whole picture emerges, the category of apocalyptic – at least in the terms I outlined at the beginning of this chapter – has itself been reinterpreted and recast. It may no longer be a body of revealed knowledge concerning the end of days when the Anti-Christ will rule for a time, Armageddon will lead to untold destruction and suffering, and God will deliver us in that great final battle. However, while it has certainly become richer, we would do well to be wary of attributing that reinterpretation to a uniquely individual creative genius, for that would be to fall into the trap of valorizing the authentic vision of the private artist. The fact that Cave himself and many of his critics are keen to stress that element of his work should be enough to trigger a decent dose of ideological criticism, directed specifically at the liberal ideology that provides the resources for such a position. But the critique of that element of Cave's music is the topic of another chapter, especially in terms of the Christology he likes to deploy.

4 Death

Entwined together in this culture of death.
(Cave 2004a)

Two abiding passions – crime and theology.
(Brown 1998)

Once again I set out to enlarge the picture produced thus far, for now total depravity and apocalyptic find another companion – death, in all its forms in Cave's music. Unlike the tendency to compartmentalize death in our (post)modern world, to sequester the elderly into compounds known as 'retirement villages', to block death through the frenzy of consuming commodified trash, to separate death from life, and for rock singers to favour lust and love, in all its triumphs, frustrations and disappointments, Cave is refreshingly, if at times scandalously, direct. In order to seek out the permutations of death in Cave's work, I distinguish between musical form and lyrical content, overlaying that distinction with another between death inflicted and death suffered. When we come to death suffered, we also draw closer to Cave's own perceptions of death, with myriad reflections on individual death and, even more importantly for my purposes, collective death. Yet the story is not complete without a consideration of death overcome and what that means for Cave's own continuous search for redemption. One final introductory observation: it is usually far easier, for obvious reasons, to focus on what happens before death, on our preparation for, fear of and terror before death – how do we face death? What are the social mores? Is it a part of life or divorced from life? What happens after death is, of course, an unknown zone, although that has not prevented more than a little speculation about what might happen on the other side of the door. My analysis of Cave on death is very interested precisely in how he deals with this divide, for most of the time he falls in with the majority, focusing on the lead-up to death. Yet I will push him and seek out what he says and sings concerning the other side of death.[1]

From Form to Content: The Sinister Song

Death looms large because it should. (Cave in Paytress 1998)

I begin with form, with a focus on the music itself, before turning to consider the content – assuming for a few moments that rough-and-ready distinction. As far as musical form is concerned, the most well-known appearance of death in Cave's corpus is in an album I have already had occasion to discuss, *Murder Ballads* (Cave 1996b). And the characteristic song genre on that album may be called the sinister song. As I will discuss in detail in the final chapter of this book, the sinister song is a confluence, with an ominous swerve, of two other major types of song in Cave's repertoire: the anarchic or discordant song and the hymn. While the anarchic song (and its closely related discordant song) is characterized by the note engaged in civil war, the hymn is dominated by a piano or an organ, muted bass, a much slower tempo, accompaniment that recalls a church choir if not the congregation itself, and conventional harmonic arrangement. In short, the hymn is a distinctly melodious other to the anarchic song. While the latter is characteristic mostly of Cave's time with The Birthday Party (1980–83) – although one may find pieces also with The Boys Next Door (1977–80) and The Bad Seeds (1984–) – the hymn emerges first via the cover versions of Spirituals on *Kicking against the Pricks* (Cave 1986a), coming into full flower with *The Boatman's Call* (Cave 1997a) and *No More Shall We Part* (Cave 2001).

Although Cave will eventually achieve a difficult and partial resolution (yet another dimension of the search for redemption) with what may be called the dialectical song, where the pseudo-redemption of the hymn opens out to an ecstatic remake of the anarchic song in a way that enables it to break though to a whole new level, the sinister song emerges in order to indicate why the hymn's offer of redemption is in vain. How? The sinister song brings about an incongruence meeting of the hymn and the anarchic song. The outcome of this perverse liaison is that the hymn undergoes portentous swerve where anarchic and discordant elements find a temporary lodging. As I will argue in the last chapter, in the sinister song the hymn takes on a menacing air that breathes life into the atonal depravity of the anarchic song. A close study of the sinister song reveals a pervasive sense of threat and premonition, where a shortened note (in contrast to the longer note of the hymn) hints at the lives repeatedly cut short, all of which is sung by a voice that is thoroughly mad, calculatingly self-absorbed, quiveringly intense and verging on orgasmic release as yet another murder is described in lascivious detail. Above all, the sinister song, in its mingling of the anarchic song and the hymn, negates any redemption that the latter may have promised. Of course, in closing down one (false) path to redemption, it opens up – at times despite itself – another, more promising, possibility.[2]

One may identify one or two precursors of the sinister song,[3] but its signature moment is the irrepressibly humorous *Murder Ballads* (Cave 1996b), where the hymn is pre-emptively put out of its misery, along with 66 murder victims (including one terrier). So we gain an initial impression that the slow pace of the hymn, with its deeply resonant voice and inescapable choir, is alive and well – as in the initial track 'Song of Joy' and followed up by 'Lovely Creature', 'Stagger Lee' and 'O'Malley's Bar'. But so too – at first incongruously – is the atonal note of the anarchic song, which jars with the feel of the hymn. Perverse laments (a variation on the hymn, in which the falling note is held in a drawn-up moment of longing and loss) also appear, such as 'Henry Lee' (a cover), 'Where the Wild Roses Grow' and 'The Kindness of Strangers'. The incongruity of the sinister song is enhanced by a feature of some of the tracks which I have already had cause to mention: the bright, major key and a dance-like, snappy rhythm – so 'Stagger Lee', 'Lovely Creature', 'Curse of Millhaven', 'Crow Jane' (somewhat less, but still noticeable) and especially 'O'Malley's Bar'. Yet even here, this item of jarring juxtaposition serves to intensify the sinister nature of the songs, celebrating violent death in a truly macabre fashion.

Death Inflicted

> Those nasty little details. (Cave in Dwyer 1995)

> All God's children they all gotta die. (Cave 1996b)

By now we have slipped into content, partly because the separation from form is always an artificial one. Here the lascivious, clinically detailed voice meshes in closely with the content. It may be the calm and creepy character who knocks on the door late one night in 'Song of Joy', narrating in uncomfortable detail the murder of his wife and daughters, all the while offering snippets from Milton's *Paradise Lost*. Or it may be the furious, almost orgasmic madness of 'Stagger Lee', or the pure pleasure of little Loretta, the mass murderer of 'The Curse of Millhaven', whose apparent matter-of-factness in revealing how many murders she has perpetrated becomes the signal of her own insanity.[4] Among all of these, the signal track is one we have already met, the long 'O'Malley's Bar' in which a regular at the local watering hole finally enacts what he has been itching to do for some time – systematically kill everyone in the bar.

Without fuss, this ballad begins as though in media res, a syncopated bass-cum-drum note introducing the full musical panoply – a muted drum, organ-like synthesisers, bass and rhythm guitar pointing towards the dominant voice; the only item that plays with the voice being a plinking piano, which in its own way highlights the sexual intensity of the rampage. But the voice is the key: thoroughly self-absorbed, humming, ahhing, sniffing, huhing whenever it gets the opportunity, offering approving moments of self-observation whenever he happens to catch a glimpse of himself in the mirror. The voice moves between crescendos of killing and quiet, almost spoken, objective observances of the scene.

Beyond the voice, three items stand out for our purposes here. First, the very length of the song (almost 15 minutes) indicates the obsessive attention to detail of each murder: O'Malley's wife looks for all the world like one of those fish with swollen lips when they sweep the ocean floor, her face raw and vicious before the narrator blows her head off; Richard Holmes sits down gingerly when shot, muttering 'no offense' and then his head goes the way of that of O'Malley's wife; an ashtray splits Jerry Bellows's head as he hugs his stool; and with the killing of Henry Davenport, the singer observes that the bullet 'entered through the top of his chest/And blew his bowels out on the floor'.

Second, the sexual charge of the murders is conveyed in extraordinary fashion.[5] Not only does his dick feel 'long and hard' at the first kill, that of O'Malley himself, after the murderer's hand had disappeared from view and brought out the gun itself (a prosthetic for his dick), but the voice itself rises to ejaculatory climaxes with each new murder. Closely related – and third – is the constant pattern of religious comments, exclamations and doctrinal observations. So we find the murderer crossing himself at the moment his hand decides to reach for the gun, a quiet blessing offered as a depraved holy time of sacrifice begins. And immediately after we are informed about the status of his cock, he observes that he is the man for whom 'no God waits' but for whom 'the whole world yearns'. With the divine mission established in this holy time, one populated by God and the ghosts of truth, a string of comparisons follow in which the victims remind our perpetrator of religious figures: Siobhan O'Malley is like the Madonna painted on a church-house wall; the bird-like Mr Brooks becomes a reminder of St Francis and his sparrows; the youthful Richardson becomes St Sebastian and his arrows. To complete the picture, an undercurrent of sin, culpability and free will becomes the theological backdrop. 'I have no free will', he sings, only to find Mr Richard Holmes accusing him of being an evil man after the death of Mrs Holmes. The reply: if one has no free will, then how can one be morally responsible? But when given the choice between using the last bullet to kill himself or surrender to the police at the end, he decides he is not ready to die quite yet.

Self-absorption, clinical attention to detail, sexual climax and religion all weave together in one of the best instances of a song in which death is inflicted. The perverse appeal of such a song lies, I would suggest, in the way it invites us into the mind of serial killer in action. Yet this intimacy has a dialectical effect, since it also creates distance from the mind revealed. One often hears the comment that the murderer in prison is not all that different from those of us who have not committed a murder, the only difference being that something has triggered a response that crosses a line from the common feelings of hatred, anger and a desire for revenge. But Cave manages to show here the workings of a chillingly unhinged mind, albeit one who may well be my neighbour, who may have lived in town for 30 years, who in a moment reveals the monstrous other of the Real when that friendly neighbour becomes a monster (see Žižek 2005).

However, this is not the only shape of the sinister murder ballad, for one or two other tracks on *Murder Ballads* open out a consistent and occasionally criticized feature of Cave's music (see Chapter 4): the violence directed to a lover in a relationship gone sour. I am interested here in a specific moment in that violence, namely when the lover dies or is (more usually) dead, often in the very recent past. We find this in 'Henry Lee', 'Where the Wild Roses Grow' and 'The Kindness of Strangers'. To add to the poignancy, these songs feature both male and female vocals: Cave along with another, somewhat innocent but tragic voice (P. J. Harvey in 'Henry Lee' and Kylie Minogue in 'Where the Wild Roses Grow'). In the vast majority of cases, the death is of the woman lover, although in 'Henry Lee' the man finds himself repeatedly knifed while leaning up against a fence being kissed by the woman who simultaneously wields a knife. The reason: he professes love for another girl in a 'merry green land'. But this song is an exception on two counts: here the man dies and the song narrates his death and then the drop into the deep, deep well.

The overwhelming pattern for these songs is that the woman dies, or more often, is already dead. The signature moment on *Murder Ballads* is the duet with Kylie Minogue, her voice full of naive innocence, a girl in the flush of a first love. 'Where the Wild Roses Grow' appears to narrate a tragic murder of passion, death by the river where the lovers meet for the last time in an affair of but four days. However, the female voice seems to speak from beyond the grave, for she tells of her own death by means of 'a rock in his fist'. And this perspective is the standard one of the morbid edge of Cave's love song, death standing at a minimal distinction from love.

These tracks might be described as murderous love songs, at least in terms of content. They recur with a gruesome regularity, as with 'The Kindness of Strangers', in which the poor and solitary Mary Bellows sets off to seek her own future. Lonely and full of hope in a cheap hotel room, she fatefully changes her mind concerning the man she has just met, Richard Slade, and invites him in. The next morning she is found 'cuffed to the bed, with a rag in her mouth and bullet in her head' – except that this line forms a chiasmus in the song. The very occasion for the song was that she was found this way at its beginning, only to return to the same moment once the story is complete.

It would be a little tedious to run through each instance of such a song, so let me identify two consistent features – apart from the fact that they concern the death of a recently deceased female lover. To begin with, this morbid edge of the love song runs across all the musical genres of Cave's work.[6] We find them in the anarchic/discordant songs of the early years,[7] the experiment with spirituals,[8] laments (which form a subset of the hymn)[9] and then in the more recent dialectical songs. Close attention to these various pieces reveals that they seem to be unable to resist the temptation to include moments of theology, as we saw already with the somewhat different 'O'Malley's Bar'. So references to God's abandonment appear – as in 'Well of Misery': 'The same God that abandon'd her has in turn abandon'd me' (Cave 1984). Or to judgement, suffered or escaped, where the perpetrator vows that 'no hangman's about to put a leash around me' (from 'Hey Joe in *Kicking against the Pricks* [Cave 1986a]). Or to remorse and thereby guilt, in which the killer now regrets deeply the loss, a sense that is merely an extension of all those songs that lament a love lost; so with the cry, 'What have I done?', as Jack realizes the implications of cutting away his shadow-become-wife in 'Jack's Shadow' (from *Your Funeral... My Trial* [Cave 1986b]).[10] Indeed, quite a few songs[11] play with this minimal difference, so that one is not sure whether the singer laments a love or a life lost. That is, until love and death come together as one in the line, 'To our love send a coffin of wood' (from *The Boatman's Call* [Cave 1997a]), for here we have the funeral of love itself. Finally, the theme of the life hereafter comes to the fore, to which I turn more fully in a moment.[12]

What may be said about these sinister songs, the murder ballads and the love songs with a morbid edge? As a way to understand this whole category of death inflicted, I draw upon the work of Adorno and Horkheimer, focusing on some relatively unknown but extremely relevant reflections on death. The most pertinent point is that when Cave writes and sings about death inflicted, he gives voice to a profound contradiction in our – that is Western – approach to death: between the mechanical process of simply being snuffed out and the sheer terror of death. For Adorno, this bifurcation is due to the pervasive effects of capitalism on our daily social lives, in which instrumental reason renders us merely replaceable items, another ready to stand in to take our place as we drop. The image is drawn both from warfare – one more to stand in the breach created – and factory production, in which we become like the tools we use. All of which shows up most sharply in genocide, for which the clinical mass murder of approximately six-million Jews (as well as gypsies and homosexuals) at the hands of the Nazis becomes the leitmotiv, marked by the single word 'Auschwitz', albeit not neglecting the drearily horrific repetition of acts of genocide (Adorno 1973 [1966]: 361–68; 2003 [1966]: 354–61; 1998 [1963/1969]: 89–103, 191–204; 2003 [1963]a: 573–94; 2003 [1969]: 674–90; 1978 [1951]: 58–60, 165–66, 231–33; 2003 [1951]: 65–67, 188–89, 264–66). Does this not remind one of the body count in *Murder Ballads*, in which one serial killer after another pile up bodies in gleeful and remorseless abandon? Here human beings are expendable, simply snuffed out as so many useless items: witness the killer's perverse attention to the detail of the deaths, whether through drowning or burning down in a house fire, with heads blasted off or shattered, and the carnage of a bullet's path iterated with curiosity and precision.

However, the dialectical catch of this approach to death is that the technical banality of death also produces a fragmentation between death and life, a cleavage that renders death strange and external to the totality of life. And so it becomes simultaneously a complete interruption, a sheer accident that somehow breaks in and destroys life. Death thereby becomes alien, a horrifying break that produces unimaginable panic (Adorno 1973 [1966]: 368–73; 2003 [1966]: 361–68; 2000 [1998]: 106–107; 2006 [1998]: 166–67). This other side of the reification of death shows up in the victims of *Murder Ballads*. The killers may dispense with their prey with barely a thought for the lives terminated, but those victims themselves face their unexpected and – apparently – accidental deaths with dread. Thus, in 'O'Malley's Bar', Siobhan O'Malley shivers in her grief, Mr and Mrs Holmes shriek in terror and Jerry Bellows closes his eyes, shrugging and laughing hysterically.

Only on the last point from Adorno and Horkheimer does Cave differ, even if in an unexpected fashion. For them, the outcome is that through the alienation – that is, making alien – of death, our society is actually pervaded by death: by blocking out death we come ever more under its pall. Horkheimer puts this in terms of the forgetting of history: by repressing death, we forget our history, especially its negative examples that serve as reminders of the horrific moments that must resolutely be resisted: 'True humanity would repeat the rite according to which the life that seeks to forget death stands all the more certainly under its scourge' (Horkheimer 1978: 211; 1991: 374). Where Horkheimer differs from Adorno, it is in terms of mechanisms we use to block that history and thereby the terror of death. Our absolute attachment to the trash of industrial and commercial production, an attachment manifested in the frenzy of consumption – so much so that one flies to New York, for instance, in order to shop – are all part of the effort to deny the reality of death (Horkheimer 1978: 210–11, 236; 1991: 373–74, 418–19; Horkheimer and Adorno 2002: 178–79; 2003 [1947]: 245–47).

One's initial impression with respect to Cave is that he too detaches death from life, quarantining it from the mundane course of our lives. For the deaths in his songs are often the result of violence, crimes committed against law-abiding and largely peaceful citizens – exactly one of the modes in which we like to characterize death, namely, as an interruption, an accident from outside, the result of extraneous forces that break into our lives. Yet here lies the dialectical point, for Cave does anything but block out such deaths, urging more policing, stricter prison sentences for perpetrators, as the dreary law-and-order politics would have it. No, he dwells at length on precisely such deaths, dissecting them, joking about them, not allowing us to forget, deny or push them from our consciousness. It is as though he focuses precisely on the extreme, accidental and violent form of death in order to bring that too into the realm of life – for all too often death is brutal; the peaceful scene of a person dying at the end of many years, surrounded by family and friends, being a utopian dream rather than any consistent reality. In short, for Cave there is no denial, no effort to forget and bury death under police, law or a mountain of commercial crap; he focuses squarely on death in a way that is difficult to disregard.

Death Suffered

> And the decomposing lover says... (Cave 2003)

Now we move over from death wreaked upon others to the experience of one's own death. As a way of introducing this other dimension of death, let me draw upon Ernst Bloch, who makes a related but slightly different distinction to that of Adorno and Horkheimer. For Bloch, the physical act of dying, which is, or rather should be, a part of life, must be differentiated from the ontological status of death: that is, 'the act of extinction is very different from the resultant state' (Bloch 1972: 255; 1968: 335). The trepidation before dying is a far cry from the horror of death: while the former may generate an occasional apprehension, death as an ontological status produces annihilating dread. Bloch suggests that the real issue for philosophical deliberation is this second category, the horror of the complete pulverization of any identity at death, that everything about us or indeed those close to us will simply cease to exist, a sense only exacerbated by the over-riding feeling that death cuts off a life that has not been fully realized, that it is an interruption, 'generally breaking, only very rarely rounding off, the human life' (Bloch 1972: 249; 1968: 329). As we shall soon see, Cave's attention is almost always focused on that ontological state of death and its anticipated annihilation.

Individual Annihilation

> I had one long hard think about dying. (Cave 1996b)

The immediate impression is that death suffered – of a solitary individual, usually the singer – is a theme that dominates the earlier material from The Bad Seeds, especially *From Her to Eternity*, *The First Born Is Dead*, *Kicking against the Pricks*, *Your Funeral... My Trial* and *Tender Prey*. A number of themes emerge from this material, such as execution for a crime, the depravity of a life that ends in a sordid death, relief and the escape offered by a death that is better than life, but above all the struggle against being forgotten after death, the struggle for memory and the threat of complete annihilation. In other words, we find a concern for the process of dying, how one approaches death and the ontological status of death itself, with a distinct emphasis on that last category.

Concerning the process of dying, often the victim is or is about to be executed for a crime that may or may not have been committed,[13] or less often he is the victim of a murder.[14] We have already encountered this category, but now Cave focuses on the victim. No peaceful passing here, for the end comes as a result of violence, at times in the context of what can only be called total depravity or a sickness unto death. For example, in the early 'Blundertown' from *Junkyard* (Cave 1982) in The Birthday Party days, we find the sordid reality of life characteristic of the drug-fuelled punk albums. This was a time when the bassist, Tracy Pew, died of an epileptic fit brought on by the cocktail of drugs and alcohol (Hattenstone 2008).[15]

How do these individuals face death? Some do so with an anticipation of release from a dreadful life, looking forward to the peace of not being pursued or persecuted any longer. Thus, in 'Swampland' from *Mutiny – The Bad Seed* (Cave 1983), a song that may well have come from the novel *And the Ass Saw the Angel* (Cave 1989), the subject of the song is caught in quicksand, desperately hoping, albeit not without some terror, that it will suck him down before his pursuers appear with bloodlust in their eyes. Or in 'Knockin' on Joe' from *The First Born Is Dead* (Cave 1985), the singer awaits execution on death row, his feelings torn between protest at the life lived and relief, since after death 'You cain't hurt me anymore'. And in 'Wanted Man' from the same album, he mentions the place where he is not on the wanted list any more, namely 'the place that I call home'.[16]

However, the dominant theme of these songs is that death simply leads to total annihilation as a person, with a struggle against the odds even to be remembered. So, in 'A Box for Black Paul' (Cave 1984), the singer searches in vain for some means to remember the executed Black Paul. Everything that Paul wrote becomes scrap on the street, the 'whole fucken lot' going 'right up in smoke'.[17] Or it may be one anonymous and veiled lover who visits the grave in the dead of night, as in 'Long Black Veil' from *Kicking against the Pricks* (Cave 1986a).[18] Even the crows eventually forget a corpse strung up on a pole once they have finished feasting on its rotting flesh ('Black Crow King' from *The First Born Is Dead* [Cave 1985]). Yet memory is a fickle beast, just as likely to throw up gruesome and unwelcome reminders, such as the carny's horse in 'The Carny' (Cave 1986b), the corpse of which floats out of its shallow grave during an apocalyptic storm as the carnival grimly attempts to leave the scene. Ultimately, one cannot control those memories, as people dig about for dirt and gossip (see 'Lay Me Low' from *Let Love In* [Cave 1994]).

That fickle memory and the ever-present threat of its loss comprise but one element of the obliteration of death. Saint Huck's river in *From Her to Eternity* (Cave 1984) becomes a metaphor for the sucking obliteration of identity brought about by the ontological status of death.[19] Alternatively, the devil may take one down, down, down into hell and oblivion ('Up Jumped the Devil' in *Tender Prey* [Cave 1988b]). Or a rock star may find that he or she suddenly undergoes what is known in the fame business as 'irrelevance syndrome', as we find in 'The Singer' from *Kicking against the Pricks* (Cave 1986a), who fears that suddenly 'nobody knows me'. Yesterday, the multitude may have screamed out his or her name and cried out for a song, but now he or she is gone, like the 'pages of a book' used to light a fire. All of which is summed up best in the penultimate line from 'Jangling Jack' (in *Let Love In* [Cave 1994]): having been shot by the barman, Jack dies slowly in a pool of blood, until at last 'he vomits and dies'.[20]

Collective Destruction

> The sky is on fire, the dead are heaped across the land. (Cave 2004a)

I had hoped that Cave would give more attention to collective death, with its more overt political overtones rather than the existential concerns of individual death. But it should come as no surprise that this is somewhat muted in his work, not least because he ascribes, as I argue in Chapter 6, to the classic liberal focus on the private individual, with unoriginal claims to raw artistic authenticity, the need to avoid 'selling out' and staying true to oneself, and even preferring heretical and very individual variations on theological themes. Indeed, the only significant way collective death appears in Cave's music is through the theme of apocalyptic, which we have already met in the previous chapter, and as an element in the total depravity of individual death – as with 'Jangling Jack' from *Let Love In* (Cave 1994) and 'Saint Huck' in *From Her to Eternity* (Cave 1984). Apocalyptic does feature elsewhere outside the material that deals with death, but here I wish to keep my focus on death.

As I argued in the preceding chapter, the three notable features of apocalyptic deal with conventional biblical apocalyptic, drugs, love songs and death. Yet only the first of these offers a properly collective dimension to death, for the other three – on drugs, love and death – simply revert to the individualistic default of most of Cave's work. And on only three occasions does a more political element creep into such songs. The first of these is – paradoxically – a celebration of drug addition, 'Mutiny in Heaven' from *Mutiny! – The Bad Seed* (Cave 1983). Here the needle itself gives him the power to grow wings and assault heaven itself in the Promethean and Luciferan rebellion so beloved by Ernst Bloch. Further, in 'We Call Upon the Author' (*Dig!!! Lazarus Dig!!!* [Cave 2008]), theodicy appears belatedly, now in terms of asking God why there is 'rampant discrimination, mass poverty, third world debt, infectious disease, global inequality and deepening socio-economic divisions'. Few and brief are such moments, enhanced by the only other moment of political analysis, with 'In the Ghetto' in *From Her to Eternity* (Cave 1984), where the hungry and angry black boy becomes a rebel on the fringe of society, only to be gunned down just as another hungry baby is born in the ghetto. Class, race, exploitation and covert, objective violence come together here for a profound analysis. The catch is that it appears in a cover song, originally from M. Davies via Elvis Presley.

Death Overcome

> The line that God throws down to you and me. (Cave 1996b)

For all his fascination, Cave is not content to remain with death itself, especially its state of ontological obliteration. Indeed, given his consistent attention to the possibility of redemption, one should expect a similar concern in relation to death. In short, he seeks an answer for what happens after we die. Appropriately for a topic on which we have no firm data, Cave explores various and not always compatible positions. In this respect he indicates in his own way that he follows neither the positive dogmatism of Christian theology, with its prefabricated places of heaven and hell, nor the dogmatic negativity of materialism, asserting with equally definitive belief that death is indeed an absolute end in which we can expect nothing beyond the body's dissolution. On this matter, Cave unwittingly follows Ernst Bloch's wise advice, namely, that one may contemplate death best by means of the image of the beginning of a journey, the destination of which, let alone the path itself, remain an open question: 'the *status viae* lies far beyond death, which hardly represents an inflexibly formative *status termini*' (Bloch 2000: 265; 1985c: 330). Those who assert that they know the definitive answer usually have another, more sinister agenda in this life.

All the same, we do find occasional moments when Cave either disdains the conventional religious assertion of a life beyond death, as with the mad buzzard, the reverend, who 'shrieked and flapped about life after you're dead' (in 'Pappa Won't Leave You, Henry' from *Henry's Dream* [Cave 1992]),[21] or despairs that we may anticipate nothing more than dismay and decay ('Dead Man in My Bed' from *Nocturama* [Cave 2003]). At times he holds out, as we saw above, the possibility of memory as the means by which the dead live on (apart from the examples cited earlier, see also 'Stranger Than Kindness' from *Your Funeral... My Trial* [Cave 1986b], in which the dead lover lives on in the one who survives). Not only is this a rather conventional and weak position, but it faces the profound objection that memory is fleeting, fickle and easily lost.

A hint of a more substantial position comes first with the suggestion that the dead – especially a lover – may call out from the grave (as with 'Long Time Man' from *Your Funeral... My Trial* [Cave 1986b]), but it is never clear, appropriately, whether this call is imagined or real, perhaps comparable to the phantom sensations from an amputated limb. Yet Cave draws most deeply from the well of Christian imagery and metaphor, from what may be described as the language of Christian myth. Here he plays momentarily with the images of hell and heaven and of the redemptive death of Christ on the cross, but is more interested in resurrection and, once again, apocalyptic. A few passing references to hell and heaven may be found,[22] as also the cross of Christ. It appears, somewhat undercover, in the Spanish hymn, 'Foi Na Cruz' (from *The Good Son* [Cave 1990]) and then in a grotesque manner with the extraordinary lines from 'Darker with the Day' (from *No More Shall We Part* [Cave 2001]):

> Inside I sat, seeking the presence of a God
> I searched through the pictures in a
> Leather-bound book
> I found a woolly lamb dozing in an issue of blood
> And a gilled Jesus shivering on a
> Fisherman's hook.

The extremity of this isolated imagery shows up a curious feature of Cave's treatment of death, especially in conjunction with Jesus: one would expect that his interest in death and Christ would include one of the central features of the Gospels, namely, the passion stories in which Christ dies and is risen. Here is a conjunction of pain, love, death and Christ that would resonate throughout his work. But he makes little to no use of that dimension of the Jesus story, preferring, as we shall see in my discussion of Christology, a sensuous, creative, imaginative and misunderstood Jesus. This image of a bloody lamb and gilled Jesus signals his disgust with that element of the story, while the rarity of such references indicates a studied avoidance of the death of Jesus.

However, on other occasions Cave plays with a more wholehearted Christian position, particularly after his own redemptive release from drugs and alcohol.[23] One has to listen a few times to ascertain that Cave has actually sung, for instance, 'He is the real, real thing' from a song like 'Let the Bells Ring' (*Abattoir Blues* [Cave 2004a]) – presumably Cave means Jesus, but once again the metaphoric nature of the language reasserts itself with the ambiguous call to pause and see 'the mystery of the Word' (*The Lyre of Orpheus* [Cave 2004a]).

The picture would not be complete without a deployment of resurrection itself, most notably on the track 'New Morning' (from *Tender Prey* [Cave 1988b]), where sadness, sorrow and narrow roads pass with the 'new day', which happens to be today.[24] Indeed, this post-apocalyptic song introduces a consistent pattern in which resurrection is wrapped up in apocalyptic, the language *par excellence* of Christian mythology (see the previous chapter). Or rather, resurrection appears in the context of post-apocalyptic scenes, after the death and destruction I noted earlier: so 'New Morning' (Cave 1988b), in which the battle is over and won, as well as the call to peace, to laying down the hammer and putting up the sword, as also in 'Carry Me' (from *The Lyre of Orpheus* [Cave 2004a]) and the full vision of a post-apocalyptic world in 'There is a Kingdom' (from *The Boatman's Call* [Cave 1997a]).

I must confess to being a little surprised at the depth to which Cave draws upon such Christian themes, given his rather heretical uses of it elsewhere. But I should not be so amazed, for it is well known, as was pointed out in Chapter 1, that Cave has a habit of reading the Bible, intensely and often, and that collection of texts contains a rich vein indeed of mythic, even utopian imagery of death, resurrection and the world to come (once again Cave comes near to that most consistent exegete of utopia, religious and otherwise, namely, Ernst Bloch).

Equally, if not more, powerful are the understated expressions of hope, usually given voice in the context of apocalyptic. These appear in Cave's most extended apocalyptic album, one that we have encountered already – *Abattoir*

Blues (Cave 2004a). As one example among many, in the midst of the may-hem depicted in 'Messiah Ward', we come across the lines, 'You can move up a little closer/I will throw a blanket over': a small gesture, perhaps, yet one that offers a glimmer of hope.[25] Or perhaps it is beauty that will save the world, a fragile aesthetic opening, drawn from a memory of Cave's long-dead father in 'Nature Boy'. But the best example would have to be the less conventional eschewing of institutions and their doctrines in 'Gates to the Garden' (from *The Boatman's Call* [Cave 1997a]):

> Leave these ancient places to the angels
> Let the saints attend to their keeping of the cathedrals
> And leave the dead beneath the ground so cold
> For God is in this hand that I hold
> As we open up the gates of the garden.

What may be said about these different explorations of the journey begun at death? Of course, the gate is itself a favoured image of death itself, the passage through to a place one does not know at all (see Bloch 2006 [1930]: 116–19; 1985 [1930/1969]: 152–56). Yet Cave refuses to take a doctrinaire position on what happens after death, appropriately exploring various options and images, for we can speak of death overcome only in figurative language, in the language of myth, which is necessarily diverse and even contradictory (see Boer 2009b). And within such language, these images jostle with one another for attention, offering different angles on death. After all, is this not appropriate for a poet and singer-songwriter?

Conclusion: Death Is Not the End?

In accounting for this consistent attention to death in Cave's work, a number of easy possibilities present themselves. To begin with, one might simply opine that Cave's fascination, if not near obsession, is unhealthily morbid; anyone who raises the topic more than once is regarded with a look normally reserved for the mentally ill. One instance: bring a camera to a funeral and you will be sternly scolded to keep it closed. Cave falls within this category (as do I by focusing on this feature of his work here), but the fact that he does so is a sign of neither morbidity nor pathology, as should be clear by now.

A somewhat different response would be to suggest that this fixation on death is not so unique to rock music, especially the varieties of punk with which Cave was more than intimate in his earlier years, let alone the near cousins of punk in the varieties of heavy metal. Love and death, *eros* and *thana-tos*, become the dual theme of rockers obsessed with their own mortality. This objection misses the point that these subgenres of rock tend to sit awkwardly with mainstream music, off to the side, cultivating their difference through a troublesome narrative of authenticity. For death is certainly not a favoured topic of the top 20 or even top 100; it rarely if ever commands large sales or downloads. Love, its disappointments and triumphs and thrills, remains the staple of such music. On death, then, Cave is distinctly in the minority; on the way he treats death he is well-nigh unique.

Another, slightly more substantial, possibility is to raise Cave's own individual experience: in 1978 his father died in a car accident when Cave himself was 19. Nothing exceedingly unusual about that, for neither deaths of fathers nor car accidents are foreign even to the lives of those in country Australia. For the teenage Cave it was, however, a deeply traumatic moment. Why? At the time it happened, Cave's mother was bailing him out of prison for some misdemeanour (petty burglary) typical of more rebellious teenagers. But Cave seems never to have forgiven himself; or rather, he has been engaged in an endless drive to atone for that death, one that happened while father and son were not talking much to one another, the one wishing the other out of his life. The problem is, of course, that Cave found himself face to face with the classic Oedipal wish-fulfilment: he may have wished his father gone, seeking to usurp his place with the mother, but when the event actually took place, the shock of the wish's own realization generated not only a lifelong trauma but also a guilt that perpetually seeks atonement.

Nonetheless, such an answer is only partially true, for I have argued for a stronger and more complete picture. To begin with, Cave's unremitting attention to death, especially through violence and crime, whether inflicted or suffered, has not the effect of reinforcing the separation of death from life (in light of Adorno and Horkheimer's comments noted earlier). The dialectical obverse is the case: precisely through his focus on even these violent modes of death, he brings death back into play, seeing it as part of life and not separated from it, for such extreme and brutal deaths are not uncommon, not accidents that break into a life; they are drearily common. In other words, Cave's attention to death goes some way towards countering the reification and fragmentation that severs death from life and renders it both a mechanical process and produces terror at its prospect. Even more, his concern with the nature of the horror-inducing annihilation in the state of death, as well as his metaphoric explorations of what may well happen after death, manifest not a doctrinaire position, whether religious or materialist, but a realistic position in which we can speak only in image, metaphor and myth.

5 God, Pain and the Love Song

Jesus only loves a man who loses.
(Cave 2008)

Not all of Cave's work concerns total depravity, apocalyptic and death, even with their moments of redemption, for now we turn to the first of two topics that at first sight appear slightly more positive – love and Christology. Yet it will come as no surprise that Cave is not one to let these subjects offer a sunny perspective on the grim items that have been our concern until now. That is, even with love and Christ, Cave tarries long with the negative, as Hegel would have it, so much so that one may well describe him as a dialectical musician.

The topic here is the love song. For most people, a mention of Nick Cave's love song evokes the soft and rather melodious pieces of the 1990s and early 2000s – 'Into My Arms', the 'Ship Song' and 'Where the Wild Roses Grow' are perhaps the best known of these. They were also the songs that gave Nick Cave and the Bad Seeds a much wider audience, for the – supposedly – ex-punk rocker had finally given away the clashing, music and harsh lyrics for the piano and harmony. It may come as a surprise to find that Nick Cave has been writing love songs ever since he began writing in his teens (that is, for almost four decades). There are a rather large number of them; Cave says that at a rough count he has written over 200, which is more than the official releases of all the songs (and even poetry) he has written.[1] And they cover all the phases through which Cave has moved with his music – some evoke the first awakening of love and its passion, others the sadness of parting, yet others pain and revenge and anger and sheer brutality.

How are we to make sense of such a range of love songs? I shall argue that two factors are crucial to the way that the love song comes together in Cave's music: God and pain (whether inflicted or received). Before I do so, however, we need to deal with a couple of reflections on the love song by Cave himself. As ever, he tries to direct the interpretation of his own material. As I have argued already in the first chapter, Cave is not the best interpreter of his own work, for he provides rationalizations of his work that distract one from analysing the 'actual behaviour' of his songs (see Adorno 2009 [2006]: 394). For example, in a lecture I have already quoted on the love song, he says, 'The Song of Solomon, perhaps the greatest Love Song ever written, had a massive impact on me.' He followed this up with: 'The Song of Solomon is an extraordinary Love Song but it was the remarkable series of love song/poems known as the Psalms that truly held me... In many ways these songs became the blueprint for many of my more sadistic love songs' (Cave 2004b: 398).

All of this may seem promising. We might distinguish between the 'Solomon Songs', which focus on the love merely between Cave and a woman (the Song of Solomon does not contain a reference to God), and the 'Psalm Songs', which include God and pain. Unfortunately, it is not so straightforward, for the combinations of pain and God in Cave's love song are far more complex. Cave has given me the key terms – God, pain and the love song, with a heavy reliance on the Bible.

Rather than engage in a pseudo-detective-hunt, where one conjures up a conclusion after deft sifting through the evidence and a flash of insight, let me lay out my position here and then explain it in some detail. The two terms of pain and God appear in a pattern of presence and absence, for a song may include or exclude pain and it may do the same with God. In other words, we have four logical possibilities: with pain and without God; with pain and with God; without pain and without God; without pain and with God. As I set out to explore the contours of each type, I begin with some general comments, only to move on and focus on a representative example.

The whole analysis actually fits within a diagram, a version of the Aristotelian square of logical opposites that was later appropriated by Greimas (1987) for linguistic analysis and Fredric Jameson (1987) in order to map out the ideological limits of a cultural product. It has four points.

$$s^1 \longleftrightarrow s^2$$
$$X$$
$$-s^2 \longleftrightarrow -s^1$$

The square is able, in visible and spatial terms, to present the logical outcome of a crucial and initial binary opposition or contradiction, often one that operates in the realm of ideology. Thus, moving beyond the initial term (s^1 in the canonical notation) and its hostile other (s^2), we now find the negatives $-s^2$ and $-s^1$, which at the same time fill out the full range of logical and ideological possibilities and are enlargements of the pair in the upper register. Yet, like that initial pair of opposites, this second couple is always at each other's throats.[2] Deploying the square for the purpose of analysing Cave's love song, the terms fall out as follows:

$$-\text{pain} \longleftrightarrow -\text{God}$$
$$\text{X}$$
$$+\text{pain} \longleftrightarrow +\text{God}$$

Each of the relations, horizontal and diagonal, give us the categories of Cave's love song: -pain and -God; -pain and +God; +pain and -God; +pain and +God.[3]

Secular Soppy Songs: No Pain, No God

> Songs that bang on about what a happy lot this human race is and everything is full of joy, that's an alternate world. (Cave in Sullivan 1998)

I begin with the type of song that we hear spewing out of the radio at all times of the day or night: the secular songs of love, where 'love' really means lust, sex and infatuation. This is where Cave differs very sharply from your garden-variety love song, for after running through more than three decades of music, one is able to find only seven of these secular soppy songs,[4] three of them coming from the unimpressive album, *Nocturama* (Cave 2003) and three from the weaker underside of *Abattoir Blues*, namely *The Lyre of Orpheus* (Cave 2004a).

Let me focus on one of them, 'Rock of Gibraltar' from *Nocturama*, which is a good example of the syrupy pieces that bands continue to spout forth as if they have discovered something jaw-droppingly new. In short, it is a good example of a bad song.

'Rock of Gibraltar' opens with:

> Let me say this to you
> I'll be steadfast and true
> And my love will never falter.
> (Cave 2003)

And 'falter' will soon rhyme with 'Gibraltar', as will 'alter' and 'altar'. This is simply bad poetry. The music is equally as bad: with a rolling pop sound, cheesy is the only way to describe it. Or it is until we realize that the whole song is tongue-in-cheek. It is as if to say, 'you want a sugar-coated loved song, well here!' On more than one occasion Cave has admitted that the critics have given the song a hard time, so much so that he feels sorry for the song. Bad songs, we might argue, need to be nurtured and encouraged, since too many people are ready to tear them to pieces. Even the little kick at the end of the song that tries to undo the naive affirmations of steadfastness, loyalty and love somehow fails:

> Could the powers that be
> Ever foresee
> That things could so utterly alter?
> All the plans that we laid
> Could soon be betrayed
> Betrayed like the Rock of Gibraltar.
> (Cave 2003)

Sadly, this effort at a twist, where the eternal affirmations of love stumble at their first hurdle, doesn't quite work. The reason is that it does not snap the mood of the song, which finishes the way it began without any noticeable change. Indeed, it is fortunate that only five of these secular soppy songs exist. It will come as no surprise that the presence of three of them on *Nocturama* did not help the album's appeal, nor did they help Cave break into mainstream appeal.

Painlessly Divine: No Pain, With God

> God isn't some kind of cosmic bell-boy to be called upon to sort things
> out for us. (Cave in Ellen 1998)

By contrast, the songs that did win over large audiences are what we might call the painlessly divine songs – those flushed with the passion, longing and life-changing moment of first love *and* the presence of God in some fashion. For Cave, this God is a very Christian one, albeit outside the Church or any conventional institution. Before focussing on the hit track 'Into My Arms' as a paradigmatic example, a few comments on the songs as a group are in order. Larger than the previous group, it is still small in number.[5] The music varies, running from the driving 'Hard On for Love' (basically a horny song that uses biblical images for a good rollicking bonk), through the thumping 'Get Ready for Love' (a raucous recovery of the anarchic songs of The Birthday Party days) and the jiggling 'Supernaturally', to the softer and more crooning remainder – 'Into My Arms', 'Brompton Oratory', 'There Is a Kingdom' and 'Gates to the Garden'. It is this last group that has really appealed to a wider audience.

So it is with 'Into My Arms', a simple piano and (very light) bass guitar combine with Cave's voice as the only other presence – a fully developed example of the hymn form in Cave's music (see Chapter 7). The video-clip that accompanied the release of the track was just as simple: Cave sat at a piano on a blank background. A careful listen or three brings out the feature I noted earlier (Chapter 1) in relation to Cave's 'word': the words almost seem to be sung in slow motion. Each word is very carefully articulated, so much so that even if one were stone-deaf it would be possible to understand them. These features are characteristic of many of the painlessly divine songs – the music is understated and minimal, the words are sung slowly and pushed up in the mix so that there is no mistake about what they mean.[6]

The song itself turns on a theological paradox (see also McCredden 2009: 172–73). Cave calls on the interventionist God in whom he does not believe to do precisely that, intervene. Mark 9:24 lurks in the background: 'Lord I believe, help my unbelief.' Even though the song begins with a disavowal – 'I don't believe in an interventionist God' – and even though he asks this God not to intervene should he believe in such a God – 'if I did I would kneel down and ask Him/Not to intervene when it came to you' – eventually he gives in. If such a God did have to intervene, then the least he could do would be to direct the woman in question into his arms. A similar paradox is pursued on a second occasion: while the first concerns an interventionist God, the second deals with angels, in which a disbelief in angels gives way to a prayer that, should they exist, then perhaps they might protect and, of course, guide his lover into his arms.

I have focused on the paradoxical shifts in the song because they bring out a feature of Cave's love songs to which I will return, namely, the elision of faith with love. Or rather, it is the fusion of the love of and faith in a woman with the love of and faith in God. Thus, as he falls in love/faith with the woman, he also falls in love/faith with God – at least as far as the song in concerned. So the first two verses begin with a parallel denial – he doesn't believe in an interventionist God or in angels – only to become a wary statement of faith – asking the interventionist God or the angels to guide the woman in question to Cave. The third verse then begins with, 'And I believe in love/And I know that you do too'. From there the two of them walk on together along the tricky path of the future.

This feature of Cave's love songs is what may be called Cave's Trinity. Not the father, son and holy spirit, but God, Cave and woman, with the outcome that God and the woman merge into one. This Trinity is extraordinarily conventional and yet at the same time touches on taboo. On the conventional side, it is by no means the first time woman has been connected with God. Worshipped, entreated and vilified, women have all too often been both deified and demonized, treated as both goddess and whore.[7]

Yet the connection is also taboo. For a distinct sense of that taboo we need to turn to the very similar 'Brompton Oratory' (it comes from the same softly personal album, *The Boatman's Call* [Cave 1997a]). Also slow and clearly articulated, the song has an ecclesiastical tempo to it – reverend, serious and a little ponderous. The bells and organ, set to a simple tempo, clearly produce a hymn-like feel to the song (see further on the hymn as a form in Chapter 7). The words, too, at least at the beginning, may as well have come from a hymn:

> Up those stone steps I climb
> Hail this joyful day's return
> Into its great shadowed vault I go
> Hail the Pentecostal morn.
> (Cave 1997a)

Soon enough, we come across a move similar to that of 'Into My Arms' – the woman and God merge into one another. Or rather, as I noted in Chapter 1, it is Christ's absence after his resurrection and ascension that Cave compares to the absence of the woman he loves. He wishes she would return just as Christ did – in the form of the Holy Spirit – to his loved ones at Pentecost.

Conventional enough, but the twist comes with the following lines:

> The blood imparted in little sips
> The smell of you still on my hands
> As I bring the cup up to my lips.
> (Cave 1997a)

A far more detailed treatment of this central track will appear in the next chapter on Christology, suffice to point out here that as the singer comes forward to partake of the Eucharist, he smells the woman on his hands. Immediately, all manner of images come to mind: are they vaginal fluids dried after some fingering? Have they been fucking just before he worships? Does the blood in little sips hint at menstrual fluid? The tactile sensuousness of the cup of wine merges with the physicality of sex, especially if we remember that a cup of wine is an ancient biblical metaphor for the vagina and its fluids (Song of Songs).

Here we touch on taboo.[8] Given the Church's long history of desexualizing Jesus and God, any sensuous and sexual connection will raise an eyebrow or two. Not for nothing has one heretical group after another turned the experience of religious faith and ecstasy into a deeply sexual one – libertarian Gnostics during the time of the early Christian Church, radical Anabaptists during the Reformation (as at the kingdom of Münster in 1534–35), Count Zinzendorf and the Moravian Brethren in the eighteenth century, mystics of various stripes and so on. To this I would add the charismatics of our own day, or at least some of them. Some years ago a woman given to the ecstasy of the spirit told me that her experience of Jesus was so deep and so intense that it was better than sex. I was never to find out whether that was the case, but the communion with God was clearly sexual and spiritual – orgasm involved both in equal and indistinguishable doses.

Thus far we have two small collections of love songs, one group without pain or God (the secular soppy songs) and another without pain but with God (the painlessly divine ones). While the first group may not be his best, the second group at least introduces us to a sensuous twist when the love song touches on matters theological. But that twist takes another turn when we introduce pain into the equation.

Painfully Secular: With Pain, No God

> No God up in the sky...could do the job that you did, baby, of bringing me to my knees. (Cave 1997a)

> When those two things get together, love and violence, it makes for some nasty song-writing. (Cave in Sullivan 1998)

The songs of painful love are by far the most common of Cave's love songs. Indeed, the next two categories spill over with songs that Cave has been writing since his high-school days. Following the earlier pattern, I make some general comments before focusing on a paradigmatic song. But now there is an addition – the text of a talk Cave gave in 1999 called, without pretence, 'The Love Song'. As I indicated earlier in this chapter, which should be read alongside my comments on Cave's 'word' in Chapter 1, I engage this piece with some suspicion.

By pain I mean the sadness of love, the disappointment it brings, the anger and desire for revenge that the more passionate among us feel; in short, the sorrow of love. Here my concern is those songs that play with this full range of pain in the midst of love but that do so without any presence of God, any touch of the divine or any hint of theology. Musically, the songs run across the considerable range of Cave in his various incarnations – The Boys Next Door, The Birthday Party, The Bad Seeds and Grinderman.[9] Here are: the crooning love songs promising murder or perhaps pondering what to do with the body; those haunting songs that face grief and loss and see no way out; the raw and crashing post-punk pieces that express the rough edges of loss; the pieces that touch on the blues and thereby speak for themselves; the rocking tunes that soothe the ear; and the gleeful, upbeat songs that are the most sinister of the lot.

However much one might admire the songs of brutal revenge, especially the ones that are slightly tongue-in-cheek, the best examples are those with a lighter touch. They hint at rather than plot the demise of the ex-lover, they seem to express everlasting love knowing full well that it is a pipe-dream. One of the best examples is 'The Ship Song' from *The Good Son* (Cave 1990). The first impression, with its slow tempo, dominant piano and meaningfully sung words, is of a heartfelt love song in the shape of a hymn. Coupled with the first lines, which then become the refrain throughout the song, we have an invitation (used more than once in weddings!) to absolute and wholehearted commitment.

> Come sail your ships around me
> And burn your bridges down
> We make a little history, baby
> Every time you come around.
> (Cave 1990).

The song carries on in a similar vein, expressing the life-changing effects of love – 'when I crawl into your arms/everything comes tumbling down' (Cave 1990) – or the desire to search further into that 'little mystery' that is at the heart of the lover.

A highly seductive song, but its catch is that it has its own less than pleasant secret. When played again and listened to more carefully, more than one person has been troubled by other parts of the song. For instance, the words, 'Come loose your dogs upon me', recur throughout the song. One listener asked me: is it 'doubts' or 'dogs'? Another didn't like the idea of dogs upon her at all. And then we find:

> Your face has fallen sad now
> For you know the time is nigh
> When I must remove your wings
> And you, you must try to fly.
> (Cave 1990)

What is happening here? Is not the ideal of love supposed to be one of mutual respect and encouragement? Are we not supposed to enable the full freedom and flowering of our partner? Not quite, suggests Cave. There is as much clipping of wings as growing them, a struggle for dominance and possession, fencing off and protection from potential rivals. Love is much like the struggle of master and slave in Hegel's famous account – a desperate, unequal and shifting power struggle.

Now Cave's love songs become interesting. If we look more closely at the images we find hints of a violent and sadistic underside. The dogs are loosed, the wings removed, and even burning bridges down evokes a scorched-earth policy more characteristic of warfare than peace and love –nothing other than a touch of the sadistic torture and brutal death that recurs through Cave's songs in myriad different ways. Indeed, most of Cave's love songs mix up sorrow, pain and love in a unique fashion that is often fuelled by anger.

Cave has often been questioned about this element of his love songs. Equally often he has given a range of answers. One is that when he remembers what a former lover has done to him, he becomes angry and gets it out of his system by writing a song. But that is a little too easy, for another, more systematic and deeper reason suggests itself. It comes from his lecture on the love song, given at the *Atelierhaus der Akademie der Bildenden Kunste* in Vienna, on 25 September in 1999 (Cave 2004b).[10] His main argument here is that true love songs cannot avoid an element of pain and deep sadness, of loss and longing. However, since the lecture is saturated with God and the Bible, I need to address the final category of pain before discussing the lecture further.

Brutally Divine: With Pain, With God

> Love as a holy sacrament, agency of redemption and instrument of torture. (Brown 1998)

In the songs of pain and divinity, many of the loose ends come together.[11] Here we find both pain and God, especially in a Christianity where the ultimate expression of God's love comes through the excruciating pain and death of Christ on a cross. Musically, the songs tend towards the softer, hymn-like side of Cave's work, although one or two are still rough and raucous echoes of The Birthday Party and early years of The Bad Seeds, especially 'Sad Waters' from *Your Funeral... My Trial* and 'Do You Love Me?', with their driving beat, as well as the sinister 'Loverman' from *Let Love In*. Overall, this group favours the slower lyrics, dominant piano and a sad, reflective and minor tone.[12]

However, rather than follow my custom thus far of immediately sinking into the detail of a representative song, let us return to the lecture I mentioned a little earlier. The basic point of the lecture, with its delightful literary flourishes, is that a proper love song is one of deep, unrequited and sad longing.[13] The sugary love songs, such as those we considered in our first section, are actually hate songs. In order to support this argument, Cave moves rapidly from topic to topic and from example to example, all of them turning on sadness. So we find the desperate effort to fill the void left by his father's death when Nick was a teenager; the sense that he is completing and living out his father's unfulfilled literary hopes; sadness and the theme of '*duende*' (the 'eerie and inexplicable sadness that lives in the heart of certain works of art'), God and Jesus Christ; the Song of Solomon and the Psalms, especially Psalm 137 and Boney M's popularizing of it; Kylie Minogue's 'Better the Devil You Know'; erotographomania (the uncontrollable urge to write love letters); an analysis of his own song 'Far from Me' from *The Boatman's Call* and then once again the search for God. Quite a mix, but it all comes back to support the argument that the love song is inherently a sad song.

All this is fascinating, more for what Cave does not say than for what he says. To be sure, God is omnipresent (in this lecture), but all his comments about God, the Bible and Jesus boil down to the simple argument that the love song is a prayer. So, Cave suggests that the love song sings God alive since God lives through the words of communication; that the love song is the sound of our efforts to rise above our earthly states and become God-like; that the song is the light of God 'blasting through our wounds'; that – as we have seen – the Song of Songs has influenced him with its rapturous love-metaphors; that the Psalms are the greatest love songs in the world; that the love song seeks to fill the silence between us and God; and that the love song serves God directly. As I said, it really is prayer, but that realization begins to make some sense of what I called earlier Cave's Trinity of woman, God and himself. Quite simply, the love song as prayer is addressed to God as much as it is addressed to the woman.

But the hint of something missing appears in the following: 'Though the Long Song comes in many guises – songs of exultation and praise, *songs of rage and despair*, erotic songs, songs of abandonment and loss – they all address God' (Cave 2004b: 397; emphasis added). And it is far more explicit when he suggests that the Psalms are 'bathed in bloody-minded violence', that they 'became the blueprint for many of my more sadistic love songs' (Cave 2004b: 398). Despite these references, there is no sustained discussion of a type of love song that is quite prevalent: the one that plans, celebrates, mourns and reflects on the murder of a lover. When he does discuss a particular song in detail, it is not one of the songs of murder and mayhem (see the fuller discussion of death in Chapter 4). No, he prefers to focus on Psalm 137, a song of exile and loss 'by the waters of Babylon', or his own song 'Far from Me' (from *The Boatman's Call*), where he can indulge in one of his favourite pastimes – autobiography.

Over against Cave's own preferences, let us consider one of these more violent songs, 'Nobody's Baby Now' from *Let Love In* (Cave 1994). Here we find that, as with 'Idiot Prayer', pain can take two forms. One is pain suffered. Much easier to write about, especially since it is about oneself, Cave stays with this easier topic in his lecture. The love song is thus about loss, sadness and longing. But the other form is pain inflicted. It may be in anger or revenge, but the pain is inflicted on the (ex-)lover. In other words, love is not merely about one's own sadness and longing; it is also about violence inflicted on another.

In 'Nobody's Baby Now', the violence is not immediately obvious. The opening invocation – the search through the Bible, through the poets and analysts and books on human behaviour – indicates a lament, a song of loss and grief and a desperate effort to understand what happened to this love affair. He cannot get that affair out of his life, it seems, for 'she lives in my blood and skin'. But then a few hints emerge, ambiguous lines that may be read in two ways. Thus, we hear the words, 'Her winter lips as cold as stone', as well as 'But there are some things love won't allow.' Cold lips may well be an attitude, a posture in love, but they may also be those of a cold corpse buried beneath a tombstone. And so we want to ask, what precisely is it that love won't allow? All of which becomes much more sinister with these lines:

> This is her dress that I loved best
> With the blue quilted violets across the breast
> And these are my many letters
> Torn to pieces by her long-fingered hand
> I was her cruel-hearted man
> And though I've tried to lay her ghost down
> She's moving through me, even now.
> (Cave 1994)

Again, the scene may well be one of a lonely soul left with a few relics of his departed object of love. But how has she departed? One gains the strong impression of an obsessive lover fingering what is left after a crime of passion. And the reason it feels so is the barely repressed violence. The letters are torn to pieces, he was a cruel-hearted man, violets are flowers that grow upon graves, and he desperately wishes to get her ghost to settle down. The genius of the song is that all this remains understated, hinted at but never quite said.

Barely repressed anger and violence run through this piece, mingling with longing and loss. But it is also a rage and hatred directed at a specific but unnamed woman – a hatred that borders on misogyny. Much of the violence in Cave's songs is directed at women; or rather, his love songs are rather conventionally about women and so when they give voice to pain inflicted on someone else, that person is invariably the woman in question. Now, Cave has been questioned about this inherent tendency from time to time and his answer varies. Sometimes, as mentioned earlier, he suggests it is due to a burning anger at a past lover, so he sits down and writes a song about it. At other times he admits it may be because he went to a private boys' school, so women have become a mystery and threat. And at other moments he says it is better to be open about such matters rather than attempt to repress them in the name of social morals; that he does actually hate this or that woman sometimes; or points to his morbid fascination with murders and the details of serial killers; or simply apologises for misrepresenting women, suggesting that he creates certain types upon whom he then dumps all of his ill feelings and suspicions (Ellen 1998, Nine 1997, Fabretti 2005, Morin 1996, Dwyer 1994). And, as we saw earlier, he also finds inspiration for such songs in the Bible and its violence. But he tends to skip the connection between violence, murders of passion and serial killers, on the one hand, and, on the other, the sense of sad longing that is essential to the love song.

The easy option here would be to take Cave to task for an implicit misogyny and dismiss his work on some ethical ground or other. Apart from being profoundly suspicious of ethics (Boer forthcoming[b]), I would suggest that the much more difficult option is to suggest that, just like sadness, loss and longing, anger and bitter hatred are actually part of love. Cave directs his anger at former women lovers, but it may just as well be directed at men – misandry – given one's sexual predilections. For is not love also a power struggle, a contest between two or more people who attempt to better one another? In love we find surveillance and suspicion, jealousy and anger, breakouts and guilt, curtailment and efforts at change, put downs and mockery – in short, various levels of emotional and intellectual violence. I would suggest that Cave brings out this difficult truth.

One last question: what has all this got to do with the other side of the equation, namely, God? This section is, after all, about God and pain. Here we come across another strange omission: for all Cave's talk of the Bible, the rage of God and soft call of Jesus, the love songs in the Song of Solomon and the Psalms, bringing God to existence through song – for where 'two or more are gathered in my name, there I am also' – for all this and more, Cave rarely if ever refers to the suffering and death of Jesus. This absence is very strange. The story of the cross is, at least according to conventional representations, a story of divine love and pain, of redemption and violence – God loved the world so much that he gave his only son to die for it. Both themes are at the centre of Cave's love songs as well. But so are the less savoury aspects. In the cross we also find the sadistic violence of love, child abuse, redemption through pain and the loving detail of an execution-style murder.

Cave's Trinity of love – God, pain and woman – has taken a rawer turn, much like a lot of his music. It refers not merely to the pain of loss and longing suffered in the love of God and/or of a woman. More importantly, it also refers to the pain inflicted, the angry and sadistic violence of love. In a sense, Cave's search has been for this difficult truth, namely that redemption may in fact come through this brutal and unwholesome side of love. Cave's Trinity embodies both erotic play and painful love.

6 Jesus of the Moon, or, Christology

> I tried to unravel the mystery of Jesus Christ, the saviour.
> (Cave 1994)

In about the year 1988, a major event in music history happened: at the same time that Nicholas Edward Cave made his first serious attempt to give up heroin he also became rather interested in Jesus. Although he would not finally kick the heroin habit until 1997 (leading to a four-year break in recording[1]), the nineties also marks a distinctive shift in his writing and music. As he put it somewhat offhandedly, we can divide his work according to the Bible: while the 1970s and 1980s may be called his Old Testament period, from the 1990s onwards it has been the New Testament: 'After a while I started to feel a little kinder and warmer to the world, and at the same time started to read the New Testament' (Hattenstone 2008). One does not need to look far to find evidence of such a reading: the introduction to the Gospel of Mark (Cave 1998), the depiction of his relationship with his long-dead father in terms of Christ and the Father (Cave 1997b: 141–42), and a string of songs with christological themes, such as 'The Firstborn Is Dead', 'Brompton Oratory', 'Messiah Ward', 'Dig!!! Lazarus Dig!!!' and 'Jesus of the Moon'. Even more, in his studio in Hove, near Brighton in England, there hangs a painting of Christ in all his suffering.[2]

So why does Cave have such a fascination with the figure of Christ? How does Cave's Christology emerge and what is its nature? Indeed, what is the function of such an interest in Cave's work as a whole? In order to answer these questions, I divide the following discussion into three areas: volume and noise, sex and seduction, and heresy. And in order to gain some theoretical traction, I bring into the discussion the work of Theodore Gracyk, Jacques Attali and Theodor Adorno's music criticism, joining the undercurrent of Ernst Bloch that runs through this book.

Before proceeding, another item needs to be addressed here. This chapter marks a shift from the major concern of the preceding chapters, which has been the written work of Cave – whether novels, poetry, plays or the lyrics for songs. Every now and then I have raised questions that deal with the music as well, especially in relation to apocalyptic and death (the sinister song), but these were summary treatments, anticipating the extensive exploration that comes towards the close of the book. That examination, which deals with nothing less than the philosophy of music, appears in its full glory in the next chapter. But here I make an initial foray into an analysis of Cave's music itself, operating with a simpler binary that suits the christological treatment and is able to carry us a reasonable distance into understanding the music. That such a binary will need a third element to render it a properly dialectical analysis is the burden of the chapter that follows.

Volume and Noise

> rock-rock-rock
> Big-Jesus soul-mates Trash-Can
> (Cave 1982)

One may take a range of approaches to understanding the changes that have taken place in Cave's music over the last three decades. One would be to follow an evolutionary path of increasing sophistication, maturity and a digging deep into the roots of rock itself to find new influences (Walker 2009). I prefer a somewhat different, more dialectical approach, at least as a preliminary effort in this chapter, with a focus on noise and volume. Anyone who takes time to listen to Nick Cave's music before the 1990s would characterize most of it with one word – noise. Of course, many influences have helped to produce that noise, such as punk, psychedelic, krautrock, experimental, proto-industrial and primitive rock, or the effect of other bands like Radio Birdman, The Saints, Young Charlatans, Crime and the City Solution, Primitive Calculators, GoBetweens, Whirlywirld, Stooges or the Cramps,[3] but the band always pushed the limits of music into noise. The earlier bands, The Boys Next Door and The Birthday Party, were punk and then post-punk bands, exploring the capabilities of amplified music to see what new noises might come out of those electronic devices. And Cave himself was the wild, pouting, self-important, drug-taking, heavy-drinking, venue-destroying, prophetic figure who would stride out on stage and let the curse of God roar through him. After The Birthday Party imploded in 1983 when the band moved from London to Berlin, Cave settled in the latter city and gathered what would become the first Bad Seeds line-up. The new members came from the underground scene in Berlin, especially Blixa Bargeld, who also played with the infamous Einstürzende Neubauten. Since Cave was heavily into drugs and alcohol, the recording procedure went roughly as follows: he would scribble down lyrics in his scratchy handwriting on rough pieces of paper, turn up at the studio and meet the other band members, and they would construct raw music around those lyrics. Other influences were to follow, such as the heavy sound of the Delta Blues and apocalyptic themes from the Bible.

However, around the year 1990, something changed in the music. Part of it was yet another change in line-up (Conway Savage and Martin Casey joined the group in the next year or two), part was due to Cave's move to Sao Paolo to follow a new love, and part was due to the influence of a long tradition of the *saudade*, love poetry that explored pain in the midst of love (see the previous chapter).[4] But now we start to find Jesus appearing regularly in the lyrics and other writings of Cave.[5] The title track of the new album from 1990, *The Good Son* (Cave 1990), draws directly from the parable of the Prodigal. An increasing number of ballads (in terms of content at least) also turned up, played slowly with lyrics clearly accentuated, speaking of love, pain and Jesus. The quieter, sadder songs of this period also enabled Cave to appeal to a wider audience: 'Straight to You' (Cave 1992), 'Foi Na Cruz' (Cave 1990), 'The Ship Song' (Cave 1990), 'Brother, My Cup Is Empty' (Cave 1992), 'Christina the Astonishing' (Cave 1992), 'Where the Wild Roses Grow' with Kylie Minogue (Cave 1996b) and 'Henry Lee' (Cave 1996b). Perhaps nothing sums up this period better than the second line of 'Nobody's Baby Now' (Cave 1994): 'I tried to unravel the mystery of Jesus Christ, the saviour.' Up until the mid-90s, these slower, quieter songs were interspersed with those that carried on the older, raucous style. But by 1997 *The Boatman's Call* appeared (Cave 1997a). Pared back to the simplest of music styles, it is a deeply introspective album that has song after song with Jesus present in some way or another: 'Into My Arms', 'Brompton Oratory', 'There Is a Kingdom', 'Are You the One That I've Been Waiting For?' and 'Idiot Prayer'. And, as we have seen in Chapter 1, towards the end of the decade, Cave (1998) wrote an introduction to the Gospel of Mark for the Canongate Bible series. The theme continues throughout the next few albums and even up to the present (Cave 2001, 2003, 2004a, 2008), although in the last couple of albums there has been an attempted resolution of the two contrasting tendencies between noise and quiet, raw sound and ordered music, anger and sadness (Walker 2009: 44), or, if you like, the Old Testament and the New (for further discussion of the musical transitions, see the next chapter).[6]

Clearly, something is going on with this confluence of a focus on the figure of Jesus and a marked change in music style. But let us stay with the music and the issue of noise, drawing upon Jacques Attali and Theodore Gracyk. In his influential work, *Noise* (1977, 1985), Attali argues that music is nothing other than organized noise. Different cultures may order that noise in different ways, but the relation of noise to order is, he argues, structurally related to wider patterns in economics and society. For Attali the emergence of noise, unstructured and cacophonous, is a signal of social unrest and economic mayhem. However, when that noise is once again channelled into recognizable patterns of music, it marks the return to ordered social patterns. Does this apply to Cave's music? Can we point to wider patterns of social unrest that show up in his music? It would seem so, especially at two points. The first comes with the disruption of punk – the 'Big One' – in the mid-70s, in which the long decade of the 1960s worked itself out at the level of culture. If the 1960s themselves may be seen as the belated response by a dominant and still colonial West to the anti-colonial and independence struggles of the 1950s,[7] Cave's turn to soft, sad songs about Jesus may be connected directly with another momentous political and economic event – the so-called 'fall' of communism in Eastern Europe. The connection is more direct than one might initially expect, for Cave had lived from 1984 to 1989 in West Berlin, leaving just before the fall of the Berlin Wall to go and live with a new love in Sao Paolo. It is no stretch of the imagination to see that one of the most significant political events of the late twentieth century also makes its mark in his music. I must say I am surprised to see myself making such a direct connection, but it seems difficult to avoid.[8] The turmoil of a personal life notwithstanding (including the struggle with drugs and the traumatic memory of his father's death in a car accident when Cave was 19), Attali's theory has some grip at this point.

What about Jesus? Does the turn to the figure of Jesus in his thoughts, reading and music also play a role? Yes it does, but not quite the way we might imagine. This is where Gracyk's unique proposal comes in. In a study that consciously avoids lyrics and focuses on all the other aspects of rock music – recording, the market, romanticization, rhythm, noise and ideology – Gracyk argues that one of the defining features of rock is its volume. Quite simply, pump up the volume, let the noise roar forth, and you have rock. Indeed, one of the great achievements of punk was to return to the raw, cacophonous effect of stun guitar-work, the absence of chordal eights and the, flat, disinterested voice of the lead singer (as with the brilliant debut single, '(I'm) Stranded', of the Australian and world's first punk band, The Saints, in 1976). It follows, then, that should one turn down the volume, pare back the music and slow down the rhythm, then we have something else. It is certainly not rock – perhaps folk music, ballad, jazz, classical, or in Cave's case, what I will call the hymn in the next chapter. In other words, there is a decided shift from about 1990 in Cave's music. To be sure, one encounters plenty of the older-style, anarchic and punk-inspired rock in the music of the early years of the 90s, but by the time we get to *The Boatman's Call*, the rock has well and truly gone (although it was not to disappear forever). Here we find hymns, sombre ballads and laments.

And the subject matter of all these new songs is both painful love and Jesus. Does this mean that Cave's New Testament turn has brought about a change in his music? Indeed, has Cave 'found' Jesus in some conversion? At a stretch, one could read some of his comments in this way. For example, Cave points out that although Jesus does not represent the whole, exclusive truth, what he does like is 'the inner rest and freedom that Christ offers' (Sierksma 1997). When he finally came to read 'those four wonderful prose poems of Mark, Matthew, Luke and John', he writes, 'I slowly reacquainted myself with the Jesus of my childhood...and it was through him that I was given a chance to redefine my relationship with the world' (Pascoe 1997). Further, in his intro- duction to Mark he points out, 'The Christ that emerges from Mark, tramping through the haphazard events of His life, had a ringing intensity about him that I could not resist. Christ spoke to me through His isolation, through the burden of His death, through His rage at the mundane, through His sorrow' (Cave 1998). In sum, 'He is the real, real thing' (Cave 2004a).[9]

However, rather than see this turn to Christ, from the spiteful God of the Old to the quiet, sad Christ of the New Testament, as the cause of Cave's evo- lution into the sad ballads of the 1990s, I would like to reverse the equation.[10] Instead of taking an idealist line in which one's inner convictions, one's 'atti- tudes' (as we hear so often), are the keys to change, I prefer to flip the whole equation over, stand them on their feet, so to speak, and connect them to the turn in Cave's music. In other words, the appearance of Christ acts as a signal of that shift. Now in case someone should object that I have dwelt too long with a Marxist argument (although there should always be 'vulgar' Marxists), in which the economic base acts as the primary cause for anything that hap- pens in the realms of ideology, culture and, above all, religion, I should point out that Cave may think that Jesus and the New Testament are a major cause. He may even feel – and there is good evidence to suggest that this is the case – that Jesus has led his music down quieter paths. But this is more like an after-effect, a reciprocal action that folds back on the reality of the music.

Sex and Seduction

> Lying there with all the light on your hair
> Like a Jesus of the moon, Jesus of the planets and the stars
> (Cave 2008)

One curious feature of these 'Jesus songs' (hymns really) has struck me for some time: more than one person has confided in me that they are extraordi- narily seductive. At one level I can well understand the sentiment, for many of them offer and ask for utter and total commitment. Above all, Cave has made a specialty of involving Jesus in a good number of love songs. Despite the fact that Cave claims he has written more than 200 love songs (see the previous chapter), some of these songs contain a specific feature that stands out – an erotic and seductive evocation of Jesus in a way that reminds one eerily of John Donne.

Here I shift to a consideration of the lyrics and I would like to exegete one track in particular, 'Brompton Oratory', which I have discussed briefly in the chapter on the love song.[11] The setting is the baroque Oratory of St Philip Neri, which includes statues of the twelve apostles in the Nave, statues originally carved in 1680 CE for the cathedral in Sienna (McCredden 2009: 168). The songwriter begins by walking up the steps of the oratory, hailing the joyful day's return. It is Pentecost and the reading comes from Luke 24, especially the verses where Christ returns to his loved ones after the resurrection. But now the song turns and the singer looks at the 'stone apostles', thinking to himself that such a joyful return is alright for some. But for him, he wishes he was made of stone so that he did not have to encounter a 'beauty impossible to define', impossible to believe or to endure. The third stanza moves to the act of communion, in which the blood is 'imparted in little sips' with the 'smell of you still on my hands'. And as he brings the cup to his lips, he reflects that no God in the skies or devil in the sea could 'do the job that you did' of bringing him to his knees. We close with him sitting on the stone steps, feeling at a loss, forlorn and exhausted 'by the absence of you'.

The song opens with the lightest of percussion, a swish on the cymbals and a soft tap on a snare drum. The only other instrument is an organ that plays in an ecclesial fashion. Indeed, as I argue in the following chapter, this track has the hallmarks of an ever-so-slightly upbeat hymn, which might conceivably make its way into the repertoire of a church choir – except that the lyrics may not be as acceptable for such a context. However, that subversive element does not show up initially. The first four lines invoke hymnody with images of the stone steps, the joyful day's return, the shadowed vault and the hailing of the Pentecostal morn.[12] Already a hint of the song's paradox of loss appears: the 'joyful day's return' runs a contrary path to the painful disappearance of a lover.

Yet this tension in the lyrics is first established in a curious disjunction between the style of music and those first words of joy. The music may be hymn-like, but it is certainly not the hopeful tones of Pentecost; more appropriate to Good Friday, perhaps, or Jesus' temptation in the desert, or the murder of the innocents. When the words kick in, we hear of climbing up to a joyful Pentecostal morn – an immediate jarring sets in. Add to this the way that Cave sings the words – mournfully slowly – and the song is full of tension.

One more tension completes the collection. The first stanza (the first four lines) evokes a collective scene of worship that the singer is about to join. We follow him as he steps upward, entering the church to what we assume to be a Pentecost worship service. Yet as soon as the second stanza begins – 'The reading is from Luke 24' – we undergo a shift from the collective to the personal, or rather from participation to observation. Suddenly, the song shifts to the singer's reporting on what is going on. The feeling of being at the beginning of a hymn has been shattered, for this is very much an individual and personal song.

Now I can return to the tension I mentioned earlier, namely between the sense of return evoked by the Gospel passage and the singer's own palpable sense of loss.[13] That loss is not stated until the last line: 'By the absence of you'. Yet it overshadows the whole song before that final line. So there is a gentle twist with the Gospel reading and the stone apostles. The words do not specify which verses from Luke 24 are read, but the various pericopes of that chapter concern the women at the tomb on the Sunday morning, the appearance of Jesus to the two walking to Emmaus, his appearance among the gathered followers soon afterwards and then the explanation of what had happened. It is quite clearly a story of return, although with Cave's own twist, 'to his loved ones'. This evocation of love jars with the stone apostles to whom he turns his gaze. Stone hearts, I wonder, or perhaps a reflection of the singer's own heart. Of course it is, for the stone apostles were once the lucky ones, but not the stone-dead heart of the singer. They found their lover coming back to them... Up until this point the song is interesting but not stunning: he goes into a church, hears a Bible reading, looks at some statues and thinks about his own sad state. Many run-of-the-mill love songs have done better. But then something new enters the song with the lines,

> A beauty impossible to define
> A beauty impossible to believe
> A beauty impossible to endure

This is the beauty he does not wish to see, a beauty that includes a hint of pain with the final word of the third line. A beauty impossible to endure is not necessarily a pleasurable one, or perhaps it is a pleasure found only through pain. But whose beauty? Is he referring to the apostles seeing the beauty of the risen Christ? Or is it Cave himself who does not wish to look upon that beauty? Or is it the beauty of the lover who has gone? We do not know quite yet, unless of course we have listened to the song countless times. What begins to happen is a merging of Christ and the loved one – the two begin to overlap, wash into one another, and the singer's passionate devotion applies to both.

Or perhaps they are one and the same – a trinity of Cave, Christ and an unknown lover that I identified in the previous chapter. But this is really only the beginning, for the abstract admiration and puzzlement over beauty passes over into physical, sensual contact, although not in the way we might expect. Blood is imparted in little sips: here we have the evocation of the cup of wine at the Eucharist, tipped gently by the priest or minister as the communicant kneels. Then he takes control and lifts the cup up to his own lips. Between these two acts is a line that shifts the whole register: 'The smell of you still on my hands'. Is this the smell of Christ? Or, as I suggested earlier, is it the smell of sex, of vaginal fluids, or perhaps of something else? If so, the sex must have been recent. Or is there a hint of something that pushes past the boundary into fetishized sex? The lines now evoke menstrual fluid, the blood in little sips slides towards pain and loss, and the cup is not necessarily a Eucharistic cup but melds with the cup of suffering mentioned in Christ's prayer in Gethsemane – 'My father, if it be possible, let this cup pass from me' (Matthew 26:39). And if we recall the Song of Songs, then the cup of wine itself becomes a metaphor for a moist, lubricated and aroused vagina.

It is never clear whether Cave sings of his lost lover or of Christ, for the Eucharist becomes a moment of sensual and physical contact with both Christ and the lover (see also McCredden 2009: 170–71). Or rather, it is a memory, a physical recovery, or even a transubstantiation of what was lost, for Christ too had gone and left his lovers behind. Does Cave hope that the act will bring back his lover? It does not seem to be the case. In the chapter on the love song, I suggested that this track broaches sexual taboo, especially in light of the Church's de-sensualization and de-sexualization of Christ, but here I would suggest that it also reminds us of the overt sexuality and passionate spirituality of the mystical tradition. One of the best examples is the twelfth-century Beguine, Hadewijch of Brabant from the Netherlands (from her seventh vision):

> On that day my mind was beset so fearfully and so painfully by desirous love that all my separate limbs threatened to break and all my veins were in travail. The longing in which I then was cannot be expressed by any language... I desired to have full fruition of my beloved, and to understand and taste him to the full. I desired that his Humanity should to the fullest extent be one in fruition with my humanity, and that mine then should hold its stand and be strong enough to enter into perfection until I content him. (Hadewijch 1980: 280)

However, another feature of this mystical and sensual tradition may pass unnoticed: the sex of the lover is never specified. We assume the singer's lost lover is female, largely because of the biographical knowledge that Cave is heterosexual. But English does not specify gender with its second pronoun (the reference to 'baby' is no giveaway). And so it is by no means clear whether the one who has gone is female or male. The boundaries between bodies, identities and gender become quite blurred as they fold over and leak into one another – and that includes Christ. Cave's Christology has become decidedly queer, transgendered and sensual.

So it is with the remaining words of the song: the lover who does far more of a job on the singer than either God in heaven or the devil beneath the sea is now both/and the sensual Christ and the lost lover. But as with so many of Cave's songs, that devotion and passion is not a source of joy. Exhausted pain washes over the end of the song, and as with Cave's best love songs, the pain is most exquisite when both God and pain are present – now in the figure of Christ.

Heresy

> A shadowy Jesus flitted from tree to tree. (Cave 1992)

Nick Cave's Christology is becoming a little heretical. Sceptical of the Church and its teaching, not given to believing in the historical veracity of the Virgin Birth or the Resurrection, and then finding a sensual and sexual Christ who has a peccadillo for threesomes is not your run-of-the-mill orthodox Christology. I would add his observations that the Christ who draws Cave in is a creative and artistic Christ who is misunderstood and shunned. This Christ embodies the struggle of faith, trying to understand what it means to live in relation to God. Christ struggles and fails, only to be abandoned by those whom he felt were closest. Elsewhere, he presents a picture of a writer's God, saying that he most certainly believes in God but that he writes God into existence anew with each song or poem. Or he suggests that God is present only when 'two or three are gathered' (see Cave 1998, Hattenstone 2008, Dwyer 1994, Pascoe 1997). Further, as we have already seen, the existential effort to come to terms with the death of his father – a devastating and 'palpable sense of loss' (Maume 2006) – in a car accident when Cave was a teenager, is articulated in terms of the relationship between Christ and the Father.

So how do we read this sensual, seductive, creative, uncertain, collective and very personal lover, Christ? What I do not propose to do is take Cave's word on all this, for he is too well known for seeking to direct interpretation of his own work (see Chapter 1). Instead, I wish to play off three theorists against one another, particularly on the question of the romanticization of rock. For Alan Bloom (1987), the wild, barbaric, Dionysian jungle beat of rock is to be abhorred. Rock releases the primal urge, encourages people to wild, indiscriminate sex, drugs, booze and rolls back the achievements of order and culture as embodied in someone like Mozart. By contrast, for Camille Paglia (1992: 19–21) the primitive urge of rock is its great appeal. Rock releases the deeply repressed side of ourselves, offering an unmediated expression of our most individual and rebellious side. Paglia argues that rock has 'sold out' by becoming commercialized, by pandering to the record companies and the market and by seeking money over genuine and unique artistic expression.

Neither position offers anything particularly new. At heart, they share the same assumption, namely that rock is fundamentally primitive and Dionysian. Bloom might want it banned and Paglia might want it released, but they are on the same ideological ground, for which Adorno's devastating criticisms – that the claim to primitiveness on behalf of popular music (especially jazz) is the purest false consciousness – are as relevant as ever (Adorno 1999 [1959]: 169–71; see Witkin 1998: 164–65). Musicians too inevitably romanticize rock in similar ways. A young band bashing it out in someone's garage (as did Cave and company in the early 1970s while still at high school) will swear never to sell out. Speculation continues as to when Bob Dylan sold out – was it when he introduced electric sound in that fateful concert in 1966 when someone was heard to yell out 'Judas' from the audience? Or did he do so when he made an advertisement for the new Cadillac Escalade in 2007? Or if a band moves from an underground recording label to one of the big multi-nationals, some will spit in disgust at the move.

However, as Gracyk (1996: 175–206) argues cogently, rock had been defined from the moment it began as a recording, commercial venture. Its aesthetic cannot be understood without such a reality. Even underground and alternative singers and groups find a place within a commercial network dominated by the market. So what are we to make of the claims to originality, to authenticity and to individual expression? Cave is one who plays the line so well, stating over and over that he is not interested in being popular or in selling albums or being relevant, is surprised and suspicious when the band is successful (he withdrew his nomination for the 1996 MTV music award for best male artist since his temperamental muse is not a racehorse); he insists on rebutting not merely the status quo but also alienating his own milieu, refusing to allow any of his music to be used for advertising, arguing that the creative process is intensely private and happens of its own accord, and that all he desires is to be true to himself – in short, pursuing the authenticity of the individual artist (among others, see Cave 1996a, Dombal 2010, Doran

2010, Pishof 2001, Casey 2001, Calkin 2001, Peake 1998, Brown 1998, Thompson 1997, Margetts 1997, Mulholland 1996, Dwyer 1994, Engelshoven 1994). What the youthful and drug-addled Cave wrote of Einstürzende Neubaten applies equally well to his own view of his own musical production:

> Through their own hard work, by *steadfast lack of compromise*, through the pain of true self-expression, through a genuine love of their medium, they have attained a sound which is first *authentic*, and which is *utterly their own*. But not for the sake of being different. They are a group which has developed its own special language for one reason – to *give voice to their souls*... This is why E. N. will remain timeless. They have always known the meaning and purpose of their medium: to give vent to the expression of the soul. (Cave 1988a: 158; see also Goldman 1998; Walker 2009: 45)

I have added the emphases, since they highlight the well-worn key terms of the authentic, individual musician: lack of compromise, authentic, utterly one's own, giving voice to one's soul. In response, it is all too easy to find examples where he has 'sold out', such as seeking out interview after interview (they now run into the many hundreds over the last three decades),[14] or becoming a commercial success with the 'Jesus songs', or singing a duet with Kylie Minogue (Cave 1996b), or being inducted into the music hall of fame.

Let me bring all this back to the heretical Christology of Nick Cave, deploying an insight from Adorno, namely, that the claim to artistic autonomy (so characteristic of high modernity) not only gives off signals about its own social and economic location but is actually a prime mode in which social reality embeds itself, precisely at the moment when art sees itself as thoroughly aloof from such reality. Indeed, in proper dialectical fashion, Adorno argues that artistic autonomy not only gives off signals about its own location, but it is also the prime mode in which social reality embeds itself, precisely when music (and art) seeks to be and thinks that it is aloof from such reality (Adorno 1999 [1959]: 1–14; 2002: 391–430; 2006 [1949]: 99–102; see Schweppenhäuser 2009: 105).[15] In Cave's case, he has said time and again that he has no time for the insipid and colourless Christ of the churches, citing his experience as a choir-boy in the Wangaratta Anglican Church. Instead, we are given a distinctive and individual picture of Christ, blending elements from here and there and offering his own original pieces to the mosaic. But this fits in perfectly well with the authentic, individual artist who seeks meaning by being true to himself. It is, I would suggest, nothing less than claim to the autonomous individual, free to express his or her own position without constraint; in a word, heresy.

Although we can trace the lineaments of such an individual back at least to Augustine, with the Enlightenment the private individual became a leitmotiv of the new ideology of liberalism. It was a very political move, for asserting the value of each individual threatened the vested interests of church, dogma, or God-given absolute power for a monarch. Following the French Revolution, in one European country after another, the claim to individual rights, to democracy, republicanism and freedom of speech in the name of those rights, was regarded as a threat to the very foundations of society. Tom Paine's widely read *Rights of Man*, written in 1791 after he emigrated from England to North America, was proscribed and burned, and those who printed and distributed it were thrown in prison. The proponents of this new liberal ideology, centred in merchant groups in the towns, were watched by the police, their presses were censored or closed down, and their leaders often had to go into exile. Yet the pattern of economic production and relations – capitalism – for which this ideology of liberalism was the most elaborate and appropriate expression was eventually to win through so that it is almost impossible for us now to imagine any other world.

The ideology of the sacrosanct individual, along with the laissez-faire capitalism that is its inseparable twin, occasionally goes into eclipse (not least in the economic crash of 2008 and the prolonged recession that followed), yet soon enough it shines out as brightly as ever after these periodic periods of darkness. Above all, it is alive and well in art and popular music, taking the form of the authentic artist who will not compromise her or his individual expression. This liberal, bourgeois tradition lies at the heart of Cave's idiosyncratic Christology.[16] I would also suggest that heresy is the best word for both this Christology and for the ideology of the authentic individual. After all, is not heresy the ability to make a choice, from *hairesis*, the ability of an individual to strike on a path of his or her own? It is not for nothing that the churches have struggled to keep heresy on the list of damnable sins, for the ideology of liberalism is so much part of our landscape that the charge of heresy these days evokes the dark and dingy times of medieval power and usually brings forth a laugh or mere curiosity that it could still be invoked.

Conclusion

> The face of Jesus in my soup. (Cave 1988b)

This heretical Christology, which I must admit has its appeal at certain points, is one that emerges out of a particular Enlightenment ideology of the sacrosanct and inviolable individual. It may mark a profound shift in the nature of

Nick Cave's music, from the crashing punk rock of the 1970s or the post-punk of the early 1980s, to the slower, quieter love songs of the 1990s and beyond. It may collapse the boundaries of gender and sex in a uniquely sensual Trinity, it may give expression to a bewildered Christ who is trying to sort out what faith means and who this 'father' really is, and it may be an artist's Christology, one that brings God to life in writing, song and the gathering of a few. But this heresy fits in perfectly well with all the other heresies that one may find. Nick Cave has 'chosen' and constructed the heresy that means most to him. I must admit that I am the last one to allow anyone else to tell me what to do or think, but I wonder whether a more iconoclastic heresy, as Adorno persistently argued (2006), would be one that challenges such an underlying ideology and its economic system.

7 Hearing Around Corners: Nick Cave Meets Ernst Bloch

> There is an intrinsically creative aesthetic which not only comments but is spontaneous, speculative. It is only in the latter's interpretation that truly 'absolute' music is established, that the envisioned, utopian castle of music reveals itself.
> (Bloch 1985b: 93)

Nick Cave and the philosophy of music – is that not an incongruous and improbably pairing? Possibly, but that is precisely what I propose to undertake in this final chapter: an interpretation of Cave's entire opus through the ears of Ernst Bloch's philosophy of music. Why Bloch? To begin with, my own attraction to Bloch runs deep, for he is one of the few philosophers who seduces me, who gets my juices flowing, who continues to excite with a startling insight. Bloch combines philosophical rigour, Marxist analysis, a thorough interest in religion and an arresting approach to music. The first three elements of his work may be reasonably well known (see Boer 2007a: 1–56), albeit not as well as they should be, but Bloch's philosophy of music remains one of the hidden gems of his work. So far, so good, but why analyse Cave's music in terms of Bloch's philosophy of music? Intimate knowledge of Bloch and thorough saturation in Cave's music reveal a close affinity between the two, especially through the dialectical features of music itself. However, in order to establish that affinity, one must also rely on a deeper appreciation, a hearing around corners, in order to gain the sense that through their very modes of expression, their musical outlook, intensity and hope, they come close indeed. Above all, they share an appreciation of both the theological and utopian, or theo-utopian dimensions of music, a crucial feature of the analysis that follows.

Before proceeding, a word on the place of this chapter in the total structure of the book is in order. To begin with, in relation to the previous chapter, this one picks up the initial analysis found there of the shifting musical forms of Cave's work, but now it moves beyond a binary analysis (although a hint of a third feature did begin to emerge) to a full-blooded dialectical analysis. In light of the book as a whole, my analysis has thus far been largely, although not exclusively, concerned with either the literary production of Nick Cave (novels, poems, plays and the like) or the lyrical content of his songs. But now, as a way of drawing the analysis to a close, I focus exclusively on the musical forms of his work, all of which present a complex pattern in search of musical redemption.

Hearing Around Corners

I begin with a concise statement of Bloch's philosophy of music,[1] with an ear cocked for what is relevant for my analysis of Cave: in the bravura 'Philosophy of Music' section that opens his *Spirit of Utopia*, Bloch offers a thorough retelling of the belated story of music by emphasizing its very human nature, recounting that story in terms of the basic category of the note and its hangers-on (hearing, voice, song, dance and rhythm), listening with a philosophical and theo-utopian ear that attempts to hear around corners.

Let me say a little more about each of these carefully weighted terms in this brief description. To begin with, Bloch's philosophy of music is a thorough retelling of the story of music. Now, at one level, Bloch assumes that music itself does not have a narrative and that it cannot be represented in conventional terms. So writes David Drew in his detailed introduction to the English translation of Bloch's musical essays: 'it is essential to his philosophical purpose that music is imageless and without narrative form' (Drew 1985: xxv), precisely so that Bloch may assume that music is philosophy, requiring the merest gloss and clarification. True enough, at least as far as this position enables Bloch to avoid the narrative pull of those forms he favours, such as song, fugue, sonata and opera. However, at another level Bloch offers a profound retelling of the story of music, now in terms of the twisting fortunes of the note and the song.

More of that in a moment, since first I wish to reprise the second phrase: the story of music is a belated one. Although he later qualifies the point,[2] Bloch argues that it is crucial for understanding music that it appears lately, as one untimely born: 'The Persians, Chaldeans and Egyptians, the Greeks and schoolmen, *all of them without any music worth mentioning*' (Bloch 1985b: 136; emphasis Bloch's).[3] Only in the last few centuries, and especially – I would add – since the explosion of the myriad forms of rock music since the 1950s, has music come into its own as a central and complex cultural form (Cave of course is part of this late flourishing). Why? Not only does it step into the role of a seemingly fading religion, but the lateness of music gives it a uniquely dialectical role in the anticipation of utopia, for it both negates and transforms, or rather sublates (*Aufhebung*) the hope embodied in religion. So too with Cave: in fact, for Cave music and religion are intrinsically bound up with one another, so much so that I begin to suspect that Bloch's dialectical analysis seems as though it were written for the treatment that follows.

Further, Bloch never tires of emphasizing that music is a distinctly human activity. Known only through that most embedded of sense receptors – the ear – and manifested first as a listening to oneself, music is what we would now call a very human construct. For Bloch, this means that the building blocks of music are – after the note – voice, song and the dance in which rhythm first manifests itself. But it also means that Bloch opposes any argument for the mathematical, supra-human and divine (Pythagoras and his myriad successors) existence of music, whether of spheres, planets or angels; or rather, he reads these in a dialectical fashion that enhances intimate human creativity in and through music. In other words, in that old opposition between technique and interpretation, between written score and performed piece, Bloch sides with the latter while seeking to transform the former. This also means that any analysis of music must resort primarily to the human act of listening rather than technical analysis of scores, for only in this way can we hear around corners (see more below). It seems to me obvious, but it is worth pointing out that in many cases with rock the score follows the performed piece, written after the fact and not as a primary moment of creativity; the musical piece emerges first in late-night strumming and humming, the pressing of a key or quiet blast on a flute. Once performed and accepted by listeners, the score appears late, demanded by those who wish to know how to play the piece.

I have already mentioned the pivotal role of the note in Bloch's philosophy, as indeed its fellow-travellers on the journey (voice, song, dance and rhythm). The note follows a varied and twisting path; or rather it cuts a very new path through what is mostly a European collection of musical forms and a German collection of musicians. While I criticize Bloch in a longer study for his very narrow focus (Boer forthcoming[a]), I also seek out the shape of his argument rather than its content, for what Bloch does with his dialectical readings of the fugue and sonata, or Bach, Beethoven and Wagner, is thoroughly recast the story of music so that in transforming its past the future begins to look decidedly different and more hopeful. In what follows, I set out to follow the note's own fascinating if diverse path in Nick Cave's work, although I do so in light of a specific concern of Bloch: the song. Why the song? Music begins, argues Bloch, with listening to our bodies, with noticing its trembling and twitching desire to dance, but also our love of singing, of singing to ourselves. Hum, whistle, tapping foot and nodding head are at the origins of music. In other words, since music is a thoroughly human affair, the note is embodied above all in the song. Now, Bloch will go on in his great retelling to distinguish between: (a) singing-to-oneself, which is manifested in the dance and in chamber music; (b) the uniform song (*geschlossenes Lied*), the secular version of which is the oratorio (with which Bloch spends relatively little time), while the sacred one is the fugue; (c) the open-ended song (*Handlungloper*), where we find the sonata, Beethoven and Bruckner, the transcendent opera, the symphony and Wagner (Bloch 1985c: 14–15; 1974: 22–23). Of course, the three are dialectically related, with singing-to-oneself as a form that is *constitutive*, the uniform song as an *impinging* type of song, expecting something more, not so that it can be discarded but be transformed, and the open-ended song as a *fulfilment* that draws the other two forms into itself, realizing their potential and transforming them in the process (*Aufhebung*). When I first read Bloch's philosophy of music and listened (again) to Cave's work, I thought that this particular argument of Bloch was the least useful, that the types of song were tied to his own very German situation. Yet, by the time I had made my way through three decades or more of Cave's music, it was precisely this analysis that provided me with some specific tools. So I began to distinguish between the anarchic or discordant song, the hymn (and its related lament), the sinister song and the dialectical song, all of which relate to one another in a pattern that is nothing other than a search – now at a distinctly musical level – for redemption.

Three items remain in my brief statement of Bloch's philosophy of music: he listens with a philosophical and theo-utopian ear, all the while striving to hear around corners. The first is obvious, especially in light of my earlier point that Bloch – the philosopher – sees music as philosophy in and of itself, needing but a touch-up here and a gloss there. However, Bloch's philosophical interest has a particular curve, for his lifelong pursuit was for a philosophy of hope, seeking not only to discover within the existing, albeit limited parameters of philosophy its own irrepressible utopian drive, but also to reconstruct philosophy with an opening to utopia (Bloch 1995, 1985a, 2000, 1985c) – hence the 'utopian ear', but theo-utopian? As any reader of Bloch's 'Philosophy of Music' soon discovers, theology is never far from the surface. And when Bloch comes to close the various sections of that work on music, particularly the work as a whole, theology comes into play, explicitly, heretically, apocalyptically, in what I like to call his theo-utopian flourishes. More than one commentator (Geoghegan 1996, Hudson 1982, Jones 1995) has become uncomfortable with this theological Bloch, preferring to see such flourishes (elsewhere in his work, for few have commented on the 'Philosophy of Music') as unfortunate slips or at best peripheral rhetoric. I cannot disagree more and cannot emphasize enough how important theology is for understanding Bloch's work as a whole, let alone his musical reflections (see further Boer 2007b: 1–56). Again the curious connection between Bloch and Cave shows itself, for theology is central for understanding Cave's work as well.

This theo-utopian ear has two dimensions. First, Bloch is astute enough to realize that the Bible and theology are laced with utopian themes, especially those relating to the last days, the eschaton and salvation, whether individual and collective, themes that he is keen to appropriate and reshape in a utopian direction. Second, we must not forget that Bloch saw music picking up the mantle of religion, a mantle that had slipped to the ground with the onset of modernity and secularism. So it should come as no surprise that eschatological themes from theology infuse his philosophy of music, for music functions as the *Aufhebung* of theology itself (once again, such a description will turn out to be apposite to Cave himself).

Finally, what does hearing around corners mean? Simply put, it is an intuitive grasp of the deeper urges and drives of music, well beyond analysing scores, techniques of production, performance and recording, or assiduously learning the 'rules' of musical (dis)harmony.[4] For Bloch, that hearing is, as we have seen, distinctly utopian, dialectical and theological. So it will not do to rely upon what musicians say about their own work, or to rest with criticizing Bloch for his obvious lacks concerning musical history, theory and technique (some of which he sought to correct in his later work), or to challenge his interpretations of composers such as Bach, Beethoven and Wagner, or indeed – as I am inclined to do – to castigate him for a very European and especially German focus (both of them anomalies within world music). Instead, the specifics become the means to a deeper insight into the very workings of music, requiring what he calls a 'clair-hearing' or 'clair-audience' in interpretation – *Hellhören*, a play on *Hellsehen*, clairvoyance (Bloch 1974: 163; see also Korstvedt 2010: 153). Elsewhere he calls it a 'metaphysics of divination and utopia [*Metaphysik von Ahnung und Utopie*]' (Bloch 1985b: 131; 1974: 154). But this also means that Bloch's approach is far more amenable to analysing material seemingly at some distance from what he does analyse – in my case, the varied collection of music created by Nick Cave.

Concerning the Wandering Path of the Note, or, Forms of the Song

With Bloch in mind, the nub of my argument may be stated briefly: the basic form of the song in Cave's work is the anarchic or discordant song (even though he worked hard in his early days to discover this form), but he attempts to resolve the internal tensions of this song through two main approaches and a few sidelines: one is the hymn and the lament (and then also a delightful perversion which I call the sinister song), and the other is the dialectical song. Always tempted by the hymn, I suggest that musical redemption is achieved – always partially – only through the dialectical garage song, in which the former anarchic song is allowed full reign. Listening with a theo-utopian ear,

I suggest that these tensions and the effort to overcome them constitute the musical shape of Cave's search for redemption.

We will soon immerse ourselves in the detail of more than three decades of music, so let me at the outset outline the major features of each type of song in which the note manifests itself in Cave's work.[5] The anarchic song, found almost entirely with The Birthday Party and a little with The Boys Next Door and The Bad Seeds, is best described as the note under internal attack, engaged in civil war or class struggle. Here the song fully exploits its closeness to noise (Attali 1985, 1977), pushing with some effort to glorious anarchic breakdown. This is, of course, the punk note, which we have already met in the preceding chapter in terms of noise and volume, for the early Cave was part of what was then (in the late 70s and early 80s) the refreshing moment known as punk.[6] Closely related, to the extent that I usually take it as part of the anarchic song, is the discordant song: defined by the note under tension, now we find the song pulled in all directions, often embodied in the various instruments of the band and the voice, but at times the tensions are manifested within each of these zones. The differences between the anarchic and discordant song are that in the former the bass line is caught up enthusiastically in the mayhem, while in the latter the bass usually tries to anchor the song, sometimes with success and at others without; the former applies mostly to The Birthday Party, while the latter is found with The Bad Seeds.

The major new direction in the twisting path of the note, as it moves from the tent of one song to another, is the hymn: characterized by a noticeably dominant keyboard, often simply a piano or organ,[7] and a muted bass line, the hymn is sung slowly, accompanied in a way that recalls a choir – or, if one prefers a more democratic bent to religious music, the congregation – and is more conventionally harmonic. With comprehensive and intimate listening (so much so that the music seems to inhabit every corner and cavity of one's head), the hymn comes through clearly as a melodious counter to the anarchic song. A sub-group of the hymn is the lament – with its own deep biblical heritage – which is virtually the same as the hymn, except that the drawn-out note falls, again and again, at the end of each phrase and line. I will suggest below that in the night of the lament we find that the note has become one of longing, held in failing anticipation.

Before we come to the third major shape of the song, I need to note one variation, if not a perversion, namely the sinister song (which we have met in Chapter 4 in the discussion of death). In brief, this song is a means by which the hymn and the discordant song meet one another. More of a one-night-stand or perhaps an occasional affair, this is a minor but intriguing song: a hymn with an ominous twist, in which discordant elements are more comfortable.

Found mostly on *Murder Ballads* (Cave 1996b), it signals that the hymn may actually offer us a false redemption, that sin always crouches at the door.

If the sinister song provides welcome relief from what quickly becomes a tiresome hymn (*The Boatman's Call* [Cave 1997a], dominated by hymns, is perhaps the least listenable of all Cave's recordings), then the dialectical song is the full, adrenalin-pumping resolution. Now we have the splendour of the anarchic/discordant song, but in a way that dialectically overcomes the discordant nature by allowing each element to flourish fully. The tempo is usually upbeat, in full rock – much like a bunch of old rockers returning to the garage of their youth and letting rip with glee. While the hymn may seem easy to find, the dialectical song is as difficult to achieve as the anarchic song: full of hard work, running the danger of slipping away again, its moments are more fleeting than one would hope. Not only does that heighten the sheer pleasure of such moments, but it is another mark of Cave's difficult search for redemption.

Anarchy...

> 'Listen to this, Dad. Did you ever play real music like this?' And Cave will reply, his knuckles whitening on the steering- wheel, 'No, son, I never played music like this.' (Calkin 2001)

> They picked scraps of punk from the garbage, fried it, put it through the blender, mashed it, beat it, cooked it again, and served it up with double-killer chilli. (Hall 1995)

Contrary to what one might expect, the anarchic song is not some primeval chaos – the *tohu vavohu* of Genesis 1:2 – which must then be shaped and formed in the creative musical act. That is to say, this form of the song is not a natural state from which one emerges and into which one easily falls once again. The early punk-oriented bands in which Cave was involved work very hard indeed to achieve the anarchic song, which comes into its own in perhaps a handful of pieces: 'Pleasure Avalanche' from *Mutiny – The Bad Seed* (Cave 1983), 'The Fried Catcher' in *The Birthday Party* (Cave 1980), 'The Dim Locator' and 'Big Jesus Trash Can' in *Junkyard* (Cave 1982), and then a fistful – 'Music Girl', 'Cry', 'Ho Ho', 'Figure of Fun', 'A Dead Song', 'Yard', 'Just You and Me', 'Blundertown' and 'Kathy's Kisses' – from *Prayers on Fire* (Cave 1981). A relatively meagre collection, is it not? And they are all gathered from a relatively short period of time, from 1980 to 1983, the era of The Birthday Party band.

Fast or slow, these examples of the anarchic song clash, whine, crunch, growl, screech and grate. Celebrating the disdain of any key register, the harsh, metallic drums smash their way through, the bass is as scatty as can be, and Cave's voice (to which I will return below) shows an extraordinary versatility, preferring cacophony over melody any day. In a word: brilliant. It is as close one might get to a glorious anarchism of the note, down to its roots in time and rhythm.

In order to see how the full anarchic song is actually quite difficult to achieve, let us consider three early collections, one the first album released by The Boys Next Door, called *Door, Door* (Cave 1979), the second the earliest recording, made of the band performing live at the Soundboard, Melbourne (Cave 1977) and the third the eponymous first album of The Birthday Party (Cave 1980). *Door, Door* involves reasonably straightforward rock, obeying most of the 'rules', with recognizable and well-slotted places for the note, a few additions (saxophone and an eerie synthesizer), but above all a driving beat that would work well in any pub. None of the numbers stand out, except perhaps 'After a Fashion' and 'I Mistake Myself' for their smoothness. In short, this album is a long way from the anarchic song that would turn up a couple of years later, for only with *Prayers on Fire* (1981) does the real punk begin.

And if we were hoping to see the anarchic song emerge in the vigour of drug-fuelled youth with *The Birthday Party* (Cave 1980), the album that announced the new band, having changed its name in between Melbourne and London, then we are in for some disappointing listening. To be sure, it is rougher and more ragged, but the bass line is strong, anchoring the songs – 'Hats on Wrong', 'Hair Shirt', 'Guilt Parade', 'Riddle House' (with a slightly more complex poly-rhythm), 'Waving My Arms', 'The Red Clock' and 'Happy Birthday' (in short, nearly the whole album) – even to the point of providing a marching beat ('Mr Clarinet'), so that one gains the impression of a reasonably disciplined note. Occasionally, guitars (under the bowed back and expert fingers of Rowland Howard, a recent recruit) and Cave's voice race frantically about, but they are always held in check by the bass line, pulled back so far that harmony threatens to break out, especially in 'Guilt Parade' and 'Waving My Arms'.

Is there any hint of the anarchic song on these albums? One solitary piece on each album offers a taste: in the midst of the rather predictable driving rhythm of 'Somebody's Watching' (on *Door, Door*), we hear some dirt in the guitar, some growling feedback that messes with the relatively clean sound of the album as a whole. But with 'The Fried Catcher' from *The Birthday Party* we finally come upon the first full anarchic song: a heavily vagrant guitar opens up, Cave's voice jumps nervously about, the bass line does come in a little, but it is certainly not there to anchor the rest; indeed, the percussion, with its clonks and bangs, ends up being as much a part of mayhem as the rest. And the close, with its feedback-dragged guitar, is brilliant.

The solitary moment of 'The Fried Catcher' would soon enough crash through to the fully anarchic album of a year later, *Prayers on Fire* (Cave 1981). But before we get there, I would like to trouble what has been a reasonably chronological path, one that awaits the emergence of the full-blooded anarchic song. For now our somewhat linear narrative is broken up by a turn back to the first recording made by The Boys Next Door, back in 1977 at the Melbourne Soundboard. Made up mostly of cover versions, this live-set sounds on first hearing like an on-stage version of the band that recorded *Door, Door*, except that the edges are rougher, with more of a touch of the anarchic song than either of the two albums I have discussed already. Thus, 'Gloria', 'My Generation', 'My Future', 'These Boots Are Made for Walking', 'World Panic' and 'Louie Louie' all manifest, as known songs, recognizable patterns for the note, yet they have been roughed up, shirts torn, smokes scrounged from passers-by on the wrong side of the tracks. At one or two moments, the note slips closer still to the anarchic song: 'I'm 18', with its slurred lyrics, twanging guitar and straying drums sounds more like the punk for which Cave *et al.* were celebrated not long afterwards. But 'Masturbation Generation' is the stand-out here, since it is both a Cave original and foreshadows the anarchic song to come – the voice is ragged, the sound 'raw' and the note excited by the sense that it is about to be let out of prison.

Fully released it certainly is, bounding out full of angry energy, in the three central exhibits of The Birthday Party: *Prayers on Fire* (Cave 1981), *Junkyard* (Cave 1982) and the double EP, *Mutiny! – The Bad Seed* (Cave 1983). Given their common ground in exploring the full anarchic possibilities of the note, I take them together. Here we find pieces full of screeching, screaming, grating, shouted lyrics that celebrate the disdain of any key, harsh, clattering drums with cymbals smashing their way through, a bass with ADHD and voices in cacophony. Three of the best examples, one from each album: in 'Ho Ho' (*Prayers on Fire*) rhythm itself disappears in the anarchism of the song; in 'Pleasure Avalanche' (*Mutiny! – The Bad Seed*) the note simply breaks down in the full anarchism of growls, feedback, erratic drums and a bass that is doing something at a good distance from the others; and in 'The Dim Locator' and 'Big Jesus Trash Can' (*Junkyard*) it becomes difficult to distinguish the various instruments as markers of the errant note, for now the sheer noise blends screaming guitar, sepulchral voice, metallic clattering of drums and bass's thumping into one crescendo of noise.

In short, they are pieces in pure self-destruct mode, engaged in musical civil war, so much so that it becomes an almost forlorn task to find any exceptions. Where exceptions do turn up we find variations on the anarchic song: for example, with 'King Ink' (and partly 'Dull Day' and 'Magic Girl' – all from *Prayers on Fire*) the bass is initially noticeably present, but now as a focus for attack from manic guitar and ruined voice. Or, with the track 'She's Hit' (*Junkyard*), we stumble across a contest between Cave's voice and Rowland Howard's guitar, with the drums working overtime for a look-in.[8]

However, once the anarchic song has been gained, one or two glimmers of new possibilities begin to show their faces, if somewhat momentarily. To begin with, in the slower tracks, 'Several Sins' and '6 Inch Gold Blade' (and the later section of 'Kiss Me Black'), once again from *Junkyard*, an errant note now encounters not a growling and screaming voice from Cave, but one with some timbre and resonance. So also with a couple of tracks from *Mutiny! – The Bad Seed*, namely 'Deep in the Woods' and 'Jennifer's Veil': here the resonant quality of Cave's voice threatens to break out, holding the song together in a way that will become dominant later with The Bad Seeds. And in '6 Inch Gold Blade' and 'Deep in the Woods' we also find the seeds of what will later become the 'sinister song' – a slow piece with a thoroughly macabre twist, madness and death quivering at its very core. Yet the full sinister song must await the hymn in order to come into its own.

Soon we pass to the discordant song, more characteristic of The Bad Seeds than The Birthday Party's anarchic song. But what is the difference? Simply put, the full anarchic song disdains the anchoring effect of the bass line, whereas the discordant song prefers to challenge the bass (a precursor appears with a song I mentioned above – 'King Ink' from *Prayers on Fire*). Is the emergence of the discordant song, then, a slight amelioration of the anarchic song and perhaps a step towards redemption? Is it a necessary transition to the dialectical song, which may well be regarded as the anarchic song that has become the *Aufhebung* of itself? Let us see.

...and Discordancy

> But he [Blixa Bargeld] was always more concerned with making his guitar sound like a dying horse, more than anything else. (Cave in Robinson 1998)

Initially, the transition to The Bad Seeds manifests little apparent change. The note is still ominous and angry, full of the reeling blows of ongoing tension or conflict. On the first three albums – *From Her to Eternity* (Cave 1984), *The Firstborn Is Dead* (Cave 1985) and *Kicking against the Pricks* (Cave 1986a) – the anarchic song seems to be in full flight, playing freely with the codes of harmony, gleefully grasping howlers and running off with the most unlikely of companions. Here too we find conflict within the note, the internal dynamics of the song pulling every way so that it constantly threatens to fall apart. For instance, in *The Firstborn Is Dead* the note clangs (bass guitar) and crashes (the stark drums) its way through an imagined southern USA, full of howling and fearful growling and occasional traces of ringing quality. Songs such as 'Tupelo' may bring the note rushing upon us, riding the thunder and heavy black clouds of an ominous storm, while 'Say Goodbye to the Little Girl Tree' or 'Knockin' on Joe' or 'The Six Strings That Drew Blood' (a piece originally written for Rowland Howard and first recorded for *Mutiny! – The Bad Seed* [Cave 1983]), with their jarring atonality, make for anything but easy listening.

All the same, some variations begin to creep into the music, the first a distinctive feature of *The Firstborn Is Dead* and the other a more general tendency. To begin with, in the album with its allusion to the slaughter of the firstborn Egyptians at the moment of flight by the mythical Israelites, we find a stark and solitary note. That loneliness has already been foreshadowed in 'A Box for Black Paul' on *From Her to Eternity*, with its laboured piano, wandering voice and occasional bass. But here its full isolation comes to the fore. Technically, the stark and ascetic loneliness of the note is due to the preference for singularity – a cymbal, solitary guitar note (no strummed chords), single, articulated piano notes and the alienated voice of Cave on 'Say Goodbye to the Little Girl Tree', or the harmonica, jarring voices and plinking piano of 'Knockin' on Joe', or the meandering uncertainty of the plodding bass and errant drum on 'Bline Lemon Jefferson'. I would suggest that here we have a prime instance of music's origins in a listening to oneself, to one's own body and its sounds (as Bloch argued). The overwhelming sense of stripped-down music and bare notes serves to emphasize Cave's voice. From that emaciated, drug-ridden body emerges a range of sounds that gives one the feeling not only of listening to Cave's own body, but that we have been given the privilege of access to that internally focused activity as well.

This solitary sparseness of this note meshes in with at least two factors: drugs and an underlying liberal ideology of the individual. With a taste for endless cigarettes, hard liquor and harder drugs – so much so it is a wonder Cave both made it to 50 and managed to give them all away – he would, until about 1997, scribble down lyrics when the muse would take him and then bring a fistful of scraps to rehearsal or the studio. As I pointed out in the previous chapter, there the band in its various incarnations would build a song, allowing their musical idiosyncrasies to show forth. (Needless to say, any musical score was far from the scene – and thereby The Bad Seeds carried on a tradition that goes back to the willed ignorance of conventional musical technique and composition of early jazz.) Indeed, at this time the band continued a pattern from the time of The Birthday Party of extreme, drug-induced performance antics. As

Walker puts it, the sheer unpredictability of the live performances meant that they were one of the 'most compelling and genuinely dangerous live acts ever to besmirch rock history' (Walker 2009: 42; see also Mulholland 1996, Miller 1988). Mick Harvey, the long-time multi-instrumentalist (with Cave from high-school days) and most introverted and quiet member of the band, confessed, 'I think I got tense before we went on because I never knew what was going to happen, or whether someone was going to get seriously hurt' (Brokenmouth 1996: 122). Needless to say, the crowds came to witness, mouths agape, such overt excess.

But it is also part and parcel with a deep allegiance to creative individuality that ties in most strongly with the ideology of liberalism that I outlined in the discussion of heresy in the previous chapter. This private individual professes not to be bound by any codes except his own, voicing (paradoxically) rather conventional desires for authenticity and rawness, disdain for critics and commercialization (the old saw of 'selling out'), listening only to the sensitive and temperamental muse. So too with the solitary note of this time, which provides an extreme musical form of the sacrosanct private individual – not a bad achievement when you are in a band, even if its name begins with your own (*Nick Cave* and the Bad Seeds).

I did promise another variation within the discordant song, which stands in some tension with this solitary note: the increasing dominance of the bass line. Indeed, this factor is the main reason for distinguishing between the anarchic and the discordant song. The full anarchic song dispenses, as we saw, with the bass and any conventional rhythm; by contrast, in the discordant song the note struggles against the controlling role of the bass and drums. For example, in 'Cabin Fever' and 'From Her to Eternity' (in the album of that name) we find a reasonably recognizable rhythm, but the note itself fights this rhythm, running off on its own only to be brought back again at the end of a very long leash. At another level, the struggle takes place within the note, embodied above all in Blixa Bargeld's anarchic guitar and Cave's deliberately tuneless singing. Both fight the rhythm, asserted with the brutal force of a grimly dominant chain gang in 'Well of Misery' and 'Wings off Flies' (in *From Her to Eternity*). Mostly, the conflict of the note is contained within these perimeters, but at times the fight spills out onto the street. Thus, in 'From Her to Eternity' and 'A Box for Black Paul', other forms of the note appear to add to its impossible struggles: a piano, a whistle perhaps, ensuring they do not agree with either guitar or voice. At only a few moments is the bass line successfully challenged: at the close of 'Saint Huck' drums and bass part company (parts of 'A Box for Black Paul' also veer into the same territory); the alliance of the bass line broken for a moment, these two now struggle with one another, along with all the others. Yet these traces of the anarchic song are few, standing out as exceptions.

In the midst of the discordant song we come across the first hint of a new direction (in contrast to a mere variation), embodied in the cover of a spiritual. In *From Her to Eternity* appears what at first seems to be a pure anomaly, namely 'In the Ghetto': a cover of the Elvis Presley song, it is a smooth, almost fully harmonious rendition with Cave's voice coming through with conventional purity. Here is the first effort at some resolution, a papering over of the conflicts everywhere else apparent; it will turn out to be the first glimpse of the hymn. Soon enough we get a full album of such covers in *Kicking against the Pricks*.[9] Cave growls and howls less, the note finds company from time to time, and one picks up hints of conventional licks every now and then, perhaps even a croon – so the opening track, 'Muddy Waters', 'Sweet Annaleah', 'Long Black Veil', 'Something's Gotten Hold of My Heart' and 'Jesus Met the Woman at the Well'. Not only does the note occasionally pause from its violent conflict, not only do we find it enjoying company from time to time (most notably with back-up vocals), but here we find the first hints of that softer note that would become the hallmark of the hymn, which coincided with Cave's mini-breakthrough into mainstream success.

What are we to make of this shift, in which half the songs seem to be putting some distance between them and the early time of the anarchic and discordant songs? Two suggestions demand some attention. First, the overwhelming effect of *Kicking against the Pricks* is that the note has been seduced by the music of the southern USA, a place Cave has never visited to any extent but one that fits his adopted 'Southern Gothic' persona. Already *The Firstborn Is Dead* had begun to look longingly southward (unless one is in Mexico or beyond), but it was a look from afar, from Berlin of all places. Now we find a fascination with the extraordinary musical creativity that arose in a situation of racism, poverty, rural struggle and powerful, ecstatic and occult religiosity. This was, of course, the period when Cave was also writing *And the Ass Saw the Angel* (Cave 1989), set in a fantastic landscape constructed from both Australian and southern US elements (see Chapter 2). The note seems to have followed Cave's gaze.

Second, the songs chosen and reinterpreted as covers bring to the fore an element concealed in the earlier, raw, solitary and conflicted time of the note: a sense of deep longing. What is longed for is as yet unclear, although the multi-voice tracks like 'Jesus Met the Woman at the Well' echo heavily the spirituals and their longing for an end to suffering, exploitation and slavery, a longing, in short, for paradise. Is all of this, then, the first step to resolution of the conflicted nature of the note? Does the longing expressed give voice to some hope, a possible path to musical redemption?

Transition

> Harvey is a dark shadow mincing here and there, standing stock still, unfurling great chunks of sound that meet fellow chunks from Bargeld and co. Under it all, Thomas Wydler, Die Haut's explosive drummer, pounds mercilessly. (Gee 1997b)

The next five albums – *Your Funeral... My Trial* (Cave 1986b), *Tender Prey* (Cave 1988b), *The Good Son* (Cave 1990), *Henry's Dream* (Cave 1992) and *Let Love In* (Cave 1994) – display a profound diversity of the note, trying out all manner of possibilities between the discordant song and the hymn. Still the discordant song has plenty of room to move, as in *Your Funeral... My Trial* (Cave 1986b), in which tracks like 'The Carny', 'Your Funeral, My Trial', 'Jack's Shadow', 'She Fell Away' and 'Scum', as well as most of the tracks on *Tender Prey* (Cave 1988b), especially the signature doppelganger of 'The Mercy Seat', hark back to the first album produced by the Bad Seeds in all its jarring juxtapositions and impossible tensions within the note. So also with later tracks like 'The Hammer Song' and 'The Witness Song' from *The Good Son* (Cave 1990), 'John Finn's Wife' and 'Jack the Ripper' from *Henry's Dream* (Cave 1992), or indeed 'Jangling Jack' from *Let Love In* (Cave 1994), each of them a great piece of discordancy, with the note pulling in all directions, all of which the bass line tries to hold together with only limited success.

The spiritual, too, hangs over some of the tracks, now expressed as what I have called the note full of deep longing, especially in 'Stranger Than Kindness' from *Your Funeral... My Trial*. While the violins provide an urgent edge, Cave's voice lingers over the words, savouring them as though he is both reluctant to give them away and yet hopes for something beyond past and present. But the spiritual cannot escape the discordant song, suggesting both the frail possibility of redemption embodied in the spiritual and the search for a new form. Thus, in 'I Had a Dream, Joe' (*Henry's Dream* [Cave 1992]), 'The Good Son' (Cave 1990) and 'New Morning' (*Tender Prey* [Cave 1988b]) both the spiritual appears, especially in their openings, along with the characteristic atonality of the earlier songs. So also 'When I First Came to Town' from the same album, in which the atonal tendencies of the verses contrast with the refrain of 'O Sweet Jesus'. All of which is shown up starkly in the two versions of 'Do You Love Me?' from *Let Love In* (Cave 1994): in the first version, we are tantalizingly promised a smooth, co-ordinated song, but as soon as the first keyboard kicks in we know we are in for a more atonal piece, which is then exacerbated by the second keyboard, twanging guitar and Cave's solo voice. By contrast, the second version (the last track on the album) slows the whole song down: the result is that the atonality is softened and Cave's voice gains its resonance, so that now the track hints at the hymn and lament we will meet soon enough. In sum, these blendings of the spiritual and the discordant song suggest that there is always a risk that salvation slips away, that the attempt of overcoming fails. In short: we sin again too quickly.

Hymn (and Lament)

> It is demythologized prayer, rid of efficacious magic. (Adorno 1998 [1963]: 2)

All this experimentation of forms, of mixing and matching, leads to perhaps the most significant new development in the song: the hymn. Its features we have already met: a strong piano or organ, a softened bass line, a significant change of the tempo and rhythm in a much slower song which is accompanied by a choir or congregation.[10] The hymn bursts into Cave's music with extraordinary purity, appearing as a simple cover, namely, the Spanish 'Foi Na Cruz' from *The Good Son* (Cave 1990). Here are the multiple voices of the choir, here the slowed down song and here, perhaps most noticeably, the congregation led by Cave's deeply resonant voice. No longer does he seek to exploit its obvious quality on the atonal shouts, screeches and growls of an early piece such as 'Big Jesus Trash Can', for now the timbre and richness of his voice follows more conventional paths of harmony. In many respects, the hymn is the natural outflow of the spiritual (which is indeed the feel of the track that follows 'Foi Na Cruz', namely, the eponymous 'The Good Son'), giving musical expression to longing, loss and faith; but it is also the musical form of the lyrical love song, or ballad as it is often called,[11] the content of which I have analysed in Chapter 5.

Now that the hymn has announced itself in full grandeur, it undergoes a number of experiments, even an occasional mutation, in relation to the other forms of the song we have met thus far. Other relatively pure examples occur, such as the profoundly seductive 'The Ship Song' from *The Good Son* (Cave 1990), again sung slowly, backed up by the choir and a lining up of the note in rich harmony. So also 'Christina the Astonishing' from *Henry's Dream* (Cave 1992), replete with an electric organ in a clear, subdued even worshipful piece, so much so that Cave sounds like a soloist in a choir, which comes in quietly to support him at some points.

Still the pure hymn in earlier material is relatively rare, scattered among a liberal supply of discordant tracks; occasionally, however, both discordant song and hymn meet in the same piece. Is this a case of struggling emergence, impurities still clinging to the hymn as it is dragged from the water, or is something else happening in the mixed instances? 'The Weeping Song' (from *The*

Good Son [Cave 1990]) seems like the former, for although the slowly sung lyrics, multiple vocals and the timbre of Cave's voice suggest a hymn, the driving bass takes it out of that realm. Two far more interesting examples come with 'Straight to You' and 'Loom of the Land' (*Henry's Dream* [Cave 1992]): much is made of the dragging note of longing as part of what sounds distinctly like a hymn, yet that form is disturbed by a constant backdrop of the discordant note. The effect is to present the hymn as an attempted resolution of the discordant song *within the same piece*. That is to say, within these tracks the larger pattern I have been tracing of the relation between discordant song and hymn appears in microcosm. That this resolution eventually fails shows up later in another combination of the discordant song and the hymn, namely, the sinister song, but its moment of close analysis needs to wait a little longer.[12]

A further and significant variation on the hymn is the lament, which we will meet more than once in the music to come. Already a small crowd of laments has gathered: 'Nobody's Baby Now', 'Ain't Gonna Rain Anymore', 'Lay Me Low' and the second version of 'Do You Love Me?' (all from *Let Love In* [Cave 1994]). All of the features of the hymn appear here, but with one noticeable difference, for the slow, carefully sung note falls whenever possible – in disappointment, sadness, loss.

Eventually, both hymn and lament lurch into dominance in *The Boatman's Call* (Cave 1997a), *No More Shall We Part* (Cave 2001) and then lays thick on the ground in *Nocturama* (Cave 2003) – spanning the time when Cave finally gave up drugs. And the effect is deadening, so much so that one must have wondered at the time whether his muse had fled with the narcotics. One might feel at times that the early anarchic song is an uncomfortable listening experience, or even that the profoundly atonal moments of the discordant song are not made for relaxation, but at least they intrigue, entice, even seduce at times. Not so the endless hymns and laments of these two albums.[13] To give one a sense of how dominant the hymn/lament is on both these albums, let me list them, beginning with the hymns: from *The Boatman's Call*, 'Into My Arms', 'Lime Tree Arbour', 'There Is a Kingdom' (sung almost completely by the congregation), '(Are You) The One That I've Been Waiting For?', 'Far From Me', 'Green Eyes';[14] from *No More Shall We Part* the hymns include 'Hallelujah' (now with violins and a choir), 'Love Letter' (more violins)', 'Sweetheart Come' (piano and some violin thrown in) and 'Gates to the Garden'; while on *Nocturama* appear 'He Wants You' and 'She Passed By My Window'. As far as the closely related laments are concerned, *The Boatman's Call* has 'People Just Ain't No Good', 'Brompton Oratory' (with full church organ), 'Where Do We Go But Nowhere?', 'Black Hair' (organ once again), 'Idiot Prayer', 'West Country Girl'. On *No More Shall We Part* we find 'No More Shall We Part', 'We Came Along This Road' and 'Darker with the Day,' while *Nocturama* contains 'Wonderful Life', 'Right Out of Your Hand', 'Still in Love'. Only two small variations appear in this collection: in 'As I Sat Sadly by Her Side' (from *No More Shall We Part*) we hear the obligatory piano, but one that hints at discordancy with its high plinking, accompanied by a relatively high voice. Slightly different is 'There Is a Town' (*Nocturama*), in which the lament must compete with a tendency to break out in stronger rhythm, bordering on rock. Yet they are half-hearted experiments, much like 'God Is in the House', which sounds much like a hymn, but now the voice rises much higher in its hint of fanaticism, irony and mockery.

No doubt the tedium of this long list will have made a reader's eyes skip with relief to the end of the paragraph; but that is precisely the effect both of the albums and their tedious songs. At least in a worship service one has some variation – a passage read from Scripture, a sermon, some movement and theatre, bread eaten and wine drunk. Not so here: nary a glorious, discordant song to be found. Given their deadening effect, the supposedly heart-felt hymn and its associated lament offer not so much a resolution of the anarchic or discordant song as a cul-de-sac.[15]

Sinister Song

> Outside the vultures wheel
> The wolves howl, the serpents hiss. (Cave 1996b)

The hymn as a failed resolution: is this merely my own instinct, a response to an oppressive listening experience? No, for within Cave's own corpus appears a thoroughly intriguing song with a darkly sinister bent – one that we have met briefly in the treatment of death in Chapter 3, but which now undergoes a more thorough interrogation. Not so much one of the major forms of the song that I have discussed thus far, it nevertheless marks a crucial moment in Cave's music, for now the hymn takes a menacing turn that once again recovers the total atonal depravity of the anarchic song. The sinister song is one full of foreboding, in which the unhurried pace of the hymn now features a shortened note, cut off before its completion (unlike the held note of the hymn or lament), all of which is overlaid by the comically mad, thoroughly self-absorbed voice. Yet the most distinctive feature of the sinister song is the way the hymn and the discordant/anarchic song blend in a way that is definitely not redemptive. Unlike the combinations I noted earlier, in which the hymn sought to overcome the discordant song and effect a redemptive resolution, the sinister song shows the breakdown of the hymn, its failed effort at redemption now taking a twist via elements of the discordant song into territory that is simultaneously humorous and ominous.

A few precursors to the sinister song appear, such as the foreboding piece, 'The Singer', from *Kicking against the Pricks* (Cave 1986a), or, from *Let Love In* (Cave 1994), the thoroughly evil 'Loverman', or the murderous 'Red Right Hand' with its cut-off note, or 'I Let Love In', in which atonality undermines the attempted resolution of the hymn. Yet the most sustained instance of the sinister song appears in *Murder Ballads* (Cave 1996b), which I have had cause to discuss in the chapter on death. The immediate impression – with the opening track 'Song of Joy', reinforced with 'Lovely Creature' as well as 'Stagger Lee' and 'O'Malley's Bar' – is that the atonal note is alive and well (one of the few items that does thrive in an album strewn with murdered bodies), struggling against the slow pace of the hymn, its resonant voice and even choir. Even the apparent hymn, the cover of Bob Dylans's 'Death Is Not the End', has an ironically macabre feel at the end of the album. And now a twisted lament or two appears: 'Henry Lee' (a cover), 'Where the Wild Roses Grow' and 'The Kindness of Strangers' are all full of keyboard, a slowed note that perpetually drops and in some cases a forlorn woman's voice (to the point of sobs in 'The Kindness of Strangers') that stands out from the choir.

Two features of the sinister song require a little more comment. First, the distinctive tone of this type of song is rendered by the mad voice, marked above all by elaborate articulation, lascivious attention to the word's own detail, the soft sound of opening lips, a quiver of excitement, as well as moments of intense crescendo and even gravelly breathing (in 'Lovely Creature'). This crazy voice runs through 'Song of Joy', 'Curse of Millhaven', 'Crow Jane' and 'O'Malley's Bar'. That last, brilliant track also reveals another dimension: the orgasmic edge of the murderer's voice as he narrates his killings. Second, the sinister song is not merely oppressive and macabre, for what clinches the sinister touch is an upbeat, dance-like rhythm, all delivered in a bright key that ensures a grim humour is never far away. This incongruously snappy feel appears with 'Stagger Lee', 'Lovely Creature', 'Curse of Millhaven', to a lesser extent with 'Crow Jane', but especially in the bravura 'O'Malley's Bar'. I am reminded of Bloch's comment on Beethoven, namely that he would overturn the conventions of minor and major keys, seeing the rules as opportunities for creativity rather than boundaries within which one must remain (Bloch 1985b: 95; 1974: 114).

The failed resolution of the hymn embodied in the sinister note would not mean the end of the hymn or the lament, for *Murder Ballads* (1996) actually appeared before the albums of hymns, *The Boatman's Call* (1997) and *No More Shall We Part* (2001). And we come across the hymn in later albums as well, as we shall soon see. So why locate the sinister song in my argument after these works? Not only does it have a logical place here, but the first two albums were recorded at the same time. The band began recording *The Boatman's Call*, but then turned their attention to *Murder Ballads*, which was perceived at the time as a side project, a less than serious way to let off steam in the face of the supposedly pure honesty of *The Boatman's Call*. Yet they are almost too keen to stress this element of *Murder Ballads*, that it was light-hearted and not nearly as much work, that they expected it to flop and were thereby surprised and perturbed at its success (Mattila 1997, Gee 1997b, Mulholland 1996, Morin 1996, Fricke 1996). Is this not precisely the point? Burdened by the searing and oppressive hymns of *The Boatman's Call*, the need to do something else, with relative ease and huge enjoyment, signals the end run of the hymn as a form of the song. In this doubled moment (one that would be repeated in another way later with Grinderman), the sinister song already reveals the failure of the hymn's resolution at precisely the moment when the latter form comes into full flower.

Dialectical Song

> You drive yourself into a state that lifts you above what is mundane in
> life, where time passes differently. (Cave in Fontaine 1997)

In contrast to the hymn, resolution or indeed redemption comes closest in what I have called the dialectical song. Lest this argument should seem like a grand dialectical flourish in which all is resolved in the end, let me underline the point that the dialectical song is as difficult, if not more difficult, to achieve than the full anarchic song. Many are the attempts, but fewer are the moments when it actually comes off, for it has a tendency to slide away into all manner of other forms. But why call them dialectical songs? In these songs the dissonance, atonality, indeed anarchic noise of the various dimensions of the note are not overcome by the appropriation of a form in which all these elements are lined up, ordered to follow the rules of harmony and thereby produce a palatable song. No, only when they are allowed to run to the full, to stretch their muscles and pump their lungs with fresh air, to go off as they will – only then do they seem to work together at another level. In other words, this resolution is achieved – in a form of the dialectic developed and deployed impressively by Theodor Adorno – not despite or by denying the anarchy and dissonance of the note, but by taking that very atonality to its very end.

Although the dialectical song comes into its own only with *Abattoir Blues* (Cave 2004a), to be followed by *Dig!!! Lazarus Dig!!!* (Cave 2008) and both *Grinderman* albums (Grinderman 2007 and 2010), initial efforts turn up – as we would expect by now – in earlier work. Let me begin with two extraordinary pieces that express the shift between hymn and dialectic song within the track itself – thereby intensifying the shift between the two types of song. They both come from *No More Shall We Part* (Cave 2001), an album that, as I noted above, continues the overwhelming drudgery of the hymn from *The Boatman's Call*. To begin with, 'Oh My Lord' threatens to be yet another hymn, thereby slipping into more of the same. Yet once the track gets under way, it draws nigh to the dialectical song, with the note pulling out of line and then threatening to shift to another level; and as it closes we get the closest yet to the dialectical song in full flight, with every element of the note thumping it out as it sees fit.[16] Even more telling is 'The Sorrowful Wife' from the same album: it begins with strong piano and violins, subdued bass and the slow and deep voice of the hymn; but then, right in the middle, the hymn stops and a solitary, repeated note on the piano opens out into a song that is everything but the hymn – a thumping, crashing, almost ecstatic dialectical crescendo!

Other early moments are not quite so momentous, but they are worth noting here to show the longish leads for what eventually emerges as a new form of the song. Already in 1986, in 'Jack's Shadow' and 'Hard on for Love' (*Your Funeral... My Trial* [Cave 1986b]), the flailing drums, enthusiastic guitar work and Cave's own screaming into the mike herald one of the first moments of the dialectical song, one that marks both an early recovery and transcendence of the discordant song. So too a few years later with 'Papa Won't Leave You, Henry' from the album concerning none other than Henry's own nocturnal imaginings (Cave 1992), for here the song manifests, through its discordant groundwork of the verses to the thumping chorus, the very process of moving from the discordant song to its transcendence in the dialectical song. And it does so by cranking up the very same elements of the discordant song until they break through to come together once again at another level. A couple of other examples include 'Fifteen Feet of Pure White Snow' (*No More Shall We Part* [Cave 2001]) and 'Dead Man in My Bed' (*Nocturama* [Cave 2003]), both on the cusp of the transition from hymn to dialectics. The former marks what I take to be the first full manifestation of the dialectical song, with the guitar plunking out a path seemingly known only to itself, the piano plunking away on its own, the drums frantic, the voice cranking up the pitch and pace, and the bass adding to the chaos rather than trying to control it (as with the discordant song). All of which one also finds in the recording that soon followed, 'Dead Man in My Bed', which appeared a year before the full flourishing of the dialectical song.[17]

These are but precursors, early efforts that perhaps arose by accident. Not so the superb *Abattoir Blues*, the first half of a double album with *The Lyre of Orpheus* (Cave 2004a). Given the importance of this album, allow me to offer a slightly fuller analysis, for here the dialectical song stands up in rampaging glory. The opening track, 'Get Ready for Love', has crazy guitar work (rhythm and lead), crashing drumming, a voice that really recovers the full acrobatics of The Birthday Party, replete with some screeching female voices (the choir with a whole new angle!). Each note goes its own direction in absolute glee – and it all comes together in a way that we have been expecting for some time. Unconstrained, the note is free to roam, and in doing so it storms over the line to the dialectical song.

Once released, the note may come back and reconstitute earlier forms: 'Cannibal's Hymn' manifests the note of longing, formally resident with the lament, but with a whole new twist: the note may play freely, running now to guitar, now to an almost twanging keyboard/synthesizer, now to a bass crescendo, now to a voice in full flight, all of which comes to a dialectical climax. 'Hiding All Away' begins with the industrial crunching sounds reminiscent of Einstürzende Neubauten, the band that excited Cave so much in the days of The Birthday Party and from which Blixa Bargeld came to join the early Bad Seeds, but from there the bass does its own thing, the guitar grinds, the drums stay with the industrial feel, and again the female voices seem to sing separately rather than as one, a counterpoint to Cave's voice. It all wants is to run in its own directions, although it hesitates for a moment, unsure whether it wishes to hold the show together as is or rise above the clashing sounds and seek another resolution, a resolution offered towards the close in a grand dialectical crescendo.

The next three tracks are among the best of the dialectical songs: 'There She Goes, My Beautiful World', 'Nature Boy' and 'Abattoir Blues', with their wrecked keyboards, trashed guitar, punished drums, voices (female again) in dissonant fullness; in short, the note is thoroughly enjoying the vast new horizons that have opened up for it. Even the choir is transformed, turning the hymn on its head. The back-up vocals to these tracks sound distinctly like gospel singers in a church choir, yet they no longer hold back, ceasing to be 'back-up' at all, for now each becomes an individual voice ringing in an almost ecstatic rapture. Among this group, 'Abattoir Blues' marks a new direction enabled by the dialectical song: blues. Yet the significance of this track is that it shows the dialectical song need not be a fast number, for here the note slows down and yet it is not a lament, hymn or sinister song. Similar is a fifth member of our group, 'Let the Bells Ring': at a slower tempo, the note can relax and do as it pleases, embodying what may be called a slow dialectics.

Perhaps the best way to summarize the dialectical song in *Abattoir Blues* is by means of Ernst Bloch's comment on Beethoven, an observation that brings the latter into the same zone as Cave and the dialectical song. Like Beethoven, in Cave we meet 'the universal spirit of music who wrecked keyboards [*der die*

Klaviere zerstrümmert], swept in like a hurricane and turned even the strongest orchestra to jelly in the face of his music's *a priori* exorbitancy' (Bloch 1985b: 30; 1974: 40).[18]

Nonetheless, the dialectical song is not as easy as it seems. Apart from the sister-album, *The Lyre of Orpheus* (Cave 2004a), which I will discuss in a moment, the other products – again a curious pair – reveal the difficulties of that song. *Dig!!! Lazarus Dig!!!* (Cave 2008) and the two *Grinderman* albums (2007, 2010) show plenty of signs of slippage.[19] Now, this is more significant than at first seems to be the case, for *Grinderman* was supposed to be a return to basics, a rock album in which Cave donned a guitar after eight weeks of self-tutoring and these ageing rockers returned to the simple pleasures of a youthful garage band, going back to the source before even The Boys Next Door. It was intended, according to Warren Ellis (a member of the original high-school band), 'to be a really open liberating thing', with the band agreeing to 'push on, relentless', so much so that Grinderman was to be the great, rejuvenating other to the Bad Seeds, in recording and performance, so much so that Grinderman provided the necessary bomb to raise *Dig!!! Lazarus Dig!!!* (which followed) to a whole new level (see Doran 2010, Petridis 2010). In short, Grinderman provides the moment of dialectical *Aufhebung*. Not quite, I would suggest.

To be sure, the first *Grinderman* album has a sprinkling of full-blooded dialectical songs: I think of 'Get It On', 'Love Bomb', 'No Pussy Blues', 'Depth Charge Ethel' and 'Honey Bee (Let's Fly to Mars)' – the last two flaying the note as much as they can. From *Grinderman 2* one might add 'Mickey Mouse and the Goodbye Man', 'Worm Tamer', 'Heathen Child' and perhaps 'Bellringer Blues'. All the same, too many tracks do not quite make the grade. '(I Don't Need You To) Set Me Free', for example, is a little too slick, missing out by bowing to conventional harmonies despite the growling guitars, manic drumming, urgent bass and voices like a pack of dogs howling on their own. And the slower songs on both albums begin to sound remarkably like harmonious hymns with frayed edges: from *Grinderman* (2007) comes the title track, as well as 'When My Love Comes Down' and 'Go Tell the Women', or even a lament, like 'Man in the Moon', full of organs and falling notes; and from *Grinderman 2* (2010), 'When My Baby Comes', 'Kitchenette' and 'What I Know', with its rough choir; so too, and perversely, does evil 'Evil' have its own, relatively harmonious, choir. In fact, the second album has slipped so much that it sounds much more like a conventional Bad Seeds effort than the first *Grinderman* album.

Dig!!! Lazarus, Dig!!! (Cave 2008) is little different. Some of the offerings are as good as the dialectical song can get, characterized – in tracks like

'Today's Lesson', 'Moonland' and 'Lie Down Here (And Be My Girl)' – by instruments that are off and away and signs that Cave's voice is even better after he gave up smoking (the last of his addictions, apart from creative work and tea). The best, however, is 'We Call Upon the Author', a piece that reminds me of that brilliant description of utopia, in which everyone can enjoy their various pathologies without repression – so also with the various elements of the note in this song.

But that is about it; the remaining numbers do not quite live up to the rigours of the dialectical song. A noticeable feature of most of the pieces is the return of a strong, unifying and anchoring bass line – a feature of the discordant song, which at times reasserts its presence, reclaiming the dialectical song and scoffing at its lofty claims. Here I would locate the opening track, 'Dig!!! Lazarus Dig!!!', as well as 'Albert Goes West', 'Midnight Man' and even the thoroughly enjoyable 'More New from Nowhere'. Alongside these efforts of the discordant song to reassert itself, the temptations of the hymn sometimes prove to be too much. Thus, 'Night of the Lotus Eaters' and 'Hold on to Yourself' have freely running elements, but they are also held together more harmoniously than the others. Above all, 'Jesus of the Moon' is the most hymn-like of all, with many of the hymn's characteristic features, with a slower tempo, piano and even violins. In sum, many of the tracks on *Dig!!! Lazarus Dig!!!* are quite tame in terms of the note's antics, for they tend to cohere rather well, with an occasional lick or errant moment soon brought back into line.

I mentioned earlier that the four collections under discussion come in two pairs, a feature that may initially suggest the dialectical song has manifested itself even in the production of albums themselves: as *Abattoir Blues* is to *The Lyre of Orpheus*, so are the *Grinderman* albums to *Dig!!! Lazarus Dig!!!* If only it were so easy. The catch is that the latter two are middling efforts, mirroring one another in their scattered achievements of the dialectical song and the good number of those pieces that do not make the grade. In other words, the dialectical hope that one might have had – that the doppelganger effort of *Grinderman 1* and *2* would give the crucial leverage for the fully fledged dialectical song in *Dig!!! Lazarus Dig!!!* – is somewhat disappointed. Does the other pair succeed – the double-album that is not a double-album, since it is two differently named albums in one cover? Again, the answer must be: not quite.

Or rather, they succeed in an entirely unexpected way: the degree to which *Abattoir Blues* is the most complete achievement of the dialectical song is the same degree to which *The Lyre of Orpheus* fails. How is this a success? The failure of one seems to provide the opportunity for the other; or, conversely, the apparent success of *Abattoir Blues* ensures that *The Lyre of Orpheus* will slide away. Only a few tracks on that latter album come close to the dialectical song, such as the slower 'The Lyre of Orpheus', as well as 'Spell', the resplendently urgent 'Supernaturally' and (less so) 'Carry Me'. The remainder make a few gestures to the discordant note – 'Breathless', 'Babe You Turn Me On', 'O Children', 'Spell', 'Carry Me' and 'Easy Money' – but they are tempted too often by the false security of conventional harmony and the hymn/lament, so much so that 'Easy Money' could well have come from *The Boatman's Call*, even to the point of the choir and strong piano in what is really a lament. Not quite a return to the hymn, but we are back with the struggle between hymn and dialectical song that characterized *No More Shall We Part*.

Voice

> Sometimes it sounds like the moaning of a dying insect. (Cave in Calkin 2001)

Inspired by Ernst Bloch's philosophy of music, even using him as a model, we come to the close of a detailed tracing of the modulations of the song in Cave's musical work. I have argued that three main forms of the song manifest themselves in that work: the hard-to-achieve anarchic and then discordant song, the effort as resolution through the hymn (and lament), its run into a dead-end, shown up by the sinister song, and then the dialectical song. Almost more difficult to achieve than the anarchic is the dialectical song, precisely because it attempts to lift the elusive anarchic/discordant song to a whole new level. However, in order to provide another angle on this assessment and as a way of offering a different summary, let me focus on the voice, that human harp (Bloch 1985b: 140–45; 1974: 202–207) which lies at the beginning of music, in which singing-to-oneself and dance become the bodily basis of all music.

The voice is, at least for Cave, the most versatile, adaptable and powerful of all the instruments. One might formulate its changing roles in two ways. A first, more traditional one would be to argue that Cave works overtime in his early days with The Boys Next Door and The Birthday Party to *conceal* the inherent quality of his voice, even though its resonance and timbre do sneak out from time to time. Perhaps the best example of concealment appears with 'Capers' (from *Prayers on Fire* [Cave 1981]), where he makes use of voice-distortion devices, giving his voice a very low, sepulchral echo. Nevertheless, resonance is never far away, as in the first official release of The Boys Next Door, called *Door, Door* (1979), in which the voice is at a higher register, sung out and pushed a little; yet he cannot conceal hints of its quality, especially in 'Shivers' with its long-held notes and tendency to drop. The same may be said for 'Several Sins' and '6 Inch Gold Blade' (from *Junkyard* [Cave 1982]) and

'Deep in the Woods' and 'Jennifer's Veil' (from *Mutiny! – The Bad Seed* [Cave 1983]) in which one hears this rich voice break through.

Very similar points may then be made regarding the days of the discordant song in the early Bad Seeds: concealment is the order of the day, through howls, screeches, narrated lyrics and so on. But Cave cannot keep hiding this remarkable voice, so eventually it simply comes out of hiding and celebrates its sheer class in the hymn. Thus, in the first appearance of the hymn in *The Good Son* (Cave 1990), with the simple track 'Foi Na Cruz', Cave's voice goes deeper, rolls along more slowly and puts itself on show. The narrative of the voice is then one of a passage from concealment to celebration, a celebration that would continue (with a perverse twist) in the sinister song of *Murder Ballads* (Cave 1996b). Here the voice is enhanced in its madness, with the creepy detail of lips parting, of humming, sniffing, articulation, obsessive attention to its own detail and ecstatic crescendos.

Then, in contrast to the voice's strained concealment in the anarchic and discordant song, to its slow riches in hymn, lament and sinister song, where it is actually constrained by the expectations of harmony and timbre, in the dialectical song the voice is – along with every other dimension of the note – finally able to run free. It may roll and shout and strain, as in the anarchic song, it may offer moments of sheer quality, but above all it runs all over the scales, breaking into territory in which no scales may be found. In sum: a pattern of concealment, harmonious richness and then release.

I did say that this is one way in which we can understand the variations in Cave's voice through the various moments of the song. The problem is that such a narrative limits quality to the second and perhaps third phases, for in the first, and at times in the last, it is concealed. So I prefer a second approach that is not so restrictive. Yes of course, in the hymn and its hangers-on, the quality of that voice is there for all to see. Yet I would also suggest that in the anarchic and discordant song that its strength is even greater. All those efforts to show the voice under attack from itself – in howls, rapid drops and rises, growls, grunts, deep breathing, narrating, yodelling, pushing to breaking point, almost like vocal extreme sports – are in many respects more telling signs of that quality. Of course, in making that argument, we have come back to the beginning, restoring and transforming the anarchic song, which is precisely what happens in the dialectical song.

Conclusion: The Dialectics of Theo-utopian Hearing

In drawing to a close this effort at hearing around the corners of Cave's music, I would like to pick up my earlier observation that a significant feature of Bloch's analysis is listening with a theological and utopian ear, or theo-utopian hearing. Such a hearing has lain behind every step of the detailed analysis of this study, but now, in conclusion, let me bring it to the fore, seeing what that means for Cave's music. Within the music itself, especially in the interactions of the different forms of the song, is what I have called search for redemption (focused here on the music, but we have already witnessed that search in other dimensions of Cave's work). In brief, the search for redemption within Cave's music follows a path that moves from anarchic/discordant song, through hymn to the dialectical song. The problem with putting it so simply is that it misses the dialectical nature of their interaction as well as the sheer hard work and very partial success of the dialectical song (as also the anarchic song).

More of that in a moment, but now an exploration of this proposal in more detail: despite all the destructive, oppositional pleasure of the anarchic and even discordant songs, they give voice to the total depravity of human existence (see Chapter 2). A realistic and not undesirable theological doctrine, for Cave at least it is not enough; the curse of God can roar only for so long. So we find, after dabbling with the spiritual and its note of longing (for salvation), the stunning turn to the hymn, trailing its heavy ecclesiological associations. The early experiments with the spiritual may be seen as precursors not merely for the hymn but especially for its variation in the lament. Although the spirituals voice a profound longing for an end to suffering, exploitation and slavery, a longing, in short, for redemption, it is a false resolution, a papering over rather than dealing with the conflict itself. We see such longing in a track like 'Stranger Than Kindness' (from *Your Funeral... My Trial* [Cave 1986b]), in which an urgent musical underlay couples with the held notes of the singer's voice, all of which would feed into the lament. One may lament the continuance of depravity and sin in the world, one may express a deep longing in the midst of suffering for salvation through the spiritual, but the worshipful note – bowing to God, woman, Christ, love or redemption itself – of the hymn offers a distinct form of redemption, for its history and context offer an institution and tradition which has made the purveying of salvation its business. Nonetheless, the musical form of the hymn offers not a resolution of the anarchic song's depravity but a complete denial; hence the stark opposition between hymn and anarchic song, one melodious, calm, featuring organ and choir, the other celebrating the note at war with itself.

In other words, the hymn has not dealt with the total depravity of the anarchic song at all; it is a false path, leading to a cul-de-sac. Lining up harmonies, softening the rhythm and highlighting an organ (or piano) and a congregation or choir is simply not enough for redemption. Cave needs another form entirely: the dialectical song in which the anarchic and discordant song is drawn up, its depravity recognized, even celebrated, and yet by allowing the anarchic song the full reign it sought but could not find, the dialectical song achieves the musical redemption Cave seeks. For the hearer, this redemption is conveyed not only through the formal transformation of the anarchic and discordant song, but also through the sheer enjoyment and enthusiasm conveyed. One senses that redemption is closest at these points, largely because the feel of these songs is one of thorough pleasure and joy – but that may also be because I am an old rocker.

As a penultimate point, let me offer an analogy with class struggle, now in terms of musical forms. I mentioned earlier that the anarchic song is a song at war with itself, engaged in civil war. Now I suggest that class struggle is a better term, with the various dimensions of the note clashing in raw violence. However, one may wish to identify and critique such struggle, but one does not wish it to remain part of the status quo – especially if one is Nick Cave. One collection of options, namely the spiritual, lament and the hymn, offer a way of dealing with this struggle, but only through compromise with the powers that be and thereby denial of the conflict (hence the lining up of the note in soft harmonies of love). But no resolution of the struggle ensues, for despite denial it continues. Not so the dialectical song, since it takes that often bloody conflict by the scruff of the neck and at least entertains the possibility that it may be overcome.

Nonetheless, that redemption takes place partially and with significant effort – a feature inherited from the anarchic song itself. That is to say, for Cave's music, redemption is never certain; one is always afraid that it may slip away, or that God may not, in the end, have decided to save us after all. And so we must work even harder, diligently watching for what is known in theological circles as backsliding.[20] The depravity of sin crouches at the door, waiting to spring in a moment of weakness, as indeed does the slick and easy salvation offered by the ecclesiological hymn. The outcome: one must work even harder for one's salvation.

Conclusion: Gates to the Garden – The Search for Redemption

> The religiosity...is neither that of the believer who is secure in his faith nor a world religion of such an idealistic nature that believing in it makes no demands on the subject.
> (Adorno 2009: 256–57)[1]

Like Beethoven, Willy Nelson and Bob Dylan, to name but a few, Nick Cave seeks an elusive redemption in and through music and literature. At various moments in the preceding chapters, I have traced the different options he has pursued. It might take place, inexplicably, in the midst of total depravity, or the grand scale of apocalyptic might provide a glimpse, or death turns out not to be the final word, or the different forms of music in the songs may struggle to achieve a moment of dialectical *Aufhebung*, but the desire is resolutely persistent. Here I shall explore those possibilities in a more systematic manner, moving from a problematic aesthetic concern with beauty to a thoroughly dialectical approach to redemption.

To begin with, a number of weaker options appear from time to time. The first is really an absence of redemption, or at least a sarcastic scoffing at its possibility. We have already come across instances where redemption is almost out of the question, whether Euchrid's deep awareness of his own depravity in *And the Ass Saw the Angel* (Cave 1989), or the sheer absence of redemption in the grim Australian outback of *The Proposition* (Hillcoat 2005), or the refusal of its possibility in the poem 'Right Now, I Am A-Roamin'' (Cave 1997b: 169–71), although this poem also hints at a dialectical dimension of redemption to which I will return below. Alternatively, the possibility of salvation becomes the subject of caricature and sarcasm, as with the mad preacher from either 'Pappa Won't Leave You Henry' (Cave 1992), who 'shrieked and flapped' about life after death, or a very similar Abie Poe, who vainly offers an end to the rains in *And the Ass Saw the Angel the Angel* (Cave 1989). Perhaps the thickest sarcasm appears in the brief play, *Salomé*, where the character after whom the play is named (although she has no name in the biblical story) scoffs at John the Baptist:

> Cleanse me, Baptist. Take this yoke, the moon, under which ah slave, the terrible Emperess of mah body. Its climate, its seasons. I am woman. Cleanse me. Wash away all that's comely. Chasten me, Baptist, with your water. (Cave 1988a: 89)

Not the strongest of redemptive options, to say the least, but some other suggestions are equally weak. Beauty is one, a possibility cherished by Cave's long-dead father, a beauty 'that is going to save the world' (Cave 2004a), or even a beauty impossible to define, believe or endure (Cave 1997a). Despite Cave's predilection for beautiful women (his current wife, Susie Bick, is no exception),[2] despite his claim that art as a world unto itself has its own beauty (King 1996), despite the observation that 'I see more beauty in life than I used to' (Anonymous 1997), it remains an effete and potentially dangerous possibility.[3] And the reason it does so is that the question of beauty – as Plato ventriloquizing through Socrates would have it, what is beauty? – betrays its class associations in the very moment of effacing them through a claim to an absolute or transcendent beauty that is universally available to all. Of course, the 'all' in question is a universality of exclusion. Compare the aristocratic English question, 'anyone for tennis?' That 'anyone' did not mean the various servants attending these toffs and their ladies, let alone the peasants down the road. So also with beauty, for the question posed by a 'Socrates' or indeed an Aristotle was explicitly aimed at the propertied, ruling class (especially its randy young men), and not the ugly, low-born, unlucky, poor, rabble-like, democratic slaves, peasants and artisans who made up the bulk of society (see Ste Croix 2006: 338–39; Boer 2010: 114–15). For those 'ugly' people – at least, from the perspective of the ruling class – beauty was a very different category indeed, one that would not have included the assumptions of their masters.

For different reasons, love too is problematic, especially in light of Cave's endless pursuit of the perfect love song (see Chapter 5). Perhaps it is merely weariness on my part, but the steady stream of self-help, philosophical and theological works that espouse some form of 'love' – usually with some social bite – as the solution to the world's problems does not inspire confidence. Of course, such works (whether from Eagleton [2007], Kristeva [1987], Hardt and Negri [2004], Žižek [2000] and on and on) all argue that the love they seek is not the superficial romantic lust of popular music and Hollywood films, but *agape*, Christian love that is costly, collective and ultimately sacrificial. Unfortunately, these philosophers sound all too much like theologians who keep asserting that 'God is love', that love is a crucial and defining feature of God, for 'God so loved the world...' The problem with these myriad invocations of love is that love so often operates with a similar universality of exclusion to the one we saw with beauty. If a preacher, philosopher or singer calls on us to love one another, or that God loves us, it so often means: do not worry about your class differences, the patterns of exploitation, the fact that the wealthy boss over there is screwing you, for we must love one another 'in Christ' (as the Apostle Paul would have it in one of his favourite phrases). In fact, Cave seems to realize the limited possibilities of love, especially in those intriguing and enticing love songs that engage with pain and God. I mean not his argument (Cave 2004b) that sadness and disappointment are parts of love, nor even that love inevitably ends in bitterness and despair, but the point that emerges in some of his better love songs: love is inseparable from hatred and pain, philogyny from misogyny, philandry from misandry.

It would be possible to invert these oppositions and argue that love emerges from hatred, philanthropy from misanthropy, but that brings us to Cave's fascination with Jesus, where redemption does seem to emerge from pain and death. The catch is that here we come across a curious paradox: the obvious point is that redemption through Christ requires pain, sacrifice of another, even child-abuse (the father surrenders the son to torture and death) and utter neglect – 'My God, my God, why have you forsaken me?' Yet this possibility comes too close to the official theological positions espoused by the churches that Cave despises, whether conservative or liberal: 'Sermons often include a lot of excessive pathetic element. Sometimes sermons contain direct lies caused by the fact that priests don't understand the bible' (Cave in McNair 1997; see also Dwyer 1994). In the midst of this avoidance and rejection, I was able to find but one exception that proves the rule. It comes from a track I discussed in Chapter 4, 'Darker with the Day' from *No More Shall We Part* (Cave 2001), where we meet a 'woolly lamb dozing in an issue of blood' and a 'gilled Jesus' twitching on a fishing hook. The isolated occurrence of this image, along with the extremity of its graphic depiction, indicates a distinct avoidance of the redemptive death of Christ peddled by the churches. All of which means that the redemptive possibilities of love are also hobbled, for love does not emerge from hatred and pain; instead, it is inevitably tied down by precisely those features it cannot escape.

In place of a redemptive Christ, Cave prefers Jesus-the-amazing-man, the one given to sensuality, creative imagination and stunning teaching, but suffering chronic misunderstanding. If one stresses the very humanity of Christ, suggests Cave, then his teachings and achievements and imagination are all the more stunning (Dwyer 1994). At one level, this appreciation of Jesus trades directly in the personality cult I criticized in Chapter 1, especially when Cave elides Christ's own story into his own carefully cultivated autobiography. In fact, the Christ with whom Cave identifies is much like himself, but in this respect Cave is by no means unique. If we take the perpetual searches for the historical Jesus, then they seem to reflect back on the researcher an image remarkably similar to the researcher herself (or rather, the image that such a person would like to be). Or if we take the images of Jesus preferred by sundry believers, agnostics and non-specialists, then they will choose an image that approximates closest to their own self-perception. In all respects – Cave included – the possibilities of such readings are produced by the Gospels, for they offer multiple and not always consistent images of that enigmatic figure known as Jesus Christ. As far as redemption is concerned, the problem is not only that Cave misses the mark by not dealing with the pain and death central to the stories of Jesus, not only that he trades on a problematic personality cult, but that this creative and artistic Jesus comes too close to the hope for aesthetic redemption through beauty.

Is redemption possible at all, at least in Cave's work? A more promising line begins to appear with the apocalyptic themes that appear from time to time, especially on *Abattoir Blues* (Cave 2004a). Having explored these in some detail in Chapter 3, I do not need to repeat that treatment here, suffice to point out that redemption becomes a possibility, an opening that suggests the world is not going completely to hell. It may be a simple act, such as getting off one's arse and doing something about it, or perhaps an act of solidarity or throwing a blanket over one who is cold and hungry. But how is this any stronger than the weak aesthetic option I criticized earlier? I would suggest it is the beginning of a more dialectical approach to redemption, one in which the overwhelming scene of apocalyptic mayhem and destruction is not as total as it at first seems, in which redemption begins to appear like the smallest cloud on the horizon, one that will soon grow to become thick with rain for a parched land.

This approach is deeply Blochian: instead of a grand call to repentance, which is the garden-variety partner to apocalyptic themes, Bloch tirelessly worked to identify the utopian moment within even the grimmest and most degraded political and economic landscape. Apart from his magisterial *Principle of Hope* (Bloch 1995), the under-appreciated *Heritage of Our Times* (Bloch 1991) offers one of the best examples of such an approach. Written in the 1930s as the Nazis were coming to power, Bloch argues that we should not surrender all the utopian imagery to the Nazis. Home and hearth, blood and soil, myth and people also have deeply progressive dimensions to them, ones that the Nazis were taking over and perverting in their own fashion. In other words, in the midst of the fascist hell, one may find shards of hope, utopian glimpses that should not be surrendered to the enemy.

More dialectical possibilities will appear in a moment, but first a question must be asked: does Cave's music become a 'mere exponent of society rather than ferment for its transformation' (Adorno 2006 [1949]: 23)? If we stress the elements of Cave's artistic creation that make him a good liberal – autonomy, authenticity, individual creativity, shunning the mainstream – the answer must be no (see Chapter 6). All he does is support the dominant cultural moment of capitalism, so much so that in pursuing his own individual agenda he replicates millions of others who do the same, thereby undergirding the status quo. But now we may deploy Bloch once more, for it seems to me that Cave may indeed offer possibilities for redemptive and utopian transformation despite himself. Now the question is not whether Cave offers an image of another society that does not resemble our current one (Adorno 2006 [1949]: 23), but whether he identifies and offers redemptive opportunities and traces within this one.

It may be that redemption is insistent even in the face of death. As we saw in Chapter 4, on this question Cave draws upon some rather conventional Christian mythical language – given that it is impossible to speak directly about what happens after death. So we find resurrection invoked, as in the tracks 'New Morning' (Cave 1988b), 'Carry Me' (Cave 2004a) and 'There Is a Kingdom' (Cave 1997a), or the powerful image of a gate to a garden (Cave 1997a), which one enters but does not know precisely what is in that garden, even if one has left the saints, angels and dead behind.

Or redemption may be unexpected and inexplicable, as we found with *And the Ass Saw the Angel* (Cave 1989) in my treatment in Chapter 2. Here the ambiguous ending – Euchrid seems to knife Beth but actually has sex with her and thereby a child is produced – is thoroughly undeserved and from an unexpected quarter, for when the child is born the debilitating rains stop and new hope comes to life in the midst of total depravity. Precisely what that hope entails, whether it will be perverted by the piously twisted Ukulites or whether it frees itself from their control, remains an open question – appropriately. Another example of inexplicable redemption appears in the short story written in the hyper-speak of southern-Gothic, 'Bline Lemon Jefferson': as he swims across the Mississippi to escape his pursuers, Jefferson goes blind, yet that blindness due to cataracts is also his redemption. Not only is his iniquity and sin washed away by the baptismal river, but the cataracts themselves become sacramental: 'an again pray let us not forget that fitted neatly in my sockets...where my eyes once shone...where my bran new cataracts small n white n round like the body of Christ... O Eucharist!... O Sacrament!... wafer thin and holy' (Cave 1988a: 131).

Redemption may also be dialectical in another sense, as we saw with the forms of song that one may trace in Cave's work. From the anarchic/discordant song, through the hymn and its negation in the sinister song, to the difficult dialectical song itself in which the anarchic song is raised to a new level, redemption emerges at a thoroughly formal level. It does not take place in reaction to or despite the earlier form of the anarchic song, but by taking that form through to its dialectical extreme, where all the elements are given free reign so that they come together once again in a way that is no longer anarchic.

One last variation, this time from the humorous song (all the better for my interpretation!), 'The Lyre of Orpheus' (Cave 2004a). The protagonist begins by pottering around in his shed with a lump of wood, a piece of wire and some glue. Down and out, he saws the wood in half, glues the two pieces end to end and attaches the wire. Absentmindedly, he plucks the string, only to find that the sound produced is so beautiful it causes him to gasp and cry out, 'O my God!' But the music produced by the harp is also destructive, killing his wife Eurydice – her eyes pop out of her head and her tongue bursts through her throat – and detonating birds in the field and causing rabbits to smash their brains out on rocks. Strumming furiously until he hits a G minor 7, Orpheus wakens God from his slumber, who promptly hurls a hammer at Orpheus, smashing out his brains in turn and sending him straight to hell – where of course he meets the newly dead Eurydice. Unable to contain his enthusiasm for the discovery of music and despite Eurydice's warning not to play 'that fucking thing' (or she would stick it up his orifice), he picks it up again. Bloch would have loved this song, for not only is music itself thoroughly dangerous, leading to death, anger and hell, but it is also the source of profound inspiration and a challenge to the White Terror of God himself, at least the God who sustains the oppressive status quo. It is, in other words, a thoroughly Luciferan and Promethean moment.

By now it should be clear what redemption actually means for Cave. I have resisted defining it until now, allowing the various senses to emerge in the discussion: redemption now becomes the dialectical response to total depravity, the ability to find gaps in apocalyptic mayhem, the refusal to allow death its famed finality, the unexpected and undeserved possibility of a better world and even a challenge, despite Cave's avoidance of politics, a possibility of overthrowing oppressive powers. But the last word goes to a myth recounted by Adorno, the story of Neck (for Nick!), taken from the Brothers Grimm and which he pondered using for a never-completed study of Beethoven:

> Here we should tell the touching legend in which, for his musical teaching, the river spirit, 'Strömkarl' or 'Neck', did not merely sacrifice himself, but also promised himself resurrection and redemption. Two boys were playing by a stream, Neck sat playing his harp. The children called to him: Why do you sit there playing, Neck? You won't be blessed for that!' Then Neck began to weep bitterly, threw away his harp and sank into the depths. When the boys got home they told their father, who was a priest, what had happened. Their father said: 'You have sinned against Neck. Go back, comfort him and promise

him redemption'. When they got back to the river, Neck was sitting on the bank, grieving and weeping. The children said: 'Don't cry like that, Neck, our father told us that you, too, have a Redeemer'. Then Neck happily picked up his harp and played sweetly until long past sunset. (Adorno 1998: 168)[4]

Notes

Introduction

1. Cultural studies readings in particular seem to come closest to caricatures of academic writing, deploying the latest buzz-words and offering superficial comments on class, social location and gender. Jayasinghe's (2009) effort to queer Cave's dancing is a case in point.
2. Embodied above all in the Blackwell Bible Commentaries; see www.bbibcomm. net.
3. The German collection, *Zur Philosophie der Musik* (1974), usefully collects all of Bloch's writings on music. The English translation (Bloch 1985b) offers only a selection from the German text. For a detailed treatment of Bloch's philosophy of music, see my essay 'Theo-Utopian Hearing: Ernst Bloch on Music' (Boer forthcoming[a]).
4. I do not wish to enter here into the extensive debate concerning Adorno's rather undialectical criticisms of jazz and popular music, but see what is perhaps the best analysis of Adorno on this matter by Witkin (1998: 160–80). Basically, Adorno argued that popular commercial music masks its commodity form through claims of innovation (which is itself part of the commodity), that its supposed primitiveness is pure ideology and that its claims to freedom are illusory.
5. See especially the analysis of Schoenberg's unfinished 'Moses und Aron', in which the ban on images is the central question for Schoenberg himself and thereby Adorno's analysis (Adorno 1998 [1963]: 225–48; 2003 [1963]b: 306–38).
6. See also the comments on Berg (Adorno 1991 [1968]: 8, 46; 2003 [1968]: 334, 382) and Gustav Mahler (Adorno 1992 [1960]: 17, 39, 145; 2003 [1960]: 165–66, 189, 287). Note also: 'Is it not the case that in the final analysis Mahler has extended the Jewish prohibition on making graven images so as to include hope. The fact that the last two works which he completed have no closure, but remain open, translated the uncertain outcome between destruction and its alternative into music' (Adorno 1998 [1963]: 110; 2003 [1963]b: 350).
7. Or as Bob Dylan put it more prosaically, 'Musicians have always known that my songs were about more than just words, but most people are not musicians' (Dylan 2005: 119).

1. Searching the Holy Books

1. The Canongate Series published booklets of selected biblical texts – in the Authorized King James version, no less – with introductions written by famous and not-so-famous people who had a distinct interest in the Bible. Cave's introduction to the Gospel of Mark is now available in an audio recording (http://

www.salon.com/audio/2000/10/10/cave) and in text on the internet (http://members.fortunecity.com/vanessa77/index700.html).

2. Or, as Eaglestone (2009: 139) puts it, the gap between the public face known as 'Nick Cave' and the 'real' Nick Cave is an impossible one to bridge, for we know much about the first but precious little concerning the second. Cave's many 'autobiographies' obviously concern the public and aesthetic figure. By contrast, Eaglestone (2009) naively takes Cave's written word at face value, especially the two lectures I discuss below, 'The Flesh Made Word' (Cave 1997b: 137–42) and 'The Secret Life of the Love Song' (Cave 2004b; see also Cave 2000).

3. For that reason I prefer to follow Adorno's advice: 'the implicit knowledge of the songwriter will succeed better by analysing his products rather than by interviewing him, because the song represents an actual behaviour, rather than his rationalization of that behaviour which an interview would be most likely to get' (Adorno 2009 [2006]: 394).

4. Note also the art exhibition-variation on such autobiography, such as the 'Nick Cave Stories' exhibition at the Melbourne Arts Centre, November 2007 to April 2008 (Barrand and Fox 2007), in which were gathered notebooks, photographs, sketches, paintings, hand-written song lyrics, portraits, books from Cave's own library and so on – all for the sake of providing an insight into the life of a multi-talented artist, offering a tauntingly unachievable effort to 'understand and describe Nick Cave's creative forces' (Barrand and Fox 2007: 4).

5. As a mere sample of autobiographical multiplication in which some or all of the same points continually reappear, see also van Splunteren (1987), Baker (2003), Pishof (2001), Calkin (2001), Brown (1998), Sinclair (1998), McNair (1997), Sierksma (1997), Gander (1994), Dwyer (1994), Dax and Beck (1999: 149), Pascoe (1997) and even Mick Harvey, the long-time friend and only other permanent member of all the bands, reiterates the same narrative: 'in the '80s you could say he was obsessed with the Old Testament. In the '90s he's obsessed with the New Testament' (Gilmour 2005: 247). For the specific discussion of Christology, see Chapter 6.

6. In case we need some assistance with the autobiographical point here, Cave provides it in an interview with Jim Pascoe: 'Well, as far as I know – I might have got it wrong myself – it's concerning Christ's returning to his disciples. At least that's what I meant. I know the Bible reasonably well, but everyone can make a mistake. But it's supposed to be where Christ, after the Resurrection, returns to his friends and shows himself to his disciples. I guess I was making a point in that song that some people have it lucky that people do return to them, and in my situation, it didn't seem like that was happening; in my...in the relationship that I'm talking about within that song it doesn't seem like that was going to happen' (Pascoe 1997).

7. For very different argument, tracing a supposed decline of Cave into personal expression through ego-psychology, that arrives at a similar conclusion concerning the dominance of the written Cave, see McEvoy (2007).

8. See also McCreden's analysis (2009: 179–81), although she does not trace the detailed web of biblical allusions.

9. Dalziell (2009) opts for third approach, preferring a deconstructionist argument that Cave ultimately realizes the word is slippery, no guarantee of communication and understanding, a feature Cave sees in Christ's own inability to be understood.

2. The Total Depravity of Cave's Literary World

1. Inadvertently, since in the only two critical analyses of the novel one gains the impression that Cave either consciously chose to write a Gothic novel and then subtly altered the genre (Hart 2009) or that he made comprehensive and consistent use of Jung's *Puer Aeternus* archetype to construct the figure of Euchrid Eucrow as the fulcrum of his appropriation of the Presley myth (Wiseman-Trowse 2009).

2. Indeed, the publication of *The Complete Lyrics 1978–2007* (Cave 2007) presents three decades of lyrics as though it were poetry, formatted with indexes of titles and first lines, as is customary for poetry collections. Needless to say, no reference is made to the music (see Dalziell 2009: 194).

3. For the sake of comprehensiveness, the relevant plays are: 'The Five Fools', 'Gun Play #3', 'Emergency Ward 11:45 P.M.', 'Maine Kelly (and Me on a Bender)', 'Garbage Hearts', 'Golden-Horn-Hooligan', 'American-Speedway-Fever-Trash', 'Greasy-Hot-Rod-Cream', 'Grease-Gun-Shooter' and 'Salomé' (all found in Cave 1988a: 68–92). The short stories: 'Bline Lemon Jefferson' (Cave 1988a: 128–34), '(I'll Love You) Till the End of the World' (Cave 1997b: 51). The relevant poems, although these have also been performed as songs: 'There Is a Light', 'The Ballad of Robert Moore and Betty Contraine', 'Right Now, I Am a-Roamin' ' (Cave 1997b: 126–28, 169–70). The film-scripts: 'King King Kitchee Kitchee Ki-Mi-O: Treatment for a Film' (Cave 1997b: 129–31) and the film *The Proposition* (Hillcoat 2005). The performance-piece essays: 'The Flesh Made Word' and 'The Love Song' (Cave 1997b: 137–42; 2004b; and as performance pieces, Cave 2000). One may also add the sense of self-loathing that pervades material from the days of The Boys Next Door and The Birthday Party, especially albums like *Prayers on Fire* (Cave 1981) and *Junkyard* (Cave 1982).

4. I follow the standard practice of referencing Calvin's works. *Inst* obviously refers to the English translation (by Ford Lewis Battles [Calvin 2006 (1559)]) of *Institutes of the Christian Religion* with section, chapter and paragraph numbers. *OS* refers to the Latin edition of 1957 (1559), *Institutiones Christianae Religionis*, edited by P. Barth and G. Niesel (Calvini 1957 [1559]). It comprises 3 volumes of *Opera Selecta*, Monachii in Aedibus: Chr. Kaiser. In this case the references are to volume, page and line numbers. See further Boer (2009a).

5. Cave himself describes it as a kind of 'hyper-poetic thought-speak, not meant to be spoken – a mongrel language that was part-Biblical, part-Deep-South-dialect, part-gutter slang, at times obscenely reverent and at others reverently obscene' (Cave 1997b: 141). But he fudges matters when he suggests that the story is through the eyes of Euchrid; that may have been the aim, but he loses his nerve at crucial points and opts for a narrator's voice.

6. All the same, he does produce some stunningly good phrases: 'A platoon of hags with ruckled faces' (Cave 1989: 81); 'until the laughter became itself a wall that you could've stacked shit against all night long and still none of it would've found its way over' (Cave 1989: 133). To his credit, Cave has explored a variety of character voices, experiments in language such as the lingo of racetrack workshops (Cave 1988a: 80–81), or the patriotic stream-of-crazy-consciousness in 'H.M.S. Britain 1982' (Cave 1988a: 124–25), or the affected southern US drawl of 'Bline Lemon Jefferson' (Cave

1988a: 128–34), which may be seen as a preparatory exercise for the voice of Euchrid in *And the Ass Saw the Angel*.

7. But see the extraordinary smoker's song 'The Friend Catcher' from *The Birthday Party* (Cave 1980).

8. Hart (2009: 103) also espies at certain points the 'deft hand of a songwriter'.

9. The novel went on to win in 2009 the *Literary Review*'s Bad Sex in Fiction award, given for the most gratuitous sex scene in a piece of literature in any one year. This is by no means the only time Cave has explored the seedier side of sex: see the banging and dribbling against the dumpster in 'Garbage Hearts' (Cave 1988a: 78), the 'big fucking greaser cocker shit' of 'Greasy-Hot-Rod-Cream' (Cave 1988a: 80) and the masturbatory climax of the beheading scene in 'Salomé' (Cave 1988a: 86–92).

10. For a brief and insightful analysis of *The Proposition*, see McCredden 2009: 175–76.

11. The overlaps between songs written around the time (and indeed after) Cave was writing the novel are many: the Birthday Party songs, 'Mutiny in Heaven' and 'Swampland' from *Mutiny! – The Bad Seed* (Cave 1983); 'Tupelo', 'Say Goodbye to the Little Girl Tree' and 'Black Crow King' from *The First Born Is Dead* (Cave 1985); 'The Good Son' from the album of the same name (Cave 1990); 'Papa Won't Leave You, Henry', 'Christina the Astonishing' and 'John Finn's Wife' from *Henry's Dream* (Cave 1992); 'Red Right Hand' from *Let Love In* (Cave 1994); and even a late piece like 'Fable of the Brown Ape' from *Lyre of Orpheus* (Cave 2004a). Of course, these songs, too, share in the world Cave builds.

12. Or indeed, which turn up at various moments to depict the sleaziness and decay of life – as in Maine Kelly (and Me on a Bender)' (Cave 1988a: 74).

13. One may detect an early model for the later Bunny Munro in the paragraph-long depiction of Abie Poe as a shifty but persuasive salesman who was adept at procuring the sexual favours of his female clients (see Cave 1989: 62).

14. In Hart's unsatisfying study of the novel, she mistakenly asserts that the quotation from Numbers 22 is a collection of biblical fragments (Hart 2009: 98).

15. More than an echo of 'O'Malley's Bar' style of madness appears in *Ass* (Cave 1989: 230–42).

16. Much like Cave, who is reputed to like collecting in a carefully ordered fashion utterly useless objects, much like Walter Benjamin's bricoleur (see Hart 2009: 107).

17. This ambivalence is signalled unwittingly in a formal problem I have noted already with the text, namely, Cave's resort to third-person narrative when the first person becomes too difficult. This tension is exacerbated with the final phase of the story, when Euchrid constructs Doghead, replete with watchtower and telescope, which provide him with an uninterrupted view of the town. However, just when the mechanisms for an omniscient first person are in place, Euchrid implodes. Here Cave's nerve deserts him, for he repeatedly opts out of Euchrid's 'ah' (for 'I') and 'mah' (for 'my') for the sake of a broader, neutral picture. The only occasion when this shift works is, as I pointed out earlier, before that madness takes hold, with the crucial doubled account of the destruction of Euchrid's swamp sanctuary, for here we have the two narratives of the same event, appearing one after the other, breaking the assumed linear narrative flow. Otherwise, the third-person narratives resemble too much the movie voice-over, signalling the fact that the director has hit a creative wall. How is this a formal signal of Cave's ambivalence over redemption? His inability to resolve

the problem of redemption manifests itself in a comparable inability to resolve his formal problem.

18.   Many thanks to Chris Partridge for suggesting this point.

3. Some Routine Atrocity, or, Apocalyptic

1.   The only critic to have noticed apocalyptic themes in Cave's work is McCredden (2009: 175), specifically in relation to 'City of Refuge' from *Tender Prey* (Cave 1988b).

2.   I must add a qualifier. Since these early breakthroughs it has become clear that oppressed groups are not the only context for apocalyptic. The (religious and political) Right in the USA is far from being a forgotten minority and yet apocalyptic characterizes its view of the world – in terms of worldview, literature and movement.

3.   I have not included the morose 'Ain't Gonna Rain Anymore' from *Let Love In* (Cave 1994), although it too speaks of storm and torrential rain. Here the storm is out in the ocean and it embodies a woman who has come and gone, leaving behind a dead calm and, as the title suggests, no more rain.

4.   Some (such as a somewhat hostile respondent to one of my earlier papers) assert that the over-riding influence on Cave is music from the southern USA with its grim spirituality and stark experience of life. One may trace some of these themes in his work, but he has never lived in the south of that strange country between Canada and Mexico.

5.   So 'Hiding All Away', 'Messiah Ward', 'There She Goes, My Beautiful World', 'Nature Boy' and 'Abattoir Blues' (Cave 2004a). Similar in tone are the grim biblical songs 'City of Refuge' (*Tender Prey* [Cave 1988b]) and its line, 'The gutters will run with blood', as well as the threatening storm of the 'The Carny' (*Your Funeral... My Trial* [Cave 1986b]).

6.   For a poem on a similar theme of giving up drugs, albeit without the overt apocalyptic tones of the two mentioned, see 'The Sweetest Embrace' (Cave 1997b: 178–79), published in the year Cave finally overcame his habit.

7.   Also in 'Kong Kong Kitchee Ki-Mi-O: Treatment for a Film' (Cave 1997b: 133).

8.   Earlier efforts appear in 'Straight to You' from *Henry's Dream* (Cave 1992) and the poem 'Sail Away' (Cave 1997b: 100–101). Here Cave meshes the loss of the passion of love with the end of the world – he sings of heaven having been denied its kingdom and chariots of angels colliding in the first and offers the repeated line 'the worst it had come true' (with variations) in the second. To my mind they are a little clumsy compared to the efforts in *Abattoir Blues*.

4. Death

1.   The sole collection of scholarly work on Cave to appear thus far is notable for the sheer absence of any discussion of death (Welberry and Dalziell 2009).

2.   An astute observer may well point out that *Murder Ballads* (1996) appeared before the full celebration of the hymn in *The Boatman's Call* (1997) and *No More Shall We Part* (2001). A more nuanced argument, which emphasizes logical location over against the pressure of linear narratives, argues that the sinister song already foreshadows the pseudo-redemption of the hymn.

3. Such as the foreboding 'Dim Locator' from *Junkyard* (Cave 1982), 'The Singer' from *Kicking against the Pricks* (Cave 1986a), and, from *Let Love In* (Cave 1994), the thoroughly evil 'Loverman', the murderous 'Red Right Hand' with its cut-off note, and 'Let Love In', in which atonality undermines the attempted resolution of the hymn.
4. To this collection should be added the poem called 'The Ballad of Robert Moore and Betty Coltraine' (Cave 1997b: 127), in which Betty blasts away husband after husband, all of whom she has apparently married at some point, as well as 'Kong Kong Kitchee Ki-Mi-O: Treatment for a Film' (Cave 1997b: 131–33).
5. See also the brief play, 'Salomé', which concerns the perpetrator of John the Baptist's beheading, where Salomé's overt sexual charge from the beheading of the Baptist comes to the fore: 'My cunt yearns for it!!' cries Salomé, while the 'negro' reports at the end, 'She said to inform you that you may eat the head but she's gunna teach her cunt to talk good' (Cave 1988a: 90, 92).
6. One may also find this persistent concern with violent, inflicted death in the poetry, notes for plays and other writings beyond the music: see 'Gun Play #3' (Cave 1988a: 72), 'Emergency Ward 11:45 p.m.' (Cave 1988a: 73) and 'Salomé' (Cave 1988a: 88–92).
7. A reasonably complete list includes: 'She's Hit' and 'Hamlet (Pow, Pow, Pow)' from *Junkyard* (Cave 1982); 'Deep in the Woods' from *Mutiny! – The Bad Seed* (Cave 1983); 'Well of Misery' and 'The Moon is in the Gutter' from *From Her to Eternity* (Cave 1984); 'Your Funeral... My Trial', 'Jack's Shadow' and 'Long Time Man' from *Your Funeral... My Trial* (Cave 1986b); 'Deanna' and 'Sugar Sugar Sugar' from *Tender Prey* (Cave 1988b); 'Pappa Won't Leave You Henry' and 'Brother, My Cup is Empty' from *Henry's Dream* (Cave 1992).
8. 'Hey Joe' from *Kicking against the Pricks* (Cave 1986a). The exception here is 'I'm Gonna Kill That Woman' from *Kicking against the Pricks* (Cave 1986a), for here the singer promises a murder. One may possibly excuse this exception since the song is a cover.
9. 'Your Funeral... My Trial' from the album of the same name (Cave 1986b); 'Slowly Goes the Night' from *Tender Prey* (Cave 1988b); 'Nobody's Baby Now' and 'Ain't Gonna Rain No More' from *Let Love In* (Cave 1994); 'People Ain't No Good' from *The Boatman's Call* (Cave 1997a), 'We Came Along This Road' from *No More Shall We Part* (Cave 2001).
10. See also 'Long Time Man' from *Your Funeral... My Trial* (Cave 1986b).
11. See also 'Jennifer's Veil' in *Mutiny! – The Bad Seed* (Cave 1983); 'She Fell Away' from *Your Funeral... My Trial* (Cave 1986b); 'Slowly Goes the Night' from *Tender Prey* (Cave 1988b); 'Nobody's Baby Now' and 'Ain't Gonna Rain No More' from *Let Love In* (Cave 1994); 'Darker with the Day' from *No More Shall We Part* (Cave 2001); 'Dead Man in My Bed' from *Nocturama* (Cave 2003); and 'O Children' from *The Lyre of Orpheus* (Cave 2004a).
12. A less explicitly theological theme is an abiding anger that lingers on and justifies the killing, as we find in 'Your Funeral... My Trial' (Cave 1986b) and 'Brother, My Cup Is Empty' from *Henry's Dream* (Cave 1992).
13. As in 'A Box for Black Paul' in *From Her to Eternity* (Cave 1984), 'Black Crow King' and 'Knockin' on Joe' in *The First Born Is Dead* (Cave 1985), 'Long Black Veil' from *Kicking*

against the Pricks (Cave 1986a), 'Mercy Seat', 'Up Jumped the Devil' and 'Mercy' in *Tender Prey* (Cave 1988b).

14. 'Stranger Than Kindness' from *Your Funeral... My Trial* (Cave 1986b), 'Jangling Jack' and 'Lay Me Low' from *Let Love In* (Cave 1994).

15. We also find this tone in 'Saint Huck' in *From Her to Eternity* (Cave 1984).

16. One may also find such a welcoming of death from a troubled life in the poem 'Cassiel's Song' (Cave 1997b: 77).

17. A similar theme is found in the opening lines of the poem, 'Faraway, So Close!' (Cave 1997b: 76).

18. See also 'Stranger Than Kindness' in *Your Funeral... My Trial* (Cave 1986b), in which memory is held by one, the survivor of a toxic love affair.

19. As does the quicksand in 'Swampland' from *Mutiny! – The Bad Seed* (Cave 1983).

20. Compare the brief note for a play called 'Emergency Ward 11:45 p.m.' (Cave 1988a: 73).

21. A similar sensibility pervades John the Baptist's ecstatic anticipation of death in the brief play, 'Salomé' (Cave 1988a: 91).

22. See especially 'Up Jumped the Devil' and 'Slowly Goes the Night' (from *Tender Prey* [Cave 1988b]), as well as 'Idiot Prayer' (from *The Boatman's Call* [Cave 1997a]), where we find the lines, 'Is Heaven just for victims, dear?/Where only those in pain go?'

23. The closeness of this experience to themes of redemption appears directly with 'Fifteen Feet of Pure White Snow' (from *No More Shall We Part* [Cave 2001]), in which the valley of the shadow of death gives way to hints of resurrection.

24. Although here we should not neglect the irony of the closing track on *Murder Ballads* (Cave 1996b) – 'Death Is Not the End'. Or indeed the dreadful prospect of being resurrected to this grim life in 'Dig!!! Lazarus Dig!!!' from the album of the same name (Cave 2008).

25. See also the death denied at the hands of all those cannibals by means of the lover seeking refuge with the singer in 'Cannibal's Hymn' (from *Abattoir Blues* [Cave 2004a]).

5. God, Pain and the Love Song

1. 'It worries me that every song I write seems to be about love' (Cave in Walker 1984: 17; see also Sullivan 1998). In light of this number, the cynic may well point out that Cave is really no different from any rock artist: the posturing, the drugs, the search for authenticity and the love songs. The large number of love songs merely reinforces how mainstream Cave really is. Since nearly all bands deal in the language and poetry of love, The Bad Seeds are not unique by any stretch. As we will see, Cave gives the love song a significant and somewhat sad and brutal shift.

2. The terminology varies: in 1987 Jameson uses s^1, s^2 and their negatives, while elsewhere he uses S, -S, and their negatives.

3. Dalziell (2009) notes the central element of pain and violence only occasionally, preferring to juxtapose love with melancholy.

4. They are: 'Mr Clarinet' from *The Birthday Party* (Cave 1980); 'Rock of Gibraltar', 'She Passed By My Window', 'Babe I'm On Fire' from *Nocturama* (Cave 2003); 'Breath-

less', 'Babe You Turn Me On' and 'Spell' from *Abattoir Blues/The Lyre of Orpheus* (Cave 2004a).

5.   There are one or two more than in the previous category: 'Wild World' from *Mutiny – The Bad Seed* (Cave 1983); 'Hard On for Love' from *Your Funeral... My Trial* (Cave 1986b); 'Mercy' from *Tender Prey* (Cave 1988b); 'Into My Arms', 'Brompton Oratory' and 'There Is a Kingdom' from *The Boatman's Call* (Cave 1996b); 'Gates to the Garden' from *No More Shall We Part* (Cave 2001); 'Get Ready For Love' and 'Supernaturally' from *Abattoir Blues/The Lyre of Orpheus* (Cave 2004a).

6.   On *The Boatman's Call* (Cave 1997a) these features become tedious, for the album is replete with such hymns (as I will argue in Chapter 7). One after another these slow, personal songs tumble from the album so that one is left wanting at least a change of pace.

7.   At this point, one may take up a more psychoanalytic path, beginning with Lacan's provocative suggestion that, like God, 'woman' does not exist. In other words, neither God nor woman can be represented, for they both belong to that inaccessible yet vital realm of the Real (Lacan 1998).

8.   McCredden (2009: 170) is content to remain with blasphemy.

9.   The full list includes: 'Just You and Me' from *Prayers on Fire* (Cave 1981); 'Six Inch Gold Blade', 'Kewpie Doll', 'Junkyard' and 'Release the Bats' from *Junkyard* (Cave 1982); 'From Her to Eternity', 'Wings off Flies' and 'The Moon is in the Gutter' from *From Her to Eternity* (Cave 1984); 'I'm Gonna Kill That Woman', 'Sleeping Analeah', 'Long Black Veil', 'By the Time I Get to Phoenix' and 'The Carnival is Over' from *Kicking against the Pricks* (Cave 1986a); 'Sad Waters', 'Your Funeral... My Trial', 'Stranger Than Kindness', 'Jack's Shadow', 'She Fell Away' and 'Long Time Man' from *Your Funeral... My Trial* (Cave 1986b); 'Deanna' and 'Slowly Goes the Night' from *Tender Prey* (Cave 1988b); 'The Ship Song', 'Lament', 'The Witness Song' and 'Lucy' from *The Good Son* (Cave 1990); 'Brother, My Cup Is Empty', 'John Finn's Wife', 'The Loom of the Land' and 'Jack the Ripper' from *Henry's Dream* (Cave 1992); 'I Let Love In', 'Thirsty Dog' and 'Ain't Gonna Rain Anymore' from *Let Love In* (Cave 1994); 'Henry Lee', 'Lovely Creature' and 'Where the Wild Roses Grow' from *Murder Ballads* (Cave 1996b); 'People Ain't No Good', 'Where Do We Go Now but Nowhere', 'West Country Girl', 'Black Hair' and 'Green Eyes' from *The Boatman's Call* (Cave 1997a); 'As I Sat Sadly by Her Side', 'Love Letter', 'Sweetheart Come', 'The Sorrowful Wife' and 'We Came Along This Road' from *No More Shall We Part* (Cave 2001); 'Bring It On', 'Dead Man in My Bed' and 'Still in Love', from *Nocturama* (Cave 2003); 'Nature Boy', 'Breathless' and 'Spell' from *Abattoir Blues/The Lyre of Orpheus* (Cave 2004a); 'Lie Down Here (And Be My Girl)' from *Dig!!! Lazarus Dig!!!* (Cave 2008). To be included here are the poems 'Girl at the Bottom of My Glass', 'Blue Bird', 'Sail Away', 'Tread Softly (in Love)', 'The Ballad of Robert Moore and Betty Contraine', 'Come Into My Sleep', 'The Bridle Path' and 'The Sweetest Embrace' (Cave 1997b: 31, 78, 100, 102, 127–28, 168, 175, 178–79).

10.   The collection of material on *The Secret Life of the Love Song and the Flesh Made Word: Two Lectures by Nick Cave* (Cave 2000) contains both the lecture itself in audio form and another talk, 'The Flesh Made Word', given for the BBC radio on 3 July 1999. The text of this second lecture, to which I have already referred in the previous chapter, may also be found in *King Ink II* (Cave 1997b: 137–42). The CD also contains some

interviews and tracks that add nothing to the printed lecture I use here. Not only does Cave have a tendency to repeat himself, again and again, he also cannot resist an interview, and interviewers have been asking him largely the same questions for a long time.

11.   To complete my catalogue, here is the complete list of the last group: 'Jesus Met the Woman at the Well' from *Kicking against the Pricks* (Cave 1986a); 'Sad Waters' from *Your Funeral... My Trial* (Cave 1986b); 'New Morning' from *Tender Prey* (Cave 1988b); 'Foi Na Cruz', from *The Good Son* (Cave 1990); 'Straight to You' and 'Christina the Astonishing' from *Henry's Dream* (Cave 1992); 'Do You Love Me?', 'Nobody's Baby Now' and 'Loverman' from *Let Love In* (Cave 1994); 'I Do Love Her So (Lime Tree Arbour)', 'Are You the One I've Been Waiting for?', 'Idiot Prayer' and 'Far from Me' from *The Boatman's Call* (Cave 1996b); 'And No More Shall We Part', 'Oh, My Lord' and 'Darker with the Day' from *No More Shall We Part* (Cave 2001); 'Cannibal's Hymn', 'Hiding All Away', 'Messiah Ward', 'There She Goes, My Beautiful World', 'Abattoir Blues', 'Supernaturally', 'Carry Me' and 'O Children' (although the last two are primarily religious, with a secondary concern with earthly love) from *Abattoir Blues/The Lyre of Orpheus* (Cave 2004a); 'Hold on to Yourself' and 'Jesus and the Moon' from *Dig!!! Lazarus Dig!!!* (Cave 2008). From the poems may be added 'Lucy', '(I'll Love You) till the End of the World', 'Sail Away', 'Faraway, So Close!', 'Time Jesum Transuentum et Non Revertentum', 'Wife', 'Little Empty Boat', 'Babe, I Got You Bad' (Cave 1997b: 50–51, 76, 100–101, 132, 164–67, 172–73).

12.   For the sake of my analysis, I have restricted this group to those songs that explicitly mention God or the Bible in some way. It is of course entirely possible that all the songs of pain are also inspired by the brutal love of the Bible. In that sense, the previous category becomes a subset of this one.

13.   Cave's own favourites are: 'Sad Waters', 'Black Hair', 'I Let Love In', 'Deanna', 'From Her to Eternity', 'Nobody's Baby Now', 'Into My Arms', 'Lime Tree Arbour', 'Lucy' and 'Straight to You'.

6. Jesus of the Moon, or, Christology

1.   Like a time-delay lock, Jesus would be fully present with the last album produced while under the influence, *The Boatman's Call* (Cave 1997a); four years later, a very similar album bridges the chasm – *No More Shall We Part* (Cave 2001). See also a poem called 'The Sweetest Embrace', which already seeks to move beyond the drugs, published in the same momentous year of 1997 (Cave 1997b: 178–79).

2.   Fifteen years earlier he had two pictures above his desk and chair: 'On the wall above the table, I have a large and beautiful print of Jesus Christ surrounded by a group of small children. He is teaching them, comforting them, arms outstretched. Above this I have a smaller print of the famous Grunewald crucifixion. Christ as the flayed and pierced martyr, the tilt of his spiked head and his outstretched arms, identical to that of the serene Jesus with the children. I love these two pictures and have had them for years' (Cave 1995). See also the references in Chapter 1.

3.   For an idiosyncratic eyewitness account of those early years, see the article by the rock music critic, Clint Walker (2009), as well as the very long interview in *Offense Newsletter* from the time of The Birthday Party (Aanstedt 1983).

4. To argue, as Walker does (Walker 2009: 44–45), that it was simply because Cave grew into musical maturity and took up the piano misses the complexity of this move.

5. One may identify an occasional earlier appearance, such as 'Big Jesus Trash Can' from the anarchic Birthday Party album *Junkyard* (Cave 1982), but these are relatively isolated before 1990.

6. The effort at resolving the tension between these two tendencies is embodied dramatically in the creation of a second, pure rock band called Grinderman in 2007. Using exactly the same line-up as The Bad Seeds, Grinderman played as a support act for The Bad Seeds. Tellingly, the label under which the eponymous album (Grinderman 2007) was released is called 'Anti-'. In the next chapter I argue that the doppelganger effort of Grinderman achieves only a partial resolution.

7. See especially Jameson's essay, 'Periodizing the 60s' (1988: 178–208), as well as Negri's argument (Hardt and Negri 2000, Negri 2008, 2008 [2003]) that resistance is not peripheral but constitutive; in other words, that Power constantly adapts to a central and constitutive resistance. For the 1960s, the upshot is that the West did not create the upheavals of that time, but that they were a response to initiatives of resistance to which it was forced to respond.

8. I am usually wary of such 'vulgar Marxist' connections between a moment in culture (superstructure) and socio-economics (base), but it certainly has its place.

9. See also, almost endlessly: 'I slowly reacquainted myself with the Jesus of my childhood...and it was through him that I was given a chance to redefine my relationship with the world... To me there are certain elements to the Christ story that are patently fiction: I don't believe in the Virgin Birth and I don't believe in the Resurrection... The story of Christ interests me in that it concerns a human being's struggle with the concept of faith, which I, myself, feel very close to' (Pascoe 1997). Or: 'The life of Christ as told in the Bible seems to me to be an encrypted, powerful story, practically a metaphor for all the tribulations humans must suffer. I believe the message of Christ is that we must shake off all those demons that stop us from reaching our potential as human beings' (Dax and Beck 1999: 149). Even more: 'I like Mark a lot because it's so urgent, he'll get the basic bones of the story down and it seems like he's really rushing to get it done and it's quite exciting in that way. I used to like Luke the most because it was much more detailed and fleshed out, and concentrating a lot on the miracles. It was very very beautifully written. John is a bit irritating and so whacked out I can't take it very seriously. But I did find myself developing a sort of relationship with Christ in a way in that I really appreciated what he had to say about things... I believe as a man he was someone who had an incredible capacity to articulate his system of ideals and I find that enormously impressive' (Dwyer 1994; see also Sierksma 1997, Morin 1996, Dunn 1994, Mordue 1994).

10. Here I disagree profoundly with Eaglestone's idealist argument that the shift to Jesus marks a shift that turns on 'the rhetoric by which we discuss God and the (dream of) an unmediated relationship with him' (Eaglestone 2009: 145). This argument leads Eaglestone to identify a shift to the New Testament and Jesus with *Your Funeral... My Trial* (Cave 1986b).

11. For the full lyrics of the song, see *The Complete Lyrics* (Cave 2007). One may also consult http://www.metrolyrics.com/brompton-oratory-lyrics-nick-cave.html or

http://www.allthelyrics.com/lyrics/nick_cave/brompton_oratory-lyrics-12165. html.

12. It is not the only time Cave has entered a church at the beginning of a song – see 'Darker with the Day' on *No More Shall We Part* (Cave 2001).

13. Absence is not an uncommon theme in popular music, which Adorno already noted in the middle of the twentieth century. He was puzzled, since in a world (already then) of modern communication and travel, the phenomenon of absence, which played so large a role in traditional art, has become less of a reality. And yet it persists, perhaps as a psychological reality in the midst of interconnectedness, of an absence in the midst of presence (Adorno 2009 [2006]: 395).

14. For a collection of but some of them, see www.nick-cave.com/interviews and www. bad-seed.org/~cave/interviews.

15. Schweppenhäuser summarizes in his typically lucid style: 'For Adorno, music does not simply mirror the socially current relation between freedom and unfreedom; it does not translate social happenings into their aesthetic counterparts. But it must be involved in what Hegel calls historical substance. Adorno writes that "Beethoven did not adapt himself to the ideology of the often-cited rising bourgeoisie of the era around 1789 or 1800; rather, he embodied its spirit. Hence his unsurpassed success." The "double character of art [as] social fact and autonomous entity" maintains in authentic works a tension between internal formal principle and social experiential content. It is a central idea of Adorno's aesthetics that artworks can absorb social content only if they are overtly autonomous, that is, if they resist external functional constraints and obey only the moods and demands emanating from the formal shaping of the material... Adorno sees this as one side of the ambivalence of artworks: they may not be subject to a heteronomous, functional definition of purpose, but are accountable only to themselves; as formal structures they are nevertheless purposefully organized. This is how artworks retain social and historical elements in mediated form; that is why they require an interpretation informed by social theory and the philosophy of history' (Schweppenhäuser 2009: 105).

16. He is, after all, the product of rural petit-bourgeoisie (his father a high-school teacher of English and Mathematics, and a former student of the private school, Caulfield Grammar, in Melbourne (Hanson and Roeser 1997). On this matter, Adorno's comment on Beethoven applies remarkably well to Cave: 'His music is the this-worldly prayer of the bourgeois class, the rhetorical music of the secularization of the Christian liturgy' (Adorno 1998: 163).

7. Hearing Around Corners: Nick Cave Meets Ernst Bloch

1. For an isolated, recent study of Bloch's philosophy of music, see Korstvedt's useful but ultimately unsatisfying study (Korstvedt 2010), for he fails to connect the fragments of his discussion in a perceptive whole.

2. In The Principle of Hope, Bloch modifies his earlier bold statement, noting the contributions to musical theory (but not practice) of Pythagoras and then later Boethius (Bloch 1985b: 213–14).

3. Or as Adorno puts it, with a specific class reference: 'To date, music has only existed

as a product of the bourgeois class' (Adorno 2006 [1949]: 100). That is, its belated arrival is tied in with the late appearance of the middle class.

4. For obvious reasons, Adorno differs from Bloch on this point, at least to begin with. For Adorno, who could hear a complex musical piece as he read the score, such reading was a necessary feature of analysis (Adorno 2002: 163–64). However, he too sees the severe limits of an approach that remains at this level, for he too seeks deeper insights, although now with an extraordinary blend of philosophical and social analysis.

5. Each of these types of song may leak into one another, so that hybrid forms often emerge (hence the regular appearance of 'often', 'usually' and 'mostly' in my account).

6. One could mount a strong argument for the origins of punk in Australia with The Saints, a band that was hugely influential for Cave and The Boys Next Door (Hanson and Roeser 1997). Even though the Ramones' self-titled album from April 1976 is usually cited as the first moment of the new genre (albeit not without pre-punk threads that run back into the 1960s), with The Saints following close behind with the self-pressed single '(I'm) Stranded' in October of that year, The Saints had been playing such material before the Ramones. For The Saints were formed in 1973, at least a couple of years before the Ramones, and as the lead guitarist, Ed Kueper, said upon hearing The Ramones, 'One thing I remember having had a really depressing effect on me was the first Ramones album. When I heard it, I mean it was a great record to an extent...but I hated it because I knew we'd been doing this sort of stuff for years. There was even a chord progression on that album that we used...and I thought, "Fuck. We're going to be labelled as influenced by the Ramones," when nothing could have been further from the truth' (Anonymous 2003).

7. The hymn is not always so comforting. For instance, in 'Sad Waters' (from Your Funeral... My Trial), the smooth tones of an electric organ emerge in the last couple of bars, reminding one of nothing less than the organ of a crematorium chapel, with its touchingly anti-septic decor.

8. Indeed, Howard's influence is strong on these albums, so much so that a good many would hold him up as an example of the purity of this music, before Cave 'sold out' later on.

9. Even from the earliest days, the subtle art of doing a cover version, full of the reinterpretation required to make such a cover succeed, has been a feature of Cave's music. In the earliest recording from the Melbourne Soundboard (Cave 1977), the ratio of covers was 60:40, including 'Gloria', Louie Louie', 'I'm 18', 'Boots', 'I Put a Spell on You' and a couple of Ramones pieces.

10. Only McCredden (2009: 173) notes the possibility of the hymn in Cave's music, but she restricts such an observation to 'There Is a Kingdom' from The Boatman's Call (Cave 1997a). But see also Sierksma (1997), where both hymn and psalm appear in a discussion of the same album.

11. Walker's simplistic claim (2009: 44) that this new phase is marked by the piano and the ballad simply does not dig deep enough, or rather, to stay with the terminology of my argument, fails to listen around corners.

12. A minor variation on this suggestion of failure appears in a very different treatment of the congregational voice of the hymn: both 'Loverman' and 'Thirsty Dog' (from

Let Love In [Cave 1994]) use multiple voices to enhance the discordancy of the note, pointing to the eventual unravelling of the hymn.

13. Kessler's study (2005) of The Boatman's Call is more enthused by this album than I am, but Kessler focuses almost exclusively on the lyrics.

14. 'Green Eyes' is worth an extra comment, since it is definitely a hymn, but with the spoken voice counterpoised to the sung voice (contrapuntal, for the recited lyrics come out of sync with the sung lyrics), all of which is undergirded by echoes of the spiritual.

15. The paradox is, of course, that it was precisely this form of the song that enabled Cave's breakthrough into a much wider popularity, although that was with a select few of these hymns.

16. 'Bring It On' from *Nocturama* (Cave 2003) follows a very similar pattern.

17. 'Babe, I'm on Fire', the last track on *Nocturama* (Cave 2003), fails to make the grade here, for it slips back into the discordant song.

18. Or, as far as the note itself is concerned: 'The extravagantly treated note, the surging sound and the constant admixture composed of tension, chaos and destiny overflow into a style of music which is largely non-melodic, which is melismatic in terms of recitative, thematic in terms of motifs and develops purely symphonically as a whole' (Bloch 1985b: 26; 1974: 35).

19. A slippage that belies the hype, especially around the Grinderman project, which was described as providing Cave with the 'opportunity to blow up his past' (Dombal 2010). Cave himself claims that 'Grinderman has opened us up to do anything and be shameless' (Dombal 2010).

20. A doctrine held in common among some strange bedfellows – Roman Catholics, revivalist Protestant movements such as the Methodists, and charismatic Protestants today. Needless to say, for true Reformed Christians there is no such fear of backsliding, for salvation cannot be lost.

Conclusion

1. Or, as Cave puts it more prosaically, 'A lot of the time I feel the presence of God quite strongly; and a lot of the time I feel a great absence' (Brown 1998).

2. See also (and almost endlessly): 'Lucy' on *The Good Son* (Cave 1990), 'Something's Gotten Hold of My Heart' on *Kicking against the Pricks* (Cave 1986a), 'Hard On for Love' on *Your Funeral... My Trial* (Cave 1986b), 'Black Hair' on *The Boatman's Call* (Cave 1997a), 'And No More Shall We Part' on the album of the same name (Cave 2001), 'There She Goes My Beautiful World' from *Abattoir Blues* (Cave 2004a) and his fascination with Kylie Minogue (!) (Dwyer 1995).

3. The weakness of this aesthetic option also bedevils the analyses of Cousland (2005) and Kessler (2005), who argue, via different paths, that Cave responds to divine absence via imaginative and creative beauty.

4. Drawn from the Grimm Brothers' *Deutsche Mythologie* (Berlin, 1876, 4th edn; repr. Frankfurt am Main: Ullstein, 1981), I, 408–409.

Bibliography and Discography

Aanstedt, Tim. 1983. 'The Birthday Party Interview'. *Offense Newsletter*, http://www.nick-cave.com/interviews.

Adorno, Theodor W. 1973 [1966]. *Negative Dialectics*. Translated by E. B. Ashton. New York: Seabury.

— 1978 [1951]. *Minima Moralia*. Translated by E. Jephcott. London: Verso.

— 1991 [1968]. *Alban Berg: Master of the Smallest Link*. Translated by J. Brand and C. Hailey. Cambridge: Cambridge University Press.

— 1992 [1960]. *Mahler: A Musical Physiognomy*. Translated by E. Jephcott. Chicago: University of Chicago Press.

— 1998. *Beethoven: The Philosophy of Music*, ed. R. Tiedemann. Translated by E. Jephcott. Stanford, CA: Stanford University Press.

— 1998 [1963/1969]. *Critical Models: Interventions and Catchwords*, ed. Henry W. Pickford. New York: Columbia University Press.

— 1998 [1963]. *Quasi Una Fantasia: Essays on Modern Music*. Translated by R. Livingstone. London: Verso.

— 1999 [1959]. *Sound Figures*. Translated by R. Livingstone. Stanford, CA: Stanford University Press.

— 2000 [1998]. *Metaphysics: Concept and Problems*, ed. R. Tiedemann. Translated by E. Jephcott. Stanford, CA: Stanford University Press.

— 2002. *Essays on Music*, ed. R. Leppert. Berkeley: University of California Press.

— 2003 [1951]. *Minima Moralia*. In *Gesammelte Schriften*, Vol. 3, 11–302. Frankfurt am Main: Suhrkamp.

— 2003 [1959]. *Klangfiguren*. In *Gesammelte Schriften*, Vol. 16, 7–248. Frankfurt am Main: Suhrkamp.

— 2003 [1960]. *Mahler: Eine musikalische Physiognomik*. In *Gesammelte Schriften*, Vol. 13, 149–319. Frankfurt am Main: Suhrkamp.

— 2003 [1963]a. *Eingriffe: Kritische Modelle 1*. In *Gesammelte Schriften*, Vol. 10, 455–94. Frankfurt am Main: Suhrkamp.

— 2003 [1963]b. *Quasi Una Fantasia*. In *Gesammelte Schriften*, Vol. 16, 249–540. Frankfurt am Main: Suhrkamp.

— 2003 [1966]. *Negative Dialektik*. In *Gesammelte Schriften*, Vol. 6, 7–412. Frankfurt am Main: Suhrkamp.

— 2003 [1968]. *Berg: Der Meister des kleinsten Übergangs*. In *Gesammelte Schriften*, Vol. 13, 321–494. Frankfurt am Main: Suhrkamp.

— 2003 [1969]. *Stichworte: Kritische Modelle 2*. In *Gesammelte Schriften*, Vol. 10, 595–782. Frankfurt am Main: Suhrkamp.

— 2006 [1949]. *Philosophy of New Music*. Translated by R. Hullot-Kentor. Minneapolis: University of Minnesota Press.

— 2006 [1998]. *Metaphysik: Begriffe und Probleme, Nachgelassenen Schriften*. Frankfurt am Main: Suhrkamp.

— 2007 [2003]. *Vorlesung über Negative Dialektik: Fragmente zur Vorlesung 1965/66, Nachgelassenen Schriften*. Frankfurt am Main: Suhrkamp.

— 2008 [2003]. *Lectures on Negative Dialectics: Fragments of a Lecture Course 1965/1966*. Translated by R. Livingstone. Cambridge: Polity.

— 2009. *Night Music: Essays on Music 1928–1962*, ed. R. Tiedemann. Translated by W. Hoban. London: Seagull.

— 2009 [2006]. *Current of Music*. Cambridge: Polity.

Anonymous. 1996. 'Nick Cave: Dark Star'. *The Big Issue* (15 January), http://www.nick-cave.com/interviews.

— 1997. Interview. *Haagsche Courant* (18 March), http://www.bad-seed.org/~cave/interviews/97-03-18_hc.html.

— 2003. 'Misfits and Malcontents'. *ABC Arts Online*, http://www.abc.net.au/arts/music/stories/s780315.htm.

Attali, Jacques. 1977. *Bruits: essai sur l'économie politique de la musique*. Paris: Presses Universitaires de France.

— 1985. *Noise: The Political Economy of Music*. Minneapolis: University of Minnesota Press.

Baker, Lindsay. 2003. 'Feelings Are a Bourgeois Luxury...' *Guardian Unlimited*, http://arts.guardian.co.uk/features/story/0,885692,00.html.

Barber, Nicholas. 1997. 'How We Met'. *The Independent* (23 March), http://www.bad-seed.org/~cave/interviews/97-03-23_ios_hr.html.

Barrand, Janine, and Jamie Fox. 2007. *Nick Cave Stories*. Melbourne: Victorian Arts Centre Trust.

Barrett, Michèle. 1991. *The Politics of Truth: From Marx to Foucault*. Stanford, CA: Stanford University Press.

Bennett, Tony, Simon Frith, Lawrence Grossberg, John Shepherd and Graeme Turner (eds). 1993. *Rock and Popular Music: Politics, Policies, Institutions*. London: Routledge.

Billings, D. K. 2002. *Cargo Cult as Theater: Political Performance in the Pacific?* Lanham, MD: Lexington Books.

Bloch, Ernst. 1968. *Atheismus im Christentum: Zur Religion des Exodus und des Reichs*. Vol. 14, *Ernst Bloch Werkausgabe*. Frankfurt am Main: Suhrkamp.

— 1972. *Atheism in Christianity: The Religion of the Exodus and the Kingdom*. Translated by J. T. Swann. New York: Herder and Herder.

— 1974. *Zur Philosophie der Musik*. Frankfurt am Main: Suhrkamp.

— 1985a. *Das Prinzip Hoffnung*. Vol. 5, *Ernst Bloch Werkausgabe*. Frankfurt am Main: Suhrkamp Verlag.

— 1985b. *Essays on the Philosophy of Music*. Translated by P. Palmer. Cambridge: Cambridge University Press.

— 1985c. *Geist der Utopie, Zweite Fassung*. Vol. 3, *Ernst Bloch Werkausgabe*. Frankfurt am Main: Suhrkamp Verlag.

— 1985 [1930/1969]. *Spuren*. Vol. 1, *Ernst Bloch Werkausgabe*. Frankfurt am Main: Suhrkamp Verlag.

— 1991. *Heritage of Our Times*. Translated by N. Plaice and S. Plaice. London: Polity.

— 1995. *Principle of Hope*. Translated by N. Plaice, S. Plaice and P. Knight. Cambridge, MA: MIT Press.

— 2000. *The Spirit of Utopia*. Translated by A. A. Nassar. Stanford, CA: Stanford University Press.

— 2006 [1930]. *Traces*. Translated by A. A. Nassar. Stanford, CA: Stanford University Press.

Bloom, Alan. 1987. *The Closing of the American Mind*. New York: Simon and Schuster.

Boer, Roland. 2007a. *Criticism of Heaven: On Marxism and Theology*. Historical Materialism; Leiden: E. J. Brill.

— 2007b. *Criticism of Heaven: On Marxism and Theology, I*. Leiden: E. J. Brill.

— 2009a. *Political Grace: The Revolutionary Theology of John Calvin*. Louisville, KY: Westminster/ John Knox Press.

— 2009b. *Political Myth: On the Use and Abuse of Biblical Themes*. Durham, NC: Duke University Press.

— 2010. *Criticism of Theology: On Marxism and Theology, III*. Leiden: E. J. Brill.

— forthcoming(a). 'Theo-Utopian Hearing: Ernst Bloch on Music'.

— forthcoming(b). *In the Vale of Tears: On Marxism and Theology, V*. Historical Materialism; Leiden: E. J. Brill.

Broadhurst, Susan. 1999. *Liminal Acts: A Critical Overview of Contemporary Performance and Theory*. London: Cassell.

Brokenmouth, Robert. 1996. *Nick Cave: The Birthday Party and Other Epic Adventures*. London: Omnibus.

Brown, Mick. 1998. 'Cave's New World'. *The Age* (31 May), http://www.nick-cave.com/interviews.

Calkin, Jessamy. 2001. 'Let There Be Light'. *The Telegraph*, http://www.nick-cave.com/interviews.

Calvin, John. 2006 [1559]. *Institutes of the Christian Religion*. Translated by F. L. Battles. Louisville, KY: Westminster/John Knox Press.

Calvini, Johannes. 1957 [1559]. *Institutiones Christianae Religionis*, ed. P. Barth and G. Niesel. 3 vols, *Opera Selecta*. Monachii in Aedibus: Chr. Kaiser.

Casey, Lee. 2001. 'Nick Cave'. *Muse* (March), http://www.nick-cave.com/interviews.

Cave, Nick. 1977. *Melbourne Soundboard*. Personal.

— 1979. *Door, Door*. Mushroom.

— 1980. *The Birthday Party*. Missing Link.

— 1981. *Prayers on Fire*. Virgin.

— 1982. *Junkyard*. Virgin.

— 1983. *Mutiny! – The Bad Seed*. Mute Records.

— 1984. *From Her to Eternity*. Mute Records.

— 1985. *The First Born Is Dead*. Mute Records.

— 1986a. *Kicking against the Pricks*. Mute Records.

— 1986b. *Your Funeral... My Trial*. Mute Records.

— 1988a. *King Ink*. London: Black Spring.

— 1988b. *Tender Prey*. Mute Records.

— 1989. *And the Ass Saw the Angel*. London: Black Spring.

— 1990. *The Good Son*. Mute Records.

— 1992. *Henry's Dream*. Mute Records.

— 1994. *Let Love In*. Mute Records.

— 1995. 'A Letter from Nick'. *Bad Seeds Newsletter* (March), http://www.bad-seed.org/~cave/ interviews/95-03_mute.html.

— 1996a. 'A Letter to MTV'. (21 October), http://www.bad-seed.org/~cave/interviews.

— 1996b. *Murder Ballads*. Mute Records.

— 1997a. *The Boatman's Call*. Mute Records.

— 1997b. *King Ink II*. London: Black Spring.

— 1998. 'An Introduction to the Gospel according to Mark'. In *The Gospel according to Mark*. Edinburgh: Canongate Books.

— 2000. *The Secret Life of the Love Song & The Flesh Made Word: Two Lectures by Nick Cave*. Mute Records.

— 2001. *No More Shall We Part*. Mute Records.

— 2003. *Nocturama*. Mute Records.

— 2004a. *Abattoir Blues/The Lyre of Orpheus*. Mute Records.

— 2004b. 'The Love Song'. *Another Magazine* 7: 397–400.

— 2007. *The Complete Lyrics 1978–2007*. London: Penguin.

— 2008. *Dig!!! Lazarus Dig!!!* Mute Records.

— 2009. *The Death of Bunny Munro*. Melbourne: Text Publishing Company.

Collins, John J. 1997. *Apocalypticism and the Dead Sea Scrolls*. London: Routledge.

— 2001. *Seers, Sibyls and Sages in Hellenistic-Roman Judaism*. Leiden: E. J. Brill.

Cousland, J. R. C. 2005. 'God the Bad, and the Ugly: The *Vi(t)a Negativa* of Nick Cave and P. J. Harvey'. In *Call Me the Seeker: Listeing to Religion in Popular Music*, ed. M. J. Gilmour, 129–57. New York: Continuum.

Covach, John, and Graeme M. Boone (eds). 1997. *Understanding Rock: Essays in Musical Analysis*. New York: Oxford University Press.

Culbertson, Philip. 2010. ''Tis a Pity She's (Still) a Whore: Popular Music's Ambivalent Resistance to the Reclamation of Mary Magdalene'. In *The Bible in/and Popular Culture: A Creative Encounter*, ed. P. Culbertson and E. M. Wainwright, 61–79. Atlanta: Society of Biblical Literature.

Dalziell, Tanya. 2009. 'The Moose and Nick Cave: Melancholy, Creativity and Love Songs'. In *Cultural Seeds: Essays on the Work of Nick Cave*, ed. K. Welberry and T. Dalziell, 187–201. Farnham: Ashgate.

Dax, Maximilian, and Johannes Beck. 1999. *The Life and Music of Nick Cave: An Illustrated Biography*. Translated by I. Minock. Berlin: Die-Gestalten-Verlag.

Dibben, Nicola. 2009. *Björk*. Icons of Pop Music; London: Equinox.

Dombal, Ryan. 2010. 'Nick Cave/Grinderman'. *Pitchfork* (20 September), http://pitchfork.com/features/interviews/7843-nick-cavegrinderman.

Doran, John. 2010. 'What's Wrong with Being Sexy? Nick Cave & Jim Sclavunos of Grinderman Interviewed'. *The Quietus*, http://thequietus.com/articles/04931-nick-cave-jim-sclavunos-grinderman-interview.

Drew, David. 1985. 'Introduction: From the Other Side: Reflections on the Bloch Centenary'. In *Essays on the Philosophy of Music*, ed. E. Bloch, xi–xlviii. Cambridge: Cambridge University Press.

Dunn, Jancee. 1994. 'Interview: Nick Cave'. *Rolling Stone* (25 August), http://www.bad-seed.org/~cave/interviews/94-08_rs.html.

Dwyer, Michael. 1994. 'Interview with Nick Cave'. *The West Australian Revue* (8 December), http://www.bad-seed.org/~cave/interviews/94-12-08_revue.html.

— 1995. 'Murder He Said'. *Australian Rolling Stone* (November), http://www.nick-cave.com/interviews.

Dylan, Bob. 2005. *Chronicles*. New York: Simon & Schuster.

Eaglestone, Robert. 2009. 'From Mutiny to Calling upon the Author: Cave's Religion'. In *Cultural Seeds: Essays on the Work of Nick Cave*, ed. K. Welberry and T. Dalziell, 139–52. Farnham: Ashgate.

Eagleton, Terry. 2007. *The Meaning of Life: A Very Short Introduction*. Oxford: Oxford University Press.

Ellen, Barbara. 1998. 'It's Hip to Be Hateful'. *The Observer* (5 May), http://www.bad-seed.org/~cave/interviews/98-05-03_observer.html.

Engelshoven, Tom. 1994. 'Kicking against the Pricks'. *OOR Magazine* (8 November), http://www.nick-cave.com/interviews.

Erskine, Noel Leo. 2010. 'The Bible and Reggae: Liberation or Subjugation?' In *The Bible in/and*

Popular Culture: A Creative Encounter, ed. P. Culbertson and E. M. Wainwright, 97–109. Atlanta: Society of Biblical Literature.

Fabretti, Claudio. 2005. 'Nick Cave: The Bad Seed of Rock'. *Onda Rock*.

Fontaine, Angus. 1997. 'Songs of Mourning'. *The Daily Telegraph* (20 November), http://www.nick-cave.com/interviews.

Fricke, David. 1996. 'Death Becomes Him, Nick Cave Acquires a Taste for Murder'. *Rolling Stone* (May), http://www.bad-seed.org/~cave/interviews/96-05_rs.html.

Friedlander, Paul. 2006. *Rock and Roll: A Social History*, 2nd edn. Boulder, CO: Westview.

Frith, Simon, and Andrew Goodwin (eds). 2005. *On Record: Rock, Pop and the Written Word.* London: Routledge.

Gander, Marc. 1994. 'Interview with Nick Cave'. *American Music Press* 22, http://www.nick-cave.com/interviews.

Gee, Mike. 1997a. 'Mick Harvey, Part 1: To Have & to Hold'. *The I Magazine* (January), http://www.nick-cave.com/interviews.

— 1997b. 'Mick Harvey, Part 2: Nick Cave and the Bad Seeds'. *The I Magazine* (January), http://www.nick-cave.com/interviews.

Geoghegan, Vincent. 1996. *Ernst Bloch*. London: Routledge.

Gilmour, Michael J. 2009. *Gods and Guitars: Seeking the Sacred in Post-1960s Popular Music.* Waco, TX: Baylor University Press.

— 2011. *The Gospel according to Bob Dylan: The Old, Old Story for Modern Times.* Louisville, KY: Westminster/John Knox Press.

Gilmour, Michael J. (ed.). 2005. *Call Me Seeker: Listening to Religion in Popular Music.* London.

Goldman, Marlene. 1998. 'The Gospel according to Nick Cave'. *Rolling Stone* (17 September), www.rollingstone.com/artists/nickcave/articles/story/5919887/the_gospel_according_to_nick_cave.

Gracyk, Theodore. 1996. *Rhythm and Noise: An Aesthetics of Rock*. Durham, NC: Duke University Press.

Greimas, A. J. 1987. *On Meaning: Selected Writings in Semiotic Theory*. Minneapolis: University of Minnesota Press.

Griffiths, Dai. 2007. *Elvis Costello*. Icons of Pop Music; London: Equinox.

Grinderman. 2007. *Grinderman*: Anti-.

— 2010. *Grinderman 2*: Anti-.

Grossberg, Lawrence. 1997. *Dancing in Spite of Myself: Essays on Popular Culture*. Durham, NC: Duke University Press.

Hadewijch. 1980. *Hadewijch: The Complete Works*. Translated by C. Hart. New York: Paulist Press.

Haefelin, Jürgen. 1986. *Wilhelm Weitling. Biographie und Theorie. Der Zürcher Kommunistenprozess von 1843*. Bern: Lang.

Hall, Matthew. 1995. 'Interview with Nick Cave'. *Puncture Magazine* (March), http://www.nick-cave.com/interviews.

Hanson, Amy. 2005. *Kicking against the Pricks: An Armchair Guide to Nick Cave*. London: Helter Skelter.

Hanson, Amy, and Steve Roeser. 1997. 'Reflections of a Bad Seed'. *Goldmine Magazine* (14 March), http://www.bad-seed.org/~cave/interviews/97-03_goldmine.html.

Hardt, Michael, and Antonio Negri. 2000. *Empire*. Cambridge, MA: Harvard University Press.

— 2004. *Multitude: War and Democracy in the Age of Empire*. New York: Penguin.

Hart, Carol. 2009. '*And the Ass Saw the Angel*: A Novel of Fragment and Excess'. In *Cultural Seeds: Essays on the Work of Nick Cave*, ed. K. Welberry and T. Dalziell, 97–109. Farnham: Ashgate.

Hattenstone, Simon. 2008. 'Old Nick'. *The Guardian*, February 28.

Hill, Christopher, Barry Reay and William Lamont. 1983. *The World of the Muggletonians*. London: Temple Smith.

Hillcoat, John (dir.). 2005. *The Proposition*. Australia: Surefire Films.

Horkheimer, Max. 1978. *Dawn and Decline: Notes 1926–1931 and 1950–1969*. Translated by M. Shaw. New York: Seabury.

— 1991. 'Notizen, 1949–1969'. In *Gesammelte Schriften*, 187–425. Frankfurt am Main: Fischer Taschenbuch.

Horkheimer, Max, and Theodor W. Adorno. 2002. *Dialectic of Enlightenment: Philosophical Fragments*. Translated by E. Jephcott. Stanford, CA: Stanford University Press.

— 2003 [1947]. *Dialektik der Aufklärung: Philosophische Fragmente*. Vol. 3, *Gesammelte Schriften*. Frankfurt am Main: Suhrkamp.

Hudson, Wayne. 1982. *The Marxist Philosophy of Ernst Bloch*. London: Macmillan.

Hüttner, Martin. 1985. *Wilhelm Weitling als Frühsozialist*. Frankfurt am Main: Haag und Herchen.

Jameson, Fredric. 1981. *The Political Unconscious: Narrative as a Socially Symbolic Act*. Ithaca, NY: Cornell University Press.

— 1987. 'Foreword'. In *On Meaning: Selected Writings in Semiotic Theory*, ed. A. J. Greimas, vi–xxxii. Minneapolis: University of Minnesota Press.

— 1988. *The Ideologies of Theory, Essays 1971–1986. II. Syntax of History*. Minneapolis, Minnesota: University of Minnesota Press.

— 1998. *Brecht and Method*. London: Verso.

Jayasinghe, Laknath. 2009. 'Nick Cave, Dance Performance and the Production and Consumption of Masculinity'. In *Cultural Seeds: Essays on the Work of Nick Cave*, ed. K. Welberry and T. Dalziell, 65–80. Farnham: Ashgate.

Johnston, Ian. 1996. *Bad Seed: The Biography of Nick Cave*. London: Abacus; orig. edn, London: Little, Brown and Co., 1995.

Jones, J. M. 1995. *Assembling (Post)Modernism: The Utopian Philosophy of Ernst Bloch*. New York: Peter Lang.

Kessler, Anna. 2005. 'Faith, Doubt, and Imagination: Nick Cave on the Divine-Human Encounter'. In *Call Me the Seeker: Listeing to Religion in Popular Music*, ed. M. J. Gilmour, 79–94. New York: Continuum.

King, Jonathan. 1996. 'Interview: Nick Cave'. *Rip It Up*, http://www.nick-cave.com/interviews.

Knatz, Lothar. 1984. *Utopie und Wissenschaft im frühen deutschen Sozialismus: Theoriebildung und Wissenschaftsbegriff bei Wilhelm Weitling*. Frankfurt am Main: Peter Lang.

Korstvedt, Benjamin M. 2010. *Listening for Utopia in Ernst Bloch's Musical Philosophy*. Cambridge: Cambridge University Press.

Krieger, Michael. 1994. *Conversations with the Cannibals: The End of the Old South Pacific*. Hopwell: Ecco.

Kristeva, Julia. 1987. *Tales of Love*. Translated by L. S. Roudiez. New York: Columbia University Press.

Lacan, Jacques. 1998. *Encore: On Feminine Sexuality: The Limits of Love and Knowledge 1972–1973*, ed. J.-A. Miller. Vol. 20, *The Seminar of Jacques Lacan*. New York: W. W. Norton.

Larrain, Jorge. 1983a. 'Ideology'. In *A Dictionary of Marxist Thought*, ed. T. Bottomore, 219–23. Oxford: Blackwell.

— 1983b. *Marxism and Ideology*. London: Macmillan.

Margetts, Jayne. 1997. '*The Boatman's Call* Interview'. *The I Magazine* (May), http://www.nick-cave.com/interviews.

Marx, Karl. 1975 [1844]. 'Contribution to the Critique of Hegel's Philosophy of Law: Introduction'. In *Marx and Engels Collected Works*. Vol. 3, 175–87. Moscow: Progress Publishers.

Mattila, Ilkka. 1997. 'Finding Nick Cave'. *Radiomafia* (18 March), http://www.bad-seed.org/~cave/interviews/97-03-18_radiomafia.html.

Maume. 2006. 'Nick Cave: The Devil's Advocate'. *The Independent* (11 March), http:// www.independent.co.uk/news/people/profiles/nick-cave-devils-advocate-469418.html.

McCredden, Lyn. 2009. 'Fleshed Sacred: The Carnal Theologies of Nick Cave'. In *Cultural Seeds: Essays on the Work of Nick Cave*, ed. K. Welberry and T. Dalziell, 167–86. Farnham: Ashgate.

McEntire, Mark. 2010. 'Red Dirt God: Divine Silence and the Search for Transcendent Beauty in the Music of Emmylou Harris'. In *The Bible in/and Popular Culture: A Creative Encounter*, ed. P. Culbertson and E. M. Wainwright, 29–39. Atlanta: Society of Biblical Literature.

McEvoy, Emma. 2007. 'Now, Who Will Be the Witness/When You're All Too Healed to See? The Sad Demise of Nick Cave'. *Gothic Studies* 9.1: 79–88.

McNair, James. 1997. 'Interview with Nick Cave'. *Mojo Magazine* (March), http://www.nick-cave.com/interviews.

Miller, Rob. 1988. 'Nick Cave: A Selective History for the Unitiated'. *On the Street* (February), http://www.nick-cave.com/interviews.

Moore, Allan F. 2001. *Rock: The Primary Text: Developing a Musicology of Rock*, 2nd edn. Farnham: Ashgate.

Mordue, Mark. 1994. 'Nick Cave's Love In'. *Juice* (May), http://www.bad-seed.org/~cave/interviews/94-05_juice.html.

— 1997. 'On Screen Interview'. *MTV (Europe)* (22-23 March), http://www.nick-cave.com/interviews.

Morin, Althea. 1996. 'MB Interview'. *Seconds Magazine* (June), http://www.bad-seed.org/~cave/interviews/96-06_seconds.html.

Mulholland, Gary. 1996. 'If Looks Could Kill...' *Timeout*, http://www.bad-seed.org/~cave/interviews/96_timeout.html.

Negri, Antonio. 2008. *Empire and beyond*. Translated by E. Emery. Cambridge: Polity Press.

— 2008 [2003]. *The Porcelain Workshop: For a New Grammar of Politics*. Los Angeles: Semiotext(e).

Negus, Keith. 2008. *Bob Dylan*. Icons of Pop Music; London: Equinox.

Nine, Jennifer. 1997. 'From Her to Maturity'. *Melody Maker* (May), http://www.bad-seed.org/~cave/interviews/97-05-17_melodymaker.html.

Paglia, Camille. 1992. *Sex, Art, and American Culture*. New York: Vintage.

Pascoe, Jim. 1997. 'Awash in a Bleak and Fishless Sea'. In *Kulture Deluxe Magazine*.

Paytress, Mark. 1998. 'Nick Cave's Art of Gold'. *Record Collector* (May), http://www.bad-seed.org/~cave/interviews/98-05_recordcollector.html.

Peake, Mike. 1998. 'Interview with Nick Cave'. *FHM*, http://www.nick-cave.com/interviews.

Petridis, Alex. 2010. '"It's OK to embarrass yourself" – Nick Cave and the Return of Grinderman'. *The Guardian* (2 September), http://www.guardian.co.uk/music/2010/sep/02/grinderman-nick-cave-bad-seeds-interview.

Pishof, Ohad. 2001. 'Interview with Nick Cave'. *Yediot Ahronot* (6 April), http://www.nick-cave.com/interviews.

Robinson, John. 1998. 'Nick Cave'. *New Musical Express*, http://www.bad-seed.org/~cave/interviews/98-05-05_nme.html.

Sample, Tex. 2010. '"Help Me Make It through the Night": Narrating Class and Country Music in the Theology of Paul'. In *The Bible in/and Popular Culture: A Creative Encounter*, edited by P. Culbertson and E. M. Wainwright, 111–25. Atlanta: Society of Biblical Literature.

Scanlon, Ann. 1988. 'Talk of the Devil...' *Sounds* (24-31 December), http://www.bad-seed. org/~cave/interviews/88-12-24_sounds.html.

Schweppenhäuser, Gerhard. 2009. *Theodor W. Adorno: An Introduction*. Translated by J. Rolleston. Durham, NC: Duke University Press.

Sierksma, Pieter. 1997. 'Sometimes I Think, This Is God's Voice Speaking to Me'. *Trouw* (18 June), http://www.bad-seed.org/~cave/interviews/97-06-18_trouw.html.

Sinclair, David. 1998. 'Cool Goth of the Old School'. *The Times* (1 May), http://www.bad-seed. org/~cave/interviews/98-05-01_timesuk.html.

Sonn, Marlena. 1992. 'Nick Cave: The Only Songwriting Genius Left'. *Village Noize* 13, http:// www.nick-cave.com/interviews.

Ste Croix, G. E. M. de. 2006. *Christian Persecution, Martyrdom, and Orthodoxy*, ed. M. Whitby and J. Streeter. Oxford: Oxford University Press.

Sullivan, Jim. 1998. 'This Time Back Nick Cave's Dwelling Mainly on Love'. *The Globe*, http:// www.nick-cave.com/interviews.

Symynkywicz, Jeffrey B. 2008. *The Gospel according to Bruce Springsteen: Rock and Redemption, from* Asbury Park *to* Magic. Louisville, KY: Westminster/John Knox Press.

Tavolodo, Marton Laszlo, and Szonyei Tamas. 1997. 'Things I Have Never Told Anyone About'. *Wanted* (August), http://www.bad-seed.org/~cave/interviews/97-08_wanted.html.

Thompson, Dave. 1997. 'Nick Cave, Alphabetically'. *Alternative Press* (May), http://www.nick-cave.com/interviews.

Thompson, Edward P. 1993. *Witness against the Beast: William Blake and the Moral Law*. Cambridge: Cambridge University Press.

Turner, Steve. 2006. *The Gospel according to the Beatles*. Louisville, KY: Westminster/John Knox Press.

van Splunteren, Bram. 1987. 'Stranger in a Strange Land'. The Netherlands: VPRO TV.

Walker, Clinton. 1984. 'The Birthday Party: Love's Lonely Children'. *The Next Thing*, http:// outta-the-black.webs.com/texts/articles/1984/the-next-thing.html.

— 2009. 'Planting Seeds'. In *Cultural Seeds: Essays on the Work of Nick Cave*, ed. K. Welberry and T. Dalziell, 31–46. Farnham: Ashgate.

Welberry, Karen, and Tanya Dalziell (eds). 2009. *Cultural Seeds: Essays on the Work of Nick Cave*. Farnham: Ashgate.

Whiteley, Sheila (ed.). 1997. *Sexing the Groove: Popular Music and Gender*. London: Routledge.

Wicke, Peter. 1990. *Rock Music: Culture, Aesthetics and Sociology*. Translated by R. Fogg. Cambridge: Cambridge University Press.

Wilson, Robert R. 1984. *Sociological Approaches to the Old Testament*. Philadelphia: Fortress.

Wiseman-Trowse, Nathan. 2009. 'Oedipus Wrecks: Cave and the Presley Myth'. In *Cultural Seeds: Essays on the Work of Nick Cave*, ed. K. Welberry and T. Dalziell, 153–66. Farnham: Ashgate.

Witkin, Robert W. 1998. *Adorno on Music*. London: Routledge.

Wittke, Karl Frederick. 1950. *The Utopian Communist: A Biography of Wilhelm Weitling, Nineteenth-Century Reformer*. Baton Rouge: Louisiana State University Press.

Witts, Richard. 2006. *The Velvet Underground*. Icons of Pop Music; London: Equinox.

Žižek, Slavoj. 2000. *The Fragile Absolute, or, Why Is the Christian Legacy Worth Fighting For?* London: Verso.

— 2005. 'A Plea for Ethical Violence'. *Bible and Critical Theory* 1.1: 1–15.

Index of Subjects

Index of Names

CPSIA information can be obtained
at www.ICGtesting.com
Printed in the USA
BVOW06s2359021216

469688BV00003B/36/P